TRIBAL

TRI

College Football and the Secret Heart of America

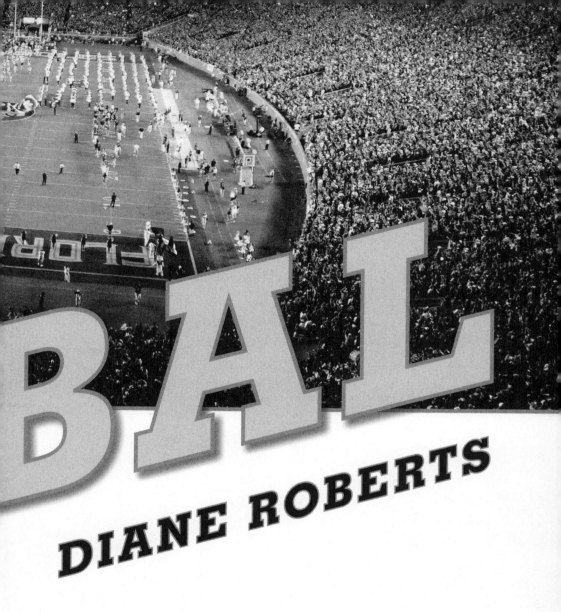

BALL

DIANE ROBERTS

An Imprint of HarperCollins*Publishers*

HarperCollins books may be purchased for educational, business, or sales promotional use. For information, please e-mail the Special Markets Department at SPsales@harper collins.com.

FIRST EDITION

Portions of chapters 1 and 4 appeared in a different form in the *Oxford American* magazine.

Designed by William Ruoto

Frontispiece © ZUMA Press, Inc./Alamy

Library of Congress Cataloging-in-Publication Data

Roberts, Diane
Tribal : college football and the secret heart of America / Diane Roberts.—First edition.
    pages   cm
ISBN 978-0-06-234262-1
1. Football—United States—History. 2. College sports—United States—History. 3. Sports and recreation—football. 4. Biography and autobiography—sports. 5. Biography and autobiography—personal memoirs.
GV950 .R64   2015
796.332/63
                                                                              2015025010

15 16 17 18 19   OV/RRD   10 9 8 7 6 5 4 3 2 1

For my football godparents,

Charlotte and Ernest Williams

And to the memory of my father,

Milton Roberts

CONTENTS

THIRD QUARTER

FOURTH QUARTER

PREGAME

"YOU'RE AN INTELLIGENT, cultivated woman," he says. "You cannot like college football. You don't like college football."

He's a historian, a distinguished scholar teaching at a distinguished university in Georgia. I'm an English professor at Florida State. We're having lunch: salads, balsamic vinaigrette, decaf, no dessert. Somehow we get onto the subject of football season in the South. He rolls his eyes. The traffic. The noise. Those awful people in awful T-shirts baying in the stands. All for a ridiculous, expensive, violent game played by overmuscled postadolescents.

I am forced to confess: I'm one of those awful people—better dressed. The sect to which I belong cleans up pretty for ball games. While the historian reads scholarly articles or composts or binge-watches *Game of Thrones*, I spend fall Saturdays celebrating the sacraments of my people, following the *ordo missae*: ESPN *Game Day*, tailgate, kickoff, four quarters, final whistle, more tailgate—the rituals of the tribe.

He's right. I don't *like* college football. Liking is warm, but not scalding; it's pleasant, something you can take or leave, not something holding you in thrall, not a force from deep in the unconscious and the gut. *Love* is closer, maybe, given that it's chemical, a brain mystery, beyond free will, beyond reason, a gaudy and ungovernable creature fed on hope and desire.

But if love implies approval, then love won't do either. College football is nasty, brutish, and long—at least three hours, four if the game's on television—a great, messy stew of energy, anger, joy, signs, portents, symbols, athletic feats, madness, and what sports announcers call "pageantry." It's the preferred sport of Republicans, climate-change deniers, and people who think every American foreign policy issue can be solved by the 101st Airborne. The game's in bed (possibly not quite the right term) with fundamentalist Christianity, anti-intellectualism, and retrograde ideas about women and people of color. It costs too much in blood and treasure: at FSU, we've unscrewed half the light-bulbs in some campus buildings and removed phones from professors' offices to save money. The library is having to cut databases and slow way down on buying books. The football stadium's getting an $81 million makeover. College football is Big Business masquerading as play, savagery sanctioned by the very institutions of higher learning founded to civilize us, a quasi-fascistic spectacle complete with uniforms, martial music, slogans, and an excess of testosterone. The crowd howls for harder hits; the boys on the field wreck their shoulders, their knees, their backs, their brains—sometimes for life. The NCAA always says it's "studying" the problem.

Yet there I am, every Saturday from late August to early January. I guess you could say I'm conflicted. I'm like those people who aren't sure they believe in the Virgin Birth and the literal Resurrection but still show up for church because they like the music and take solace in the liturgy. I'm a Seminole lifer: I grew up in Tallahassee, looking forward to the rhythm of fall Saturdays, making potato salad for the tailgate, making sure for the fourteenth time that we had the tickets and the parking pass and the corkscrew, singing the fight song and spelling F-L-O-R-I-D-A S-T-A-T-E (proving that education in Florida is not completely a lost cause), settling in to experience the ecstasy and terror of the contest.

Believe me, I've tried to abjure the realm of college football. I fully expected to outgrow it, though my mother (age eighty-three) and my football godparents (ages eighty-five and eighty-six) have yet to do so. During the ten years I lived in England, I figured my college football obsession would wear off. It didn't. On Monday mornings in the Common Room, I'd snatch the *International Herald Tribune* out of the blameless hands of whatever economics grad student was trying to look at the stocks, and check the score from Saturday's games. This was in olden times, before the Internet, before smartphones. An international call would have cost at least twenty bucks, so it had better be a crisis before I rang home. Like during the annual FSU-UF game.

The United States is the only nation sufficiently deranged to make a life-and-death matter of college sports. The United States is the only country in which so-called student-athletes can generate billions of dollars in profit just by excelling at running, tackling, blocking, throwing, and catching. Not that the "student-athletes" are getting rich. The NCAA, the universities, the licensers of "official" college-branded merchandise, Nike, Under Armour, sports broadcasters—they're the ones doing well off college football.

But long before the money, before the dedicated college-football channels and Web sites and radio shows, before the live Signing Day and Heisman extravaganzas and the NFL draft and tailgating and skyboxes, there was passion and violence and pain. The game was never a simple pastime: by 1869, when Rutgers and Princeton met for what's considered the first official college football game, it had already become a trial of honor, loaded with dramatic importance. On October 30, 1897, the *Red and Black* newspaper said of that afternoon's contest between the University of Georgia and the University of Virginia, "Every man on both teams realizes the fact that there is much at stake, and each one will enter the game with a determination to win or die."

Win or die. Seventeen-year-old Richard Von Albade Gammon, on defense for Georgia, leaped to tackle Virginia halfback Julien Hill. Von, as he was known, missed. He fell hard, chin-first on the ground. He died of massive head trauma later that night. Georgia canceled the rest of its season. The legislature in Atlanta passed a bill outlawing football in the state. The governor was about to sign it. Then he received a letter from Mrs. Rosalind Gammon, Von's mother, urging him to spare football. Von's "love for his college and his interest in all manly sports, without which he deemed the highest type of manhood impossible, is well known by his classmates and friends, and it would be inexpressibly sad to have the cause he held so dear injured by his sacrifice. Grant me the right to request that my boy's death should not be used to defeat the most cherished object of his life."

Back in 1980 Florida State beat number-three Nebraska 18–14 on the road. Thousands of students drained into the streets, screaming in happy surprise, pounding Miller Lites and passing around bottles of Jim Beam, hugging, hooting, jumping up and down like mad children. I sat on the hood of my sorority sister's birdshit green Chevelle, yelling, "F-S-U! F-S-U!" The Strip, the section of Tennessee Street lined with vital FSU institutions, such as the thick-crust pizza place, the four-for-one cocktail place, and Mike's Beer Barn, had become a parking lot of honking horns and wholesale violations of Florida's open-container law. The cops just watched. We sang the fight song. We tried to sing the Alma Mater, though most of us couldn't get past "High o'er the towering pines, our voices swell. . . ." We hollered "We won! We won!" till our throats hurt, though every soul making a ruckus that night was a good thousand miles from Lincoln, Nebraska, where the actual winning took place, and none of us did anything to help the Seminoles win, unless you count wearing our lucky socks while listening to the game on the radio. But the victory belonged to us, too, as much as the team. We all belong to the same self-selected clan. We exult and we suffer as one.

I was never a cheerleader or a majorette. I never played the game. I sat in the stands. Yet college football is central to my identity as an American. I grew up in a two-team town where football is as ubiquitous and unremarkable as air, yet as important as the sun. Florida A&M University is small, historically black, and historically good at football: the Rattlers won eight black college national championships between 1938 and 1961. Florida State University is large, historically white, and became seriously and consistently good at football in the 1980s, winning national championships in 1993, 1999, and 2014. Football is the axis on which Tallahassee turns; we arrange our lives around the power of the season—even people who despise the game and refuse to notice who's winning think twice about venturing into town on a home-game weekend, unless they enjoy driving five miles an hour amid packs of revelers bedecked in the colors and symbols of their people as they perform mysterious hand signals and chant the name of their college over and over on their way to the stadium or the bar.

Around here, nothing, not even a constitutional crisis, trumps football. In the middle of the presidential election vote recount of 2000, former secretaries of state, Pulitzer Prize–winning columnists, $600-an-hour lawyers, political operatives, and reporters for outlets from Buenos Aires to Bonn suddenly found themselves kicked out of their hotels and turned into the street. The Florida Gators were coming up from Gainesville to play the Seminoles, and all the rooms had been booked up a year in advance.

Some people still think it's just a game.

I can criticize college football; anyone with a functioning prefrontal cortex can. And should. Look at the money: in 2014, Ohio State's football program was the most valuable, worth $1.1 billion. That was before the Buckeyes won the national championship in 2015. FSU, the 2014 national champion, looks poor in comparison, coming in at $326 million. To put that in context, the entire appropriation from the state legislature to fund Florida State, one of its two "preeminent" institutions of higher education, was $398 million in 2013–14. That's for just about everything besides football: professors, paper, books, computers, air conditioning, campus cops, roof repair, reading labs, paper clips, flower beds, desks, janitors, grad students.

The National Collegiate Athletic Association, college football's multibillion-dollar governing body, is frequently useless and often venal. At a congressional hearing in the summer of 2014, Missouri senator Claire McCaskill lit into NCAA head Mark Emmert on the

NCAA's feeble response to sexual violence committed by athletes: "I feel sorry for you," McCaskill said. "I can't even tell whether you're in charge or whether you're a minion [of the universities]. If you're merely a monetary pass-through, why should you even exist?"

Why indeed? The NCAA's power, like that of the Wizard of Oz, exists only to the extent people believe in it. Between players voting to unionize and courts heaping scorn on the NCAA's conveniently lucrative definition of *amateurism*, keeping players as poor and hungry as Dickensian orphans—they often don't have the money to order a pizza on the weekend or a buy a shirt without a swoosh on it—the NCAA begins to look like the last days of the Roman Empire.

I've often wished I could love baseball instead. Baseball wears an air of innocence and simplicity; it's the game of the nation's childhood— pastoral, redolent of springtime, green shoots, and hope. It doesn't require body armor, and its players rarely suffer brain damage. Over-educated people like me are supposed to like baseball—the favored sport of National Public Radio–heads and *New Yorker* writers. Either baseball or the Tour de France. Poetically minded sportswriters, romantics, and foreigners celebrate baseball as the soul of the nation. They quote Walt Whitman: "It's our game—the American game," they quote Saul Steinberg: "Baseball is an allegorical play about America, a poetic, complex, and subtle play of courage, fear, good luck, mistakes, patience about fate, and sober self-esteem." But the truth is, baseball represents how America wants to see itself; football, specifically college football, represents America as it really is: not a Field of Dreams but a consecrated battleground where we celebrate violence and hypermasculinity, usually in the name of Jesus.

I can't quit college football. It's like a bad boyfriend: you hate that he's so right-wing, his table manners embarrass you, he's barely read a book, and you don't want your mother to meet him, but damn, he's so fine and makes you feel so good (when he isn't making you feel so bad), you just can't help yourself.

Have you ever seen a hundred thousand devotees of the University of Alabama football team urging, in high-decibel unison, "Roll, Tide,

Roll!" Or eighty thousand Seminoles performing what's known as the Tomahawk Chop while singing what purports to be a Native American war chant? There's more than a touch of Nuremberg Reichsparteitag about it. Seriously: Ernst Hanfstaengl, born in Munich, kin to the illustrious Sedgwick family of New England, and a 1909 graduate of Harvard, became part of Hitler's inner circle in the 1930s. Hanfstaengl wrote martial music for Hitler and, he claimed, used the rhythm of the cheer "Harvard! Harvard! Harvard! Rah! Rah! Rah!" for the infamous "Sieg heil! Sieg heil!" One day he played his friend Adolf some of the Crimson's most adrenaline-rousing marches: "I had Hitler fairly shouting with enthusiasm. 'That's it, Hanfstaengl, that is what we need for the movement, marvelous!' and he pranced up and down the room like a drum majorette."

I accept and embrace my Inner Barbarian. The world is divided into Us versus the Forces of Evil as manifested in the other team, my colors versus the rest of the spectrum, my team versus yours, beauty versus ugliness. During football season, you are either with us or against us. College football harks back to a never-never time of moral clarity, a time when we didn't need to think, just cheer, when we cherished our prejudices. During the 1970s and 1980s, Alabama–Penn State games were habitually cast as battles between Johnny Reb and Billy Yank, though it was the University of Florida Gators who actually affixed Confederate battle flags to their helmets when they played Penn State in 1962. Human beings love to pick a side.

The game can be so beautiful, you see. Watching Rashad Greene get under a long ball or Dalvin Cook juke left, right, left, left, running under and around to make fifteen yards, gives me immense pleasure. You could argue that ballet displays the same gorgeous athleticism, and it does. So I'll admit that violence is part of the pleasure too. America is the land of redemptive violence.

We may be entering the end-times of football. Not that the game will disappear anytime soon. Too much money involved. The NFL will carry on raking in profits while trying to divert attention from brain injuries. Universities will continue to tout "tradition" and "pride" as the marching band blasts out the fight song and cheerleaders high-kick on the sidelines and the alumni write checks. People will still insist football prepares players for the Game of Life or makes a boy into a man.

It may be that when it comes to football, America is like Saint Augustine, who, in his *Confessions*, asks God to make him chaste, just not yet. We know the game will have to change. Just not yet, not this season.

FIRST QUARTER

Chapter 1

TRIBAL BOUNDARIES

I'M SITTING ON THE 40-YARD LINE in the fitful November sunshine, watching Florida State smack Syracuse upside the head, knock their legs out from under them, and talk bad about their mamas. The Seminoles have the Orange down 28–0, and it's still the first quarter.

A few minutes before kickoff, Bobby Bowden appeared in the flesh at Doak Campbell Stadium, a smiling eminence, mingling at midfield with Heisman winner Charlie Ward, Pro Hall of Famer Derrick Brooks, and other members of his 1993 squad. Bowden hadn't been within shouting distance of the field named for him since the university administration and the big boosters forced him to resign. The vain, old country-boy King Lear sulked for three years before he agreed to come celebrate the twentieth anniversary of his—and Florida State's—first national championship. Three years during which he appeared in church pulpits or at celebrity golf tournaments, even a football game at the despised University of Florida, but never here at FSU, never on the holy ground of the team he made famous. After the hugging and grinning, Bowden took the flaming spear from FSU mascot "Osceola"—a white boy in greasepaint and long, black hair extensions—held it aloft, then thrust it into the turf. The eighty-three thousand of us in the stands cheered and whooped, forgiving the old man for having presided over our team's decline and for acting as if Tallahassee would have collapsed into a heap of red dust without him. Today we even applauded his hard-eyed wife, who famously dared FSU to sack Bobby: "You know, we don't need the university as much as they need us. If they want to pull that trick, we'll just shake the dirt off our feet and go to Europe or go on a long cruise or something."

Despite that, Ann Bowden stood next to her husband on the field before the game, smiling tepidly and waving in the direction of the bleachers. Cruises and trips to Europe cost money. The university had recently agreed to pay Bobby a stipend of 250 large in 2013 and again in 2014 to show up, be entertaining, help grease the big donors, who—despite the disastrous play calling during his last few seasons, his insistence on hiring that dim bulb of a son as offensive coordinator, and his monarchal determination to choose his own successor—still wanted to shake his hand. The Bowdens posed for pictures with Charlie Ward, who still calls them Coach and Ma'am. Ann Bowden inclined her head, gracious as a duchess. Pinned to the lapel of her pantsuit jacket was a large gold brooch shaped like a hatchet.

Today is Homecoming 2013, and the Seminoles are one big tribe again: us against the world, maybe with a third national championship on the way. By the end of the second quarter, the score's 38–0. Panting on the sidelines, the Orange look freshly squeezed. FSU's been whipping everybody by silly margins, sometimes forty, fifty, sixty points. These are unseemly numbers, though Jameis Winston, the brilliant, absurdly accurate, high-scoring quarterback usually comes out of the game in the third quarter, giving the second string a chance to score. Greed, you know, is a deadly sin.

A few rows down, a couple of girls, teenagers, in garnet and gold T-shirts and garnet and gold Mardi Gras beads, have made poster-board signs they hold up every time FSU makes a first down or whenever a TV camera points in their direction, pivoting from the field to the stands behind them and back to the field. One sign says, JAMEIS IS IN-NOCENT; the other says, I 5TILL BELIEVE, the S turned into a 5, Jameis Winston's number.

It's like this: a young woman, an FSU student named Erica Kins-man, says Jameis Winston raped her. It happened almost a year ago; the police and the university didn't think it worth mentioning until the *Tampa Bay Times* and *TMZ* heard some whispers and chased them up, discovering that she actually called the police in December 2012. The cops knew about the accusation; the FSU Athletic Department knew about the accusation. They didn't seem to feel the state attorney would be interested, not until Jameis Winston had retained a high-priced jock lawyer, anyway. State Attorney Willie Meggs found out about all this on November 13, 2013, three days before the Homecoming game. By then, the Seminole Nation had made up its mind: Famous Jam-eis could not be guilty. He's one of us—and we're nice people. Good people. The editor of the Tallahassee newspaper agonized in print, wishing the story would go away, but since horrid "national media out-lets," which do not "care a whit about our community, our university, our team or the young man many of us—me included—have learned to care about," had jumped on the scandal like a murder of carrion crows, he supposed his paper had to mention it.

Over the next couple of weeks the *Tallahassee Democrat* will run almost daily assurances that the evidence against Jameis is thin, dis-sertations on how tough it is to prove sexual battery, and lamentations over the unfair way big-city types depict "our community." Seminoles become more and more outraged. Not at Jameis Winston: At the newspapers. At television. At everybody. It's been fourteen years since Florida State won a national championship—can't we leave this until January? The Internet heaves with conspiracy theories: Erica Kins-man's lawyer graduated from the University of Florida, FSU's arch-rival. Perhaps someone at the University of Alabama, Florida State's likely opponent in the national championship game, put her up to it. Could Miami be involved? I mean, talk about *trashy* . . . Hell, maybe it's Barack Obama's fault.

Not so long ago, a black man accused of raping a white woman—or even looking at her the "wrong" way—might be lynched. But Jam-eis is no ordinary black man. He's a Heisman Trophy candidate. The heart of the Seminole team. So we attack the young woman: she must be jealous of his *real* girlfriend, a basketball player at Rice University in Texas; she must be some gold digger desperate for attention. We trash her on social media, calling her crazy, a whore, a skank, a liar. She's no longer on campus: she says she got death threats. Her sorority house had to hire security guards.

Perversely, this thing can almost dress itself up as racial progress, bucking America's long, ugly history of assuming the black man's guilt. *Newsweek* called it "*To Kill a Mockingbird* turned upside down": Erica Kinsman as the pathetic Mayella Ewell, Jameis Winston as the stoic (and innocent) Tom Robinson. The racism that has plagued the United States since the Constitution first counted a slave as three fifths of a white person has mutated like a virus, finding a new way to invade the body politic. Instead of rising up to protect White Womanhood, the Football Nation defends our African American Sports Hero.

At halftime, young women from the Seminole Tribe of Florida, real Native Americans from the South Florida reservation into which the US government's ethnic cleansing pushed them, not elective Seminoles like me and most of the rest of the crowd, crown the Homecoming Chief (who is black) and Homecoming Princess (who is white) with authentic Seminole headdresses. Before the Seminoles of Florida started advising the university, the princess wore a floor-length Sioux war bonnet, some in the marching band wore Navajo headbands, and the mascot sported fringed leather buckskin breeches last seen on an ululating "Apache brave" in a B movie. The mascot used to be called Sammie Seminole; in the late 1970s, he got a ferocity makeover and became Savage Sam. Now he's Osceola, named for the great war leader of the Second Seminole War. He rides a historically incorrect Appaloosa horse called Renegade, but his costume was designed on the rez. This, too, counts as progress.

By the fourth quarter, a good chunk of the spectators have left their seats, gone off to bars, barbecues, and other purveyors of fine wines and spirits. A good chunk of FSU's first string has left the field, too, standing on the sidelines while guys so far down the depth chart they could practically mine coal make sure poor Syracuse can't snag more than a lone field goal. In the end, the score is 59–3; Jameis Winston has thrown twenty-one passes and completed nineteen. Analysts on the sports shows will call his accuracy and efficiency "unnatural." They'll praise his poise. Then they'll turn to the question of the rape and stop smiling: what if it's true?

What if he did it? I talk to people completely convinced he's guilty as sin: he's a football player. Football players are arrogant; they treat women like dirt. I talk to many more people completely convinced he didn't do it. She's in it for the money, they say, though when Erica Kinsman named Jameis Winston as her attacker, he had yet to take a snap in a college game.

I struggle. Like everybody else, I watch Jameis Winston on the field, playing with such infectious joy, it uplifts my spirit. He smiles sweetly when talking self-effacingly to reporters, giving credit to the team as a whole. He's got charisma: remember his pregame speech at number-three Clemson? "We ain't leaving here without a victory! Hey, my brothers—put a smile on your face. We're Florida State!" It wasn't Henry V at Agincourt or Winston Churchill just before the Battle of Britain, or even Bluto at the Delta house, but it did produce a 51–14 win.

We think we know him. We do not know him. Most of us have never even met him. And never will. Five seconds while he autographs your jersey doesn't count. He could be a fine young man. He could be a rapist. We will never know. And in terms of football, it doesn't matter. For me, he's the walking archetype of my conflicted soul: a great player or a rotten little shit? A great game or a waste of time, money, and young bodies?

This is how much football means: I once traveled with the University of Alabama football team to an away game in Oxford, Mississippi. Unlike ordinary mortals on the public highway, the Crimson Tide stopped for no red light. No stop sign, either. The buses rolled through the night, patrolmen in front, patrolmen in back, sirens yowling like a pack of back-alley dogs, intersections blocked in every village and hamlet between Tuscaloosa and Tupelo so that the players, coaches, trainers, and hangers-on (like me) could arrive without pausing for so much as a road-crossing possum. Outside the Citgo stations and the Free Will Baptist churches, barbecue shacks, and hardware stores, people in red satin jackets and UA caps would lift up small children to watch the buses streak by. At the time, I thought this must be what it's like to ride with the president or the queen of England.

But it's older and stranger than that, a throwback to when there were sacred kings, holy bodies who bore the collective soul of the race. That night rolling through northern Alabama, it struck me those people's skim-milk faces and blue eyes probably haven't changed much in the two thousand years since their ancestors, wrapped in tartan, gazed with bloodthirsty adoration upon the holy oak–crowned embodiment of their hopes and desires. Some ancient hunger, far beyond the love of a contest in which somebody wins and somebody loses, moved them to stand outside at ten p.m. to watch the team ride by on a bus or line up to see the quarterback off to battle the Ole Miss Rebels. He's the sacred king, the savior, the special one. We behave as though his touch can cure scrofula or whatever disease you get from living in a little Southern town whose name nobody can spell.

Chapter 2

WHO THE HELL ARE WE?

WE BLEED ORANGE AND BLUE or orange and white or crimson and white or cardinal and gold, physiologically improbable, sure, but then college football has its own biology unknown to Linnaeus or Darwin: "Her mama was a Tiger, her daddy is a Gamecock, but what with her marrying a Deacon and moving to Austin, I reckon the young 'uns'll be Longhorns."

Professional football has fans: you're a Packers fan, a Dolphins fan, a Saints fan. Yes, *fan* is short for *fanatic*, and yes, pro football people feel passion and loyalty. Nevertheless, you're at one remove from the mad nucleus of that identity. "Your" team could move and morph; they do it all the time. The Rams left Cleveland for LA, then settled in Saint Louis. The Houston Oilers bailed on the city that lent their name some cred, turfed up in Memphis, and finally landed in Nashville as the Tennessee Titans, a reference, perhaps, to that city's full-scale replica of the Parthenon. Not that Pallas Athene was a Titan (she belonged to the usurping Olympian clan), but what's a little fuzzy mythology between season-ticket holders?

In the college game, hundreds of thousands of grown people travel long distances to sit for hours on hard metal bleachers and engage in sacramental cheering and singing, suffering and rejoicing over a bunch of armor-clad boys the size of cows crashing into each other on a field. Many (not all, mind you) will admit the existence of some things more important than football: war, famine, terrorism, deforestation, the birth of children, the death of parents, high blood pressure, low self-esteem, the Islamic State, near-Earth asteroids, Ebola, rising sea levels—complicated stuff. Yet people who can't be bothered to show up at the polls on Election Day or recycle their plastic bottles follow their football clans from Kickoff Classic Labor Day games in Atlanta to bowl games in Dallas, unfazed by the soul-sapping heat of September or the iron cold of January. Devotion to college football is more fundamental than mere fandom: it's as if you carry your team breed in your mitochondrial DNA. You're not a Bulldog fan or Buckeye fan; you actually *are* a Bulldog or a Buckeye. Not quite literally, of course. But some mystical imprinting occurs, some molecular-level shamanistic transformation. You run with the Wolfpack, strut with the Gamecocks, roll with the Tide; you're a Trojan, a Spartan, a member of the Auburn Family or the Seminole Nation. You are a citizen of a country with invisible borders. In the psychic fiefdoms of college football, we are like medieval villagers, certain that while we are righteous folk, that bunch over in the next hamlet are witches.

We are who we are because we are not *those assholes* who support Notre Dame or Tennessee or Oregon: we are better-looking, smarter, *way* cooler. Our team is virtuous, brave, strong; their team is full of cheats and thugs. If their team wins, bad things happen. The moral order disintegrates. Chaos ensues. If our team wins, the universe vibrates with joy.

This is what college football is about: not the statistical minutiae or the personalities of "student athletes" (yeah, I'm laughing, too—or crying) who may or may not win awards or go pro or enter the ministry or get arrested. They come and go. Even the demigods of the game, the coaches, come and go. College football is about the affirmation of your kindred, a bond or link that can transcend even the familial. In his book *Rammer Jammer Yellow Hammer*, Warren St. John tells the now famous story of the couple who skip their daughter's wedding ceremony because she, perhaps testing their affection and loyalty, chose to get married on the day Alabama plays Tennessee. The daddy explained: "We told her, 'Just don't get married on a game day, and we'll be there, hundred percent,' and she went off and picked the third Saturday in October, which everybody knows is when Alabama plays Tennessee, so we told her, 'Hey, we got a ball game to go to.'"

Alabama and Tennessee border each other, mirror each other, and naturally harbor a visceral mutual hatred. It's energetically vicious, joyously irrational: two poor, put-upon states perpetually characterizing each other as a bunch of witless hillbillies, accusing each other of crimes against decency and hopeless bad taste. As University of Alabama student Irvin Carney explained in a 2007 video, now a beloved ornament to Hate Tennessee Week, UT is "low-down" and "dirty." He doesn't like their mascot or their premises or their color: "I'm not a dog person. Neyland Stadium looks like a garbage-truck workers' convention. Tennessee's color is that throw-up orange. It's not an orange you can sit with. It's that puke, inside-of-a-pumpkin orange. And I don't like pumpkins."

College football divides the world into Us and Them, validating Us and disparaging Them. College football allegiance overrides many of the usual divisions—at least, temporarily. In the stadium, tribe trumps race. That lady in the jersey sitting next to you might be the quarterback's mother, though at big-time football colleges, there are proportionally many more African Americans in pads and helmets than eating boiled peanuts in the stands or kicking back in the skyboxes. Those white Bulldogs or Tigers or Spartans or Longhorns might not live next to black folks or have black friends who come for dinner, but from the way they name-check Ja'Vonn and Mario, Kermit and Isaiah, the boys on the field, you'd think they were talking about favorite nephews. Football cuts across geography, too: a cane-syrup Mississippi Delta accent heard among the board-flat vowels of Notre Dame Stadium might bring on a friendly question or two, but as long as that person's wearing green and cheering the right plays, he's Irish. And, speaking of religion, the Christians in the stands—mainline, evangelical, or those who don't exactly go to church but still get worked up about the "War on Christmas"—are OK with Islam so long as its adherents can run like Nebraska's Ameer Abdullah.

Americans are at least as adept as older cultures at dividing people up into categories of approval or disapproval: look at the South. Four centuries of race obsession has honed our genius for taxonomy. In the eighteenth and nineteenth centuries, black people weren't simply black people; they came in all sorts of varieties, mixtures to which white people attached names: mulattoes, quadroons, octoroons, sacatras, and griffes. Southerners now apply the same rage for definition and exclusion to social class, gender roles, sexuality, membership in clubs and groups, and, of course, college. Cocktail shaker in the glove compartment of the Jeep? Probably went to LSU. Wears pearls in bed? Went to Randolph-Macon. Owns a kilt? Sewanee. Camo in church? Texas A&M. Keeps saying he could have gone to Yale? Duke. Knows a suspicious amount about livestock? Auburn.

No wonder college football took root with such lush and creepy vigor in small-town America. It's our essential sport. The South, the Midwest, the rural, and many of the not truly urban burgs (Baton Rouge, Dallas, Iowa City) throughout the country that still operate like large villages, slow to change their thinking on race, gender, sexuality, and the divinely favored goodness of America, all love college football. It's the metaphor that keeps on giving, a game played by twenty-year-old boys raised to the level of some ultimate battle, some titanic struggle, for dominance, pride, joy, a championship or maybe a postseason trip to the Poulan Weed-Eater Independence Bowl or the Tostitos Fiesta Bowl. It's possible to live in Seattle or LA or New York and never notice that Washington or USC or, bless their hearts, Columbia, is playing at home Saturday, but in a college town, football season infects the place like an outbreak of swine flu: even if you don't get the fever, you cannot help knowing it's raging. You hear people playing the fight song out of their apartment windows, see the car flags fluttering as you drive, jostle your way through crowded grocery store aisles as the faithful, decked out in their colors, load up on Pringles and Bud Light Platinum for the tailgate, then holler "War Eagle!" or "Go Big Red!" across the parking lot. Get within a mile of the stadium and you will smell ribs smoking, steaks grilling, the acid pong of mustard, and the sour stink of beer spilled on the sidewalk in the sun. The normal rules of chemistry and physics, to say nothing of civil society and the highway code, are suspended: in Tuscaloosa parking is so scarce—for cars, anyway, the RVs sprawl over about half an acre each—that somehow a Cadillac Escalade and a Range Rover can both squeeze into a single space. In Athens, the bars and liquor stores open extra early on the theory that being drunk by nine a.m. gives you plenty of time to sober up before a noon kickoff. On game day, your heart beats faster; you escape from the petty worries of the quotidian—grades, jobs, the mortgage, the marriage—and enter the epic, elemental, Us versus Them.

Sitting in the stands of Doak Campbell Stadium of a Saturday afternoon, I am quite aware that many of my fellow Seminoles embrace worldviews different from mine. I know by their bumper stickers that they hate Barack Obama and Hillary Clinton, worry that Mexicans, enviro-nuts, gays, feminists, and Marxists are taking over the country, and think (hope!) Jesus is in the process of packing his bags for the return trip to earth. Yet we can have a conversation about football. The game's hardly going to bring about the Millennial Kingdom where the wolf and the lamb hang out, the lion goes vegetarian, and we don't study war no more. Still, it gives Red and Blue partisans a friendly way to relate as human beings, even enjoy each other, while the twenty-year-old kids on the field risk permanent brain damage.

If someone breaches the decorum, wears her READY FOR HILLARY T-shirt or sports his JEB! 2016 button or says something party political, there may well be a look of disdain, a clenching of the gluteal muscles. At the FSU-Virginia game a few days after Republicans whomped Democrats in the 2014 midterms, a couple of young gents disturbed the propriety of section 35, loudly celebrating the reelection of Florida governor and Batboy lookalike Rick Scott. A man down the row said, also loudly, that he couldn't stand Rick Scott and labeled him a carpetbagger. A full and frank exchange of views ensued, punctuated by other people saying, "Hey, watch the ball game!" and was eventually halted by a lady with gold-sprayed feathers in her hair shouting, "Y'all quit acting like Gators!"

There was a little silence, followed by a noncombatant offering a cheerful, bipartisan, "How 'bout them 'Noles!" Good order was restored.

I knew I was a Seminole before I knew I was white or a Presbyterian or even a girl. I knew I was a Seminole before I knew what a Seminole was. It meant I wasn't a Gator. Not that I was clear on what a Presbyterian was, either. I knew it wasn't the same as a Baptist. Baptists stuck their hands in the air to pray, and asked perfect strangers if they were "saved." Gators boasted and preened and said "Go Gators!" to perfect strangers.

Here in the postcolonial, postindustrial, postmodern, postfeminist, post-heterosexist, not quite postracial world, identity is as vexed a business as it ever was. We brood over it, Hamlet-like. College football takes the edge off this painful self-examination, offering a kind of energetic clarity. *Who the hell are we?* If you tailgate in the Grove, the answer is, of course, "Flim-flam, bim-bam, Ole Miss, by damn!" If you head to the Swamp of a Saturday afternoon, you affirm the creed: "It's *great* to *be* a *Flo-ri-da Gator*! I said, it's *great* to *be* a *Flo-ri-da Gator*!" Toting rolls of Charmin's finest two-ply at Toomer's Corner, you greet co-religionists with "War Eagle!" instead of "Hello." Stampeding with the Thundering Herd, you holler, "We are Marshall!" In Chapel Hill, you ask, rhetorically, "If God isn't a Tar Heel, then how come the sky's Carolina Blue?" We throw a "Hook 'em, Horns" to affirm our position as a worshipper in the Cult of Bevo, though when at George W. Bush's second inauguration his daughter Jenna pressed her thumb, ring, and middle fingers together, holding her index and little fingers erect, people watching across the globe, people who never spent autumn Saturdays liquored up at Darrell K. Royal–Texas Memorial Stadium, thought she was making the ancient sign of the devil.

Who the hell are we? Jean-Paul Sartre declared, "Existence precedes essence." But if Jean-Paul Sartre'd ever been to an Alabama-Auburn game, he'd have understood that belonging to the Tide or being a Tiger is rarely a choice. As a respected pollster at the Capital Survey Research Center in Montgomery put it in 2011, "It's almost genetic, a cultural process rather than a free-will choice." The fundamental nature, the soul of the tribe, is prior; the mother who nourishes us—the *alma mater*—comes before us, the fount of self, identity, being. We cheer, therefore we are.

Football identity is often determined by inheritance, marriage, or educational history. Sometimes a person from a football-deprived culture takes up with the local university team—you can't avoid 'em, so you might as well join 'em. Actual attendance at an institution of higher learning is not required. Close to three fourths of Alabamians have no college degree, yet three fourths of Alabamians say they've given themselves either to the University of Alabama or Auburn University. Most of the people who greet each other with "War Eagle!" or "Roll, Tide!" have no interest in the intellectual life of either university; they would probably dislike much of what goes on in the classroom: queer theory, evolutionary biology, and history professors insisting that yes, slavery was the central issue in the Civil War.

Occasionally—very occasionally—football identity is chosen as an act of rebellion. My father graduated from the University of Florida. He proudly sported a UF Phi Beta Kappa key, and an orange Gator golfing sweater. He never played football: he was too small, and what they used to call "delicate," with bad lungs, a deformed spleen, a mysterious blood disease. Yet he understood its power. Football—playing it, watching it, pontificating about it—was what Southern white men did, now that jousting and dueling were no longer in vogue.

In the still quasi-feudal days from the turn of the twentieth century till well into the 1950s, there was a decorum to everything: whether you attended the Episcopal church, the Presbyterian or the Baptist; what door you used at the State Theatre or where you sat on the city bus. "Negroes" went to Florida A&M, white girls to the Florida State College for Women, and white boys to the University of Florida. Way down at the bottom of the peninsula, on the far side of a vast river of grass, the private, palm-shaded University of Miami belonged to some other world. The Hurricanes played the University of Havana more often than colleges from the Old Confederacy.

Beginning in 1946, soldiers who'd been in Europe or the Pacific came home to Florida armed with the GI Bill, looking for a college education. If they were black, they had little choice: FAMU or Bethune-Cookman. Florida was still Jim Crow's southernmost province. But the Florida State College for Women found it had to make room for white men. The University of Florida would then admit white women. UF alumni worried over what this might mean for their standing in the Southeastern Conference. Some suggested letting UF go coed, then keeping FSCW single-sex. That would mean no rival team siphoning off football talent, plus more girls to choose from, some tucked away in Tallahassee, some right there in Gainesville.

However, Governor Millard Caldwell, who had attended Mr. Jefferson's university up in Virginia, ignored the traditionalists. In May 1947, he signed a decree transforming FSCW into the Florida State University and UF into a coed institution. In 1950, when my father enrolled at UF, nearly all state legislators were Gators. Most of the cabinet, the senate, and the supreme court were Gators, too. Gators controlled the citrus industry, the phosphate mines, the cattle land, the legal profession, the medical profession, damn near everything except Big Sugar. That was Cubans. UF had the professional colleges, the engineering school and the law school. For a young white man on his way up, UF was the right place from which to graduate, the right team to support, the right alums with whom to play golf, drink beer, and shoot the shit. FSU was where you went to get a wife.

My parents married in 1954. In those days, the wife adopted both her husband's last name and his college football team. Thousands of FSU grads or, if they were a few years older, alumnae of the Florida State College for Women, had to suppress their natural loyalties and cleave to Gatordom. My mother was no exception; a proud graduate of Florida State University, she learned all the words to "We Are the

Boys of Old Florida" so she could sing along with everyone else at the beginning of the fourth quarter.

Still, things were changing. Florida State began to play football and Daddy began to take notice. Perhaps he'd tired of Gator vanity, Gator hegemony, Gator arrogance. Perhaps my mother was the in-house subversive, turning him toward Florida State, reminding him that after the baby was born, he'd have to drop a bunch of cash on sitters whenever they took off for an all-day excursion from Tallahassee to Gainesville. And so, like Martin Luther fed up with papal authority and the rigidly literal understanding of transubstantiation, he rebelled, declaring himself a Seminole. To his Gator friends, it was apostasy: Spurn the noble colors orange and blue? Disavow the scourge of Georgia, Tennessee, and South Carolina? Turn your back on the home of Mister Two-Bits, the insurance salesman who'd been making the cheer add up to a dollar since 1949? Leave UF's "noble Gothic walls" and "lovely vine-clad halls" where "palm and pine are blowing" and "southern seas are flowing"? Had the man lost his mind?

The distinction between Seminoles and Gators, obvious to Seminoles and Gators, isn't immediately apparent to those who are neither. Seen from space—or even, say, from Cleveland—FSU and UF look very much alike. Because they are. Until 1905, they were more or less the same institution, one called the Seminary West of the Suwannee, in Tallahassee, the other called the Seminary East of the Suwannee, first in Lake City, then Gainesville, both planted in the old hammocks of North Florida, a place spiritually, socially, economically, and culturally as different from the lands south of Orlando as a farm from a nightclub. Unless you're a student, an alumnus, a local, or an adept in the ways of the SEC and the ACC, you might struggle to distinguish them. They resemble each other about as much as Castor and Pollux, Chang and Eng, Ronde and Tiki, both bell-towered, castellated red-brick aspirants to Oxbridge Gothic, set amid live oaks festooned with Spanish moss, and populated by people who savor their vowels.

Yet to those of us living in the psychic fiefdoms of college football, the 150 miles between Gainesville and Tallahassee might as well be

150,000 light-years. Seminoles are as unlike Gators (at least according to Seminoles and Gators) as Cain and Abel, Bosnians and Serbs, Sunni and Shia, Ulster Catholics and Ulster Protestants. You may not be able to detect the difference, but we sure as hell can. It's like in *Star Trek* when those beings look humanoid, same as you and me, then you notice there's something about the eyes—a little reptilian, perhaps—and the skin, a greenish cast. In a moment of crisis, the creature reveals itself as a formless blob of ravening hideousness with no sense of sportsmanship and a bizarre admiration for Steve Spurrier.

Gators and Seminoles each think the other capable of any atrocity, all manner of depravity, criminality, and unnatural practices. Gators claim FSU is rotten with scandal, citing the time in 1994 when sports agents bought FSU players six thousand dollars' worth of athletic footwear, inspiring the not remotely affectionate nickname Free Shoes University. Seminoles remind Gators that head coach Charley Pell and his assistants committed no fewer than fifty-nine infractions, from spying on rivals to paying players, so many that the NCAA took back their 1984 SEC Championship Trophy and banned them from TV and postseason bowls for two years. Seminoles say the answer to the question, *What does a seven-course dinner in Gainesville consist of?* is *A six-pack and a possum.* Gators say, *What did FSU freshmen get on their SATs? Drool.* Each team will tell you the other plays on natural grass so that the Homecoming Queen has somewhere to graze.

Chapter 3

AT THE CREATION

FOOTBALL IS OLD. Old as dirt. It may have begun in China, or in Greece, where it was called *episkyros*. *Harpastum*, a Roman game, also has solid claim as football's progenitor. Perhaps the Legions taught the Celts how to play: the Irish call it *caid*, the Welsh, *cnapan*—people have been playing some kind of football in the British Isles since at least the seventh century. William FitzStephen, a priest who worked for Thomas à Becket, described a pickup game in 1170:

> After lunch all the youth of the city go out into the fields to take part in a ball game. The students of each school have their own ball; the workers from each city craft are also carrying their balls. Older citizens, fathers, and wealthy citizens come on horseback to watch their juniors competing, and to relive their own youth vicariously: you can see their inner passions aroused as they watch the action and get caught up in the fun.

That's pretty close to what you see now (minus the horses) on Saturday afternoon at Sanford Stadium, in the skyboxes at Michigan's Big House, Death Valley, or the Varsity Club at FSU: "older citizens, fathers, and wealthy citizens" trying to recapture their youth.

They loved their football out in the medieval boondocks, too. Village A would challenge next-door Village B to a match. The villages and the territory between the villages, including streams, woods, pastures, barns, whatever, constituted the "field" where they'd kick or carry or throw a ball made of wood or leather or maybe an inflated animal organ through the door of the other village's parish church.

I'm happy to report, this is still going on. In Ashbourne, Derbyshire, if you're born north of Henmore Brook, you're an Up'ard; south of the little river, you're a Down'ard. The Up'ards face off against the Down'ards every year on Shrove Tuesday, playing for honor, glory, and the sheer fun of vandalism. Wise shop owners board up their windows accordingly. The game begins when some distinguished person—in 2003 it was the Prince of Wales—throws a ball off the bridge in the middle of town. It ends at 10:00 p.m. on Ash Wednesday. Everybody plays—men, women, children—and the goals are markers on the sites of two old mills three miles apart. The rules say you may stick the ball up your shirt or down your trousers and run like hell, but you may not: 1. Use a bag or motorized vehicle to get the ball to the goal; 2. Play in a graveyard; 3. Murder anyone.

They're not joking about the killing: In the Year of Our Lord 1280, at a football game in the Northumberland village of Ulgham, one Henry, son of William of Ellington, ran smack into another player's dagger, stabbing himself to death. Three hundred years later, violence was still rife. Philip Stubbs's 1583 *Anatomie of Abuses* describes "football playing" as "a bloody and murthering practice rather than a fellowly sport."

Since folk football games mostly took place in the spring, some scholars think they were a fertility rite, a celebration of the sun's return, and an opportunity for aggressive boy-girl horseplay. Nothing says sexy like grappling in the freezing mud over a pig's bladder. The cultivated upper classes disparaged football. Too rowdy. In 1314, King Edward II banned the game in London. Edward III banned the game nationwide in 1349; Edward IV banned it again in 1477, declaring that if people needed recreation they should practice archery, which, at least, trained them for the next war against France. In Scotland, the Football Act of 1424 decreed "na man play at the fut ball." People played anyway.

Football became an issue in the culture wars of the sixteenth and seventeenth centuries, along with (to use Stubbs's list of degeneracies) curled hair, lace, bright colors, Maypoles, and Christmas. Football games led to "envy, malice, rancour, choler, hatred, displeasure, fighting, brawling, contention, murther, homicide and great effusion of blood." William Shakespeare didn't sound friendly toward the game, either: Kent, in *King Lear*, calls an uppity servant, "you base football player." Manchester municipal authorities complained in 1608 that "the ffotebale" meant "glasse windowes broken yearlye and spoyled by a companie of lewd and disordered persons."

Death and property damage notwithstanding, consider this: without football, America might not exist, not the America we know. Football was one big reason our Puritan forebears flounced off to the New World in the first place. See, some Puritan preachers in the north of England tried to stop people playing sports on the Sabbath. Then King James, he of Bible fame, ups and publishes his 1618 best seller, *The Book of Sports*, in which he decrees that while bear baiting and bowling are not fit for Sundays, the Lord has no problem with Christians beating the crap out of each other playing ball—as long as they do it after church, unwittingly preparing the way for the NFL.

Weird, considering how things turned out in America, but our Pilgrim Fathers (and Mothers) regarded football as a menace to the Christian life. Obsessive Sabbatarians, they chose to leave the country rather than put up with the king's casual treatment of the Lord's Day and encouragement of a barbarous game. Off they went to Holland and then to what would become New England, searching for a country free of Maypoles, Christmas, and football. Especially football. Unfortunately for them, they'd turfed up on a continent that had been ball-game crazy for three thousand years.

The "football" played by the First Nations of North and South

America is not the same game we play now, though it still involves a great deal of violence in getting a ball to a goal. The Maya game was rather like racquetball without racquets, crossed with soccer and mob football: you played it with your hips, your forearms, feet, and knees on huge stone ball courts, found from Peru to Arizona, which connected the spheres of the living and the dead, the mortal and the divine. Sometimes the game was a substitute for war; a losing player could be sacrificed; reliefs at Chichen Itzá illustrate ceremonial beheadings after the final score, a practice some SEC coaches probably wish would come back into fashion.

Like contemporary inhabitants of the United States, the Meso-americans thought the game contributed to the harmony of the cos-mos. The *Popol Vuh*, the great compendium of Mayan myth, tells how at the dawn of creation, the hero brothers Hun Hunahpu and Vucub Hunahpu made so damn much noise playing, they irritated the gods down in Xibalba, the Underworld. The gods challenged the brothers to a game, won, dismembered both of them, and buried their bodies under the sacred ball court. Somehow Hun Hunahpu's head ended up in a tree (wild kick?), and when a divine maiden walked past, he spat on her hand, impregnating her with the twins Hunahpu and Xba-lanque, who grew up to be the Peyton and Eli Manning of ancient Mexico. The gods offered to play them, too, but this time the twins prevailed. They dug up their father and uncle, placing them in the sky as the sun and the moon.

No place was safe from the ball game: in 1676, Father Juan de Paiva, a priest at the Spanish mission of San Luis de Talimali in the red hills of North Florida, described the Apalachee iteration of it:

A leading man throws the ball in the midst of all of them, who are erect and with their hands raised. It falls into the hand of someone. And they fall upon one another at full tilt. And the last to arrive climb up over their bodies, using them as stairs. . . . aiming kicks without any concern whether it is to the face or to the body.

They "pull at arms or legs with no concern as to whether they may be dislocated or not, while still others have their mouths filled with dirt." Wearing nothing but loincloths, the players go for the ball and each other, usually resulting in a pileup with "four or five stretched out like tuna; over there are others gasping for breath, because, inasmuch as some are wont to swallow the ball, they are made to vomit it up by squeezing their windpipe or by kicks to the stomach."

The very soil of Tallahassee holds the memory of ball games reaching back more than a thousand years: I guess we come by our obsession honestly. Except for the ball swallowing and the lack of decent pads, this sounds like your average Saturday afternoon at the Doak, less than a mile as the perfect spiral flies from the old field where the Apalachee blocked, tackled, passed, and ran for the goal as the people cheered, and Father Juan recorded the action for the sports fans back home.

Chapter 4

CLEAN, OLD-FASHIONED HATRED

IN "ON THE PLEASURE OF HATING," William Hazlitt says: "Nature seems (the more we look into it) made up of antipathies: without something to hate, we should lose the very spring of thought and action."

Anyone acquainted with politics, reality television, or sports knows the truth of this. Hazlitt goes on: "Life would turn to a stagnant pool, were it not ruffled by the jarring interests, the unruly passions, of men. The white streak in our own fortunes is brightened (or just rendered visible) by making all around it as dark as possible; so the rainbow paints its form upon the cloud."

College football's animating hatreds get passed down like junk DNA. Some prefer to concern themselves with eccentric and downright nasty acts of internecine warfare. After Alabama lost to Auburn in the last breath of the ball game in 2013, one woman shot another woman, apparently for being insufficiently distressed over the Crimson Tide's bad luck. And when Rashaan Evans, a highly recruited outside linebacker from Auburn High School, committed to the University of Alabama in 2014, spurned Tigers accused his parents of "not raising him right" and openly wished he'd tear his ACL.

Everyone's heard the story of the two beloved live oaks at the corner of College and Magnolia, right across from Toomer's Drugstore, the trees murdered by a rabid Alabama supporter. Bitter over both the Tide's one-point loss to the Tigers in 2010 and the placing of a Cam Newton jersey on the statue of Bear Bryant, Harvey Updyke drove to Auburn and poisoned the trees with Spike 80-DF, a powerful herbicide used to clear rangeland and blast weeds off highway shoulders. This was a vicious strike at the heart of War Eagledom: when Auburn won a game, frat boys, sorority girls, and GDIs (goddamn independents), grown folks, teenagers in burnt orange and navy blue, and "dirt road alumni" who might never have graduated high school, much less a four-year college, gathered there to perform one of those acts of ritual vandalism beloved of the small-town South—not shooting a stop sign or tagging an overpass, but hurling hundreds of rolls of toilet paper into the knurred old brown branches of Toomer's Oaks. The toilet paper would hang there like a fat snowy fringe until the wind carried it away or the rain dissolved it or university maintenance guys with fire hoses blasted it off.

The custom of TP-ing Toomer's Corner reaches back into antiquity, which is to say, 1972, the year the Tigers beat the Crimson Tide by running in two blocked punts for touchdowns in the last minutes of the fourth quarter. The resulting bumper stickers crowed, PUNT, 'BAMA, PUNT. War Eagle elders recall how College and Magnolia heaved with revelers, and Toomer's Oaks turned from green to white amid the joy of victory over the mightily despised Tide, then ranked number two.

This, people, is hatred. Hazlitt would have understood. He did not have a position on Alabama and Auburn (they didn't play their first game till 1893), but he hated Tories and toffs and idiots. He embraced the exquisitely irrational hatreds of sports, too. His essay "The Fight," about the bare-knuckle boxing match between Bill Neate and Tom "Gas-Man" Hickman in 1822, reads like New Journalism, its author humming with ale- and adrenaline-fired aperçus about the fans and the food. The actual fight, which goes down in a Berkshire cow pasture, occupies less than a quarter of the essay: the real story is Hazlitt's burgeoning dislike of Hickman, the defending champ. "The Gas" is cock of the walk, the überdog, irritating Hazlitt with his "conscious air of anticipated triumph" and his parading about "superciliously" sucking oranges.

"In the first round," Hazlitt says, "everyone thought it was all over." Hickman dominated, as everyone—especially Hickman—assumed he would. But as the rounds wore on, the momentum shifted. Perhaps Hickman was overconfident. Perhaps Neate was underrated. In any case, Neate reared up and started landing bone-jarring punches until "the Gas-Man was so stunned in the seventeenth or eighteenth round, that his senses forsook him." Neate won: "Great, heavy, clumsy, long-armed Bill Neate kicked the beam in the scale of the Gas-Man's vanity." Justice was done and a strutting, toplofty orange sucker humiliated. We don't know if the Gas-Man then plotted to trample Neate's prize rosebushes, but we'd hardly be surprised if he did.

Some people claim to appreciate sporting contests for the athleticism or the pageantry or some such quasi-aestheticist crap. They say they don't care who wins and who loses. It's all in how the game is played.

This is, of course, bullshit. These people could be watching Ali v. Frazier, the Heat v. the Magic, Oxford v. Cambridge, or the Longhorns v. the Aggies and none of it would light a fire in their innards. Beauty-of-the-competition types secretly consider sports beneath their notice, the opiate of the masses to be endured for the sake of being polite to one's less cultivated friends, though those friends do throw great parties. Such people are missing the point. Pleasure in sports depends largely upon winning, and winning is made much brighter, like Hazlitt's rainbow, by hating your opponent. The relationship between the Georgia Institute of Technology and the University of Georgia is semiofficially called "clean, old-fashioned hate." As if that's perfectly rational.

When Georgia and Georgia Tech played for the first time in 1893, the atmosphere was like when the Orange Order marches down the Garvaghy Road. Tech won 28–6, despite Georgia fans hurling rocks from a newly plowed field at the Yellow Jacket players. The next day's

Atlanta Journal quoted a cheesed-off Bulldog complaining that Georgia Tech had employed ringers: "a medical student, a lawyer, and an insurance agent among them, with here and there a student of Georgia's School of Technology thrown in." That was true: the guy who scored all four of Tech's touchdowns was a thirty-three-year-old US Army doctor named Leonard Wood.

There's never been a nanosecond of detente between UGA and Tech: the Bulldogs yell, "And to hell with Georgia Tech!" in "Glory," sung to the tune of "John Brown's Body" (or "The Battle Hymn of the Republic," take your pick). The Yellow Jackets devote an entire (alarmingly violent) verse to the Bulldogs in their "Up with the White and Gold":

> *We'll drop our battle axe on Georgia's head,* chop!
> *When we meet her, our team will surely beat her.*
> *Down on old Georgia's farm there'll be no sound*
> *When our bow-wows rip through the air.*
> *When the battle is over, Georgia's team will be found*
> *With the Yellow Jackets swarming around!*

Back then, the game was more or less rugby, and more or less a semi-organized riot: no NCAA, no high-hit penalties, no "unsportsmanlike conduct." Occasionally, weapons were involved. In 1902, South Carolina beat Clemson 12–6. That was bad enough for the chippy cow-college lads, who hated the toffee-nosed, planter-class students at Carolina, but then a gaggle of SC supporters commenced to parading through Columbia with a poster of a Gamecock cock-a-doodle-dooing over an abject Tiger. Honor affronted, Clemson cadets marched to the enemy campus, armed with swords and bayonets. SC students hunkered down behind a wall, sticks and pistols at the ready. Coaches, preachers, cops, and faculty finally negotiated a peace, but the SC-Clemson game was suspended until 1909.

Ancient humiliations live on. And on. At their inaugural match in 1897, Ohio State lost to Michigan 34–0, creating a foundational hatred that reached its fullest flowering in the 1970s. Woody Hayes, the famously bellicose head coach of the Buckeyes, refused to utter the name of Michigan, referring to it as "that state up north." According to Buckeye folklore, Hayes and some of his coaches were driving back to Columbus after a game in Michigan and needed to gas up the car. Hayes snarled, "No, goddamnit! We do not pull in and fill up. And I'll tell you exactly why we don't. It's because I don't buy one god-damn drop of gas in the state of Michigan! We'll coast and *push* this goddamn car to the Ohio line before I give this state a nickel of my money!"

The nation's social and intellectual elites weren't immune from football tribalism either. Late nineteenth- and early twentieth-century games between Harvard and Yale, Yale and Princeton, Princeton and Penn were so brutal, the *New York Times* editorialized in horror: "The record of French duels for the last dozen years fails to show such a list of casualties as this one game of football produced." And lest you think sectarian violence a relic of the leather-helmet era, in 2006 the Florida International University Golden Panthers, overrun and outscored by the Miami Hurricanes, resorted to punching and kicking the Miami holder after another successful extra-point kick. Miami defenders, in-cluding the man-mountainous (six-eight) Calais Campbell, charged in; an FIU player hit Campbell, and both benches cleared. A'mod Ned, an injured FIU running back, hobbled off the sidelines and started whacking Hurricanes with his crutch.

The sports commentariat call these clashes "rivalries." They are not rivalries, any more than the Cathars v. Pope Innocent III, the Israelis v. the Palestinians, or He-Man v. Skeletor are rivalries. They're death matches, vendettas, originating from painful loss, epic turf battle, or grievous insult (real or imagined), which degenerate into knee-jerk revulsion. College football operates like simpleminded nationalism: Americans hate the French because they refused to support our frivo-lous invasion of Iraq (remember "Freedom Fries"?); the English hate the French, too, and the French hate the English, what with *les rosbifs* burning Joan of Arc in 1431 and buying up half the Dordogne in the

1980s. The Greeks hate the Turks and vice versa: they've been all in each other's business since Helen of Sparta ran off with the King of Troy's pretty-boy son. The searing anger Florida State Seminoles feel for Florida Gators or the vigorous loathing Texas A&M Aggies harbor for Texas Longhorns—Aggies address themselves to Bevo, the blameless steer who happens to be a Longhorn, shouting "Saw Varsity's horns off! Saw Varsity's horns off!"—feels like a blood feud germinated in the Middle Ages, something akin to the Battle of Kosovo in 1389, that gore-soaked Ottoman slapdown about which Serbs still sulk, or Bannockburn, the last time the Scots managed to beat the crap out of an English army, invoked today with flags saying "1314" at Scotland v. England football (that is to say, soccer) matches.

Much as we hate to admit it, hatred is, at some lizard brain level, fun. Profitable, too. The 2012 Alabama-Auburn game, with more than 100,000 in the stadium and another 40,000 ticketless but happily tailgating, brought an estimated $18 million to Tuscaloosa. Tallahassee hosts the FSU-Florida game every even-numbered year and nets maybe $11 million. Nearly 90,000 bodies elbow into Doak Campbell Stadium (official capacity 82,300); thousands more go to the bars and still more to private parties and barbecues. They declare their allegiance to one university or the other on their bodies, their babies, their homes, their food, their vehicles, and their pets with T-shirts, sweatshirts, polo shirts, dog jackets, cat collars, bumper stickers, beer cups, picnic napkins, coolers, stadium seats, lap blankets, doormats, tea towels, caps, beads, bedsheets, bandannas, fight-song noisemakers, saltshakers, car flags, seat covers, vanity license plates, RV banners, tablecloths, ties, iPhone covers, golf clubs, golf balls, beach towels, shot glasses, cutting boards, koozies, sippy cups, sock monkeys, wet wipes, Christmas ornaments, music boxes, necklaces, cuff links, foam fingers, hot sauce, grill covers, toy chests, cake pans, garden gnomes, umbrellas, ponchos, pajamas, pasta, key chains, headbands, handbags, mouse pads, coolers, coasters, clocks, lampshades, mailboxes, luggage tags, zipper pulls, bottle openers, temporary tattoos, garters, boxer shorts, lace knickers, money clips, bedroom slippers, in orange and blue or garnet and gold, all with a university license, all adding up to billions of dollars nation-wide. You can wipe your backside with UF- or FSU-branded toilet paper and, when you die, be laid out in a school-colors casket, branded from cradle to grave.

I know what you're thinking: what about love? Love of team, of tribe, the amour propre that gives life to sports partisanship, the thumping joy in your chest when your boys intercept a pass or score on an eighty-yard run, the delight of an exquisitely executed kickoff return, the swell of pride at your alma mater, your colors, your fight song, your mascot—yes, love's important in football. Risky, too, as love always is, but instead of trusting one man with your heart, you're trusting it to several dozen. And most of them are nineteen, twenty, and twenty-one years old. Mad, bad, dangerous.

Love is more irrational than hatred; it's dopamine-pumping, endorphin-laced batty, shutting down the parts of the cerebral cortex associated with judgment, sober prudence, reason. Hatred has other, more sophisticated talents. Semir Zeki of the Wellcome Neurobio-logy Lab did a study in 2008 wherein people looked at images of other people they claimed to despise. The medial frontal gyrus, right putamen, premotor cortex, and medial insula lit up like a Broadway marquee. Dr. Zeki observed: "A marked difference in the cortical pat-tern produced by these two sentiments of love and hate is that, whereas with love large parts of the cerebral cortex associated with judgment and reasoning become de-activated, with hate, only a small zone, lo-cated in the frontal cortex, becomes de-activated."

So hatred, even pointless, uninformed hatred of people you will never encounter in real life, is less unhinged than love. In romantic, familial, or tribal love, you tolerate unfortunate or even maddening traits—smelly feet, playing golf, a constitutional inability to defend the option—but hatred likes to dance with the analytical faculties. You need to exercise judgment, as Dr. Zeki says, to figure out how "to harm, injure or otherwise extract revenge."

Revenge is not, despite the old Klingon proverb, a dish best served cold. Sometimes it tastes sweetest when it's as hot as a silver chafing dish full of artichoke crab dip at a tailgate in the Grove. On October 4, 2014, the scene in Oxford Mississippi's Vaught-Hemingway Stadium resembled that night in 1989 when exhilarated young Germans poured over the Berlin Wall. University of Mississippi students began jumping down from the stands onto the field, risking torn khakis, twisted ankles, and spilled bourbon. The Crimson Tide isn't the equivalent of the Red Army, of course; not quite, though both Bear Bryant and the Red Army liked to talk about the beloved Motherland. Still, payback is payback and joy is joy, rare enough in human life that when it erupts, authority should honor it.

Authority did—pretty much: the state troopers and cops allowed the Rebel faithful to rush their own field hooting and hollering and holding their crimson shakers high, dancing and laughing and taunting: "Roll, Tears, Roll!" Boys and girls fell on the grass and kissed as if the End of the World was at hand. Joy, life, affirmation.

And booze. Each goalpost was suddenly festooned with boys, girls too, some (from the Delta, surely) riding sidesaddle. It's not that easy, bringing a pair of uprights down. The more ambitious boys stood up on the crossbar, taking selfies while trying to use their weight to pull the thing loose from its base. One flop-haired young gent in a regimental tie flung off his blazer and pumped the left upright while other boys sat astride, thrusting back and forth in a weirdly sexual motion, until the goalpost fell, slowly, inexorably, oh baby, oh yes! calling, "Are you ready?"

They dismantled the posts and bore them aloft, first to the Grove, where Ole Miss boosters toasted the goalpost guys, handing out beers, offering swigs of Maker's Mark. A portion of one yellow-painted post took up residence among the trees and tents, while the other proceeded down University Avenue to the town square, past the Confederate Soldier statue, pausing at various bars like a happy version of the Stations of the Cross, a Via Felix.

In the other Oxford, the one in England, after one college beats all the other colleges in rowing, they carry a boat up from the river and through the ancient town, thumping it and bellowing before they take it to the front quadrangle and burn it. Burning things is a traditional expression of triumph, as when the English whipped the Spanish Armada in 1588. Or when the West Virginia Mountaineers whipped Baylor in 2014. The cops used tear gas on all those drunk white people in Morgantown setting dumpsters and sofas alight in the street, throwing bottles and yelling like conquerors. The last time they rioted like this was when Osama Bin Laden was killed.

In the sixty-two gridiron encounters with the University of Alabama played before 2014, Ole Miss had lost fifty-one times. The last time Ole Miss whipped the Tide was in 2003. That's a lot of suffering, a lot of resentment, anger, and humiliation, fermenting since 1899 in a culture richly accustomed to nursing deep historical grievances. The Rebels hate Alabama. Despise them. Not the way they despise LSU or Mississippi State, of course, but profoundly, energetically. Snotty, entitled Alabama flaunting their baker's dozen of national championships (they claim it's actually fifteen), their huge Death Star of a stadium, their stupid houndstooth hats—Jesus, Bear Bryant's been dead for more than thirty years—their expectation of winning, always winning, as if they own the SEC, as if they own college football, I mean they name-check the fucking 1923 Rose Bowl in their fight song.

In Alabama, the fourth-poorest state in the nation, they smile and say, "At least we're not Mississippi."

On the rare, beautiful, occasions when Ole Miss wins, how can you blame the Rebels for taunting the Tide, turning Alabama's very Alabama-ness back on them? The Crimson Tide stole the rhythm of Ole Miss's famous "Hotty Toddy" chant, 'bamafying it with *Rammer Jammer* (the name of a defunct student magazine) and the state bird, the yellowhammer, which rhymed nicely with Alabama, as in "Give 'em hell, Alabama!" It's still called the "Ole Miss Cheer," and the etiquette of its use is complex: It should be played only twice, near the end of a game, and only when victory is certain—unless it's the Auburn game. Or a championship game. It must never be played before kickoff, except when the Alabama-Tennessee game is in Knoxville. The pep band rides around on a boat on the Tennessee River the night before, playing it whenever they see a craft flying an orange Vols flag.

But the night of October 4, 2014, it was the Rebels shouting, "Hey 'Bama! Hey 'Bama! We just beat the hell out of you!" According to the Rebels, it was justice, delicious payback. Of course, justice and happiness in college football have the longevity of a mayfly: three weeks after the euphoria in Oxford, the third-ranked Rebels lost to the even more despised LSU Tigers in Baton Rouge. Quarterback Bo Wallace, the golden-haired, blue-eyed hero of the Alabama game, threw an interception with nine seconds left. Disgusted by his monumental screwup, he fled the field with time still on the clock.

What would Faulkner have thought of the Festival of the Most Holy Goalpost? There's an Ole Miss football player in *The Hamlet*, his 1940 comic novel about the rise of the ghastly Snopes family, a brilliant running back named Labove. He's a poor boy from the hills who outfits his entire family in purloined cleats. Labove doesn't love the game; to him it's nothing but carrying "a trivial contemptible obloid across fleeing and meaningless white lines." Still, it pays his tuition, and Labove's so good that he gets his picture in the Memphis paper after the Mississippi State–Ole Miss game. Not that he cares. He's crazy in lust with a country schoolgirl. After he tries (and fails spectacularly) to rape her, he runs off in shame, leaving behind his beloved volumes of Thucydides and Horace.

Faulkner's own sport was fox hunting, though he once wrote a rather rococo essay on ice hockey for *Sports Illustrated*. Football—"the football"—as characters in *The Hamlet* would have it, didn't much interest him. One of the brighter bulbs of Frenchmen's Bend, Mississippi, says of the game, "I hear it ain't much different from actual fighting."

Fighting. Whatever else it might be, the United States is not one nation indivisible. As for liberty and justice, we can't even agree on a working definition for those words. The July 2013 Atlantic/ Aspen American Values Survey reveals that America is more polarized than ever: 61 percent say we've become either "somewhat more divided" or "much more divided," underlining a Pew Charitable Trusts poll, which finds that increasingly over the past twenty-five years, we pick a side and stick with it. We are a country of clans: Democrat or Republican, secular or churched, city or country, grilled or fried, boxers or briefs, Marvel or DC, MSNBC or Fox, Peroni or PBR, pro-choice or anti-abortion, cat or dog, and, out in those storied hinterlands sometimes called the *real* America, we are Volunteers or Razorbacks, Wolverines or Fighting Irish, Rattlers or Rebels or Wildcats. College football has been passionately, uncompromisingly, *us* and *them* for a hundred years. The rest of the culture is just now catching up.

During a 1960 road trip, John Steinbeck observed: "Sectional football games have the glory and the despair of war, and when a Texas team takes the field against a foreign state, it is an army with banners."

By "foreign state," Steinbeck means Arkansas. Or Louisiana. But it could as easily be a team from a couple of counties away. Football, not diplomacy, is the continuation of war by other means. It's a minor miracle that furious bands of Tigers did not march on Tuscaloosa when Toomer's Oaks finally died in 2013. All the foresters and dendrologists, all the horticulturalists and professors of silvics, couldn't stanch the poison. On April 20, 2013, Auburn TP-ed the trees one last time. Thousands of students, alums, and nostalgists swarmed Toomer's Corner, some inscribing farewells or the Auburn Creed ("I believe that this is a practical world and that I can count only on what I earn. Therefore, I believe in work, hard work") on their rolls before they hurled them high in the skeletal branches. People who had collected acorns years before and grown Toomer's seedlings in their front yards, TP-ed their trees in solidarity. A former Auburn fullback named Tellie Embery said, "I just wanted my kids to get a chance to do this one time before it changes, because it's truly something else. It's still beautiful to see the tissue flowing in the wind."

The original Toomer's Oaks have been sawed down, chopped up, and taken away to be transformed into holy relics, precious as splinters of the True Cross, but much cheaper. For $29.95, you get a photo of the oaks, matted and framed and "delivered without a front panel so one can touch the Authentic Oak!"

Alabama is America's second leading producer of wood pulp, and home of Georgia-Pacific, Gulf States, and Kimberly-Clark, makers of fine bathroom papers. Somebody ought to write a learned article on the symbolic uses of toilet paper by devotees of Alabama's two major institutions of higher learning: at AU they throw it; at UA they tape it to a box of detergent impaled on a stick, creating a pictographic representation of the cheer "Roll, Tide, Roll!"

One of the charges brought against poisoner Harvey Updyke was desecration of a venerated object. While his lawyer argued that Toomer's Oaks did not meet the standard for venerated object and requested "this Honorable Court to take judicial notice that the oak trees in question are routinely rolled with toilet paper," everybody, Bammer or Barner, knew better. Oaks are holy. Tuscaloosa calls itself the Druid City—*drus* is "oak" in ancient Greek—maybe because of some deep-lodged folk memory of the god in the oaks of Ireland or Zeus's grove at Dodona, where the priestesses would "read" the oracular rustling of the wind in the leaves.

Such is the power of the oaks that they could—for a month or two—transcend the cell-level hatred between Alabama and Auburn. A few weeks after Updyke confessed to poisoning Auburn's sacred trees, some UA alumni started a charity called Tide for Toomer's and raised $50,000 for the oaks' medical care. A couple of months later, when a murderous tornado hit Tuscaloosa, Auburn returned the favor with Tigers 4T-Town and Toomer's for Tuscaloosa.

The people of the Tide were genuinely grateful to the people of the Plains, and it was, after all, spring, when the hatred lies not dormant, exactly, but at least in a state of drowsiness. The tornado had yanked some of Tuscaloosa's old oaks out by the roots, throwing them down on streets and cars. It hacked the branches and tops off others. There was a picture circulated of a live oak that once would have been thirty or forty feet tall, broken off at ten feet and split like a divining rod. Somebody had tacked a UA flag on it.

Here's the sad truth: for every donor to Tide for Toomer's, there were probably five guys posting stuff on ESPN.com like "Why didn't he just go ahead and poison that fucking eagle??? RTR." Or this unrepentant columnist for Capstone Report, an elaborate pro-Alabama site with exhaustive coverage of SEC football and photos of Crimson Tide majorette booty, snarking: "Updyke took from the Auburn Fambly one of their most prized traditions: Throwing butt paper in trees following an Auburn win, or a meaningful Alabama loss. And I for one am glad he did it. Hurl the insults at me if you will, but you are lying if you're an Alabama fan and you say you're saddened by what he did."

Back to normal, then. In June 2013, Updyke was released from the Lee County lockup, rocking a set of Yosemite Sam whiskers. He's on probation until 2018 and banned for life from Auburn; indeed, he's forbidden to attend any collegiate sporting event anywhere ever until the end of time. His lawyer said, "He can't go to a Louisiana Tech track meet. I mean, he can't go *anywhere*."

Updyke's silvicide will never be forgotten, not as long as oaks stand, not as long as there's football, not as long as there's toilet paper. For all the pious talk of unity and sportsmanship, Auburn will recall the original trees, the mind growing them bigger, making them older, prettier, finer, endowing them with personal legend—the first kiss under Toomer's, the epic breakup under Toomer's, the epiphany in which the Meaning of Life and the Order of the Universe burned cold and bright as a star under the kind, old branches. And Auburn will transmit hatred of Harvey Updyke like a legend of ancient persecution. Updyke's crime will become part of the long story of perfidious Alabama. The Crimson Tide will continue to express official disapproval of Updyke: he's vulgar, white-trashy; he behaves the way Alabama fans say Auburn fans behave. Yet when they spotted Updyke on Bourbon Street the night before the 2012 Sugar Bowl, they wanted their pictures taken with him. Updyke is Alabama's id, its unfettered, mullet-sporting, g-dropping inner redneck, for whom hating Auburn is practically a sacrament.

In 2012, Updyke called Paul Finebaum's radio show—he'd originally confessed his sin on air eighteen months before. Now notorious, banned from the Alabama campus, he claimed he'd been beaten up, yelled at, threatened with death. He was penitent, sort of, acknowledging he'd hurt people and looking to history for an exculpatory story. He reminded Finebaum about "Tommy Lewis and the '54 Cotton Bowl. He came off the bench and tackled the Rice player. They asked him, 'Why'd you do it?' He said, 'I just have too much Bama in me.'"

Then Updyke signed off: "Roll, damn Tide."

Chapter 5

BIG GAME

OCTOBER 8, 1966: Florida State takes the field against the University of Florida. So far this season, FSU has lost a close one (to Houston), and won an even closer one against a rival everybody said they couldn't beat. As *Tallahassee Democrat* sports columnist Bill McGrotha put it, the Seminoles "rose up and stuffed press clippings down Miami's not-so-invulnerable throat here Saturday night."

None of that matters. This is the Gator game, the serious test, the game that governs the emotional climate for at least the next twelve months. FSU boasts some marquee talent in soon-to-be All-American flanker Ron Sellers, but Florida has Steve Spurrier, the favorite for the Heisman Trophy, quarterbacking the Gators as though he's auditioning for the part of Mephistopheles: icy and ruthless. Last season he put up two hundred or more yards in every game he played. This afternoon, Spurrier throws for three touchdowns. No interceptions. FSU leads the game several times, but it doesn't matter; Spurrier keeps coming back, relentless as a rash.

The Gators in the stands wear buttons that say, NEVER, FSU, NEVER.

Fourth quarter. The Seminoles trail 22–19. With seventeen seconds to go, FSU has the ball on the Florida 45. Ron Sellers is laid out on the bench, sucking air after a wallop to the solar plexus. Lane

Fenner, who hasn't played a down all season, goes in. He's six five, a junior, majoring in geology. He's a bit of a rebel; Coach says he "doesn't like rules." He's supposedly some kind of bohemian: they say he took ballet; they say he refused to join the Fellowship of Christian Athletes; they say that when the Seminoles were in El Paso preparing for the Sun Bowl, he went missing for a while and was finally found in a cave, examining the rocks.

Seminole QB Gary Pajcic calls full-right, 82, Z-up. Fenner hauls ass deep, beating two defenders, as Pajcic crafts a forty-five-yard pass as lovely and sure as a young mullet leaping in a freshwater spring. Fenner reaches, nabs the ball, and half-falls into the end zone, scoring six for the Seminoles.

Except he doesn't. Or, to be more correct, one Doug Moseley, the Southeastern Conference field judge, says he doesn't. The catch is ruled "no catch." Ref says Lane Fenner does not have control of the ball when his feet go down. Lane Fenner begs to differ. Later, the film confirms it; the pictures in the papers confirm it; Fenner's in bounds, across the goal line. In a just universe, in a universe not run by Gators, it's six points. It's a Seminole win.

You have to understand: It still bothers us. We still talk about it. As part of the ritual of dread, hope, and anger the week before FSU plays Florida at the end of November, Florida newspapers revisit the Catch and the Bad Call so often the picture of Lane Fenner in the end zone is seared into the brains of Seminoles young enough to be Lane Fenner's grandchildren. The Great Injustice happened half a century ago, but so what? You can still rouse the Irish to hot rage over the Battle of the Boyne in 1690.

Consider Thomas Kent "T. K." Wetherell, FSU class of '68, a man with a pretty impressive postgraduation career: professor, politician, speaker of the Florida House. Before all that, he was a Seminole wideout; he played in the 1966 game; and no, he is not over it. Moseley's call was sheer effrontery: "You can see the catch. You see the goal line. You see the sideline. He's two feet in bounds."

The University of Florida's not over it, either. Down at the capitol, Governor Lawton Chiles, one of those UF supporters so all-in they're called Bull Gators, used to make it his business to torment T. K. Wetherell—then in the House of Representatives—every blessed year just before the UF-FSU game, cackling, "Fenner was in. We knew it. You knew it. But you still lost."

When Wetherell became president of FSU in 2002, he retaliated, ordering the official team histories to "adjust" the score of the 1966 game to 25–22, as if the touchdown had been allowed. He had the famous photos of Fenner's touchdown blown up and hung in the president's mansion and in the president's box at Doak Campbell Stadium. The urinals in his executive men's room had strategically placed orange and blue Gator heads. When his dear friend quarterback Gary Pajcic died of a rare form of viral encephalitis in 2006, forty years on, Wetherell made the usual correct pronouncements about Pajcic as a father, a citizen, a lawyer, and a good man, but did not hold back on reminding the world of Pajcic's mighty throw and Fenner's catch: "By God, it was in bounds," said Wetherell. "It was in bounds then and it's in bounds now."

Mere hours after the 1966 game, somebody printed thousands of copies of the Fenner photo. It spread around Tallahassee like hookworm, showing up in dorm rooms and living rooms and state offices, taped to the insides of lockers and the outsides of mirrors, on telephone poles and by cash registers in diners and gas stations. At the bottom: "Lest We Forget."

"Lest We Forget" is the motto inscribed on all those Daughters of the Confederacy-sponsored memorials to the rebel dead of the Civil War. The phrase comes from the refrain of Rudyard Kipling's 1897 poem "Recessional": "Lord God of Hosts, be with us yet, / Lest we forget—lest we forget!"

God knows what Kipling, gloomily warning the British Empire against the sin of pride in the year of Queen Victoria's Diamond Jubilee, or the Daughters, who revised America's bloodiest war into a defeat so stirring and so romantic it more or less morphed into a victory, would think of a college football team kidnapping this solemn phrase to memorialize a win unjustly snatched away by the dark forces of refereedom. On second thought, the Daughters of the Confederacy would love it. The South breeds grandiosity like pond water breeds mosquitoes. Most of our plantation "mansions" might have been bare-board cottages with dirt yards, but their owners named them after English castles or novels by Sir Walter Scott; your ride may be an '84 Trans Am or a Subaru BRAT, but it's pimped out, raised up on tires taller than a quarter horse and wearing more spangles and furbelows than a Cotton Queen contestant. And that's not simple fruit salad: it's got grated coconut, so we call it ambrosia, the Food of the Gods.

I had one of those "Lest We Forget" pictures of Lane Fenner when I was little. My father might have given it to me; I don't remember. I kept it in a Romeo y Julieta cigar box along with my other Seminole relics: ticket stubs, the little gold metal footballs out of my mother's Homecoming corsages, the playing-card-size FSU schedules with the picture of Steve Tensi or Fred Biletnikoff on the back, the faded garnet ribbon printed vertically in gold: GO TO HELL GATORS.

I remember—I think I remember, anyway—my parents coming home from the 1966 game, my father in a door-slamming temper, my mother, who had a lot of experience dealing with post-loss hissy fits, paying the babysitter and hustling her out the door, the house quiet in the early autumn evening. Only church to look forward to tomorrow and Daddy watching *The Bill Peterson Show* on TV so he could yell at the coach. Who could not, of course, hear him.

By the next FSU-Florida game, the one in Gainesville in 1967, my father was dead, and I inherited his tickets.

SECOND QUARTER

Chapter 6

OLD-TIME RELIGION

I'D SWEAR FEATHER BOAS were involved, though that may be a post hoc delusion. There was definitely bumping and grinding. As the University of Alabama's Million Dollar Band played "Just a Closer Walk with Thee"—not the earnest version everybody knows, but some syncopated, Blaze Starr–at–the–Sho Bar, down-and-dirty arrangement—the Crimsonettes flung their batons on the grass behind them and danced, offering first one sequined hip, then the other, miming the slow, stripperish peeling off of long evening gloves.

Not that anyone would confuse Crimsonettes with red-hot mamas, despite their tight sparkly outfits, despite their attempts at come-hither pouts. Booty-shaking to a jazz funeral song made famous by the Selah Jubilee Singers qualifies as one of those moments of glorious incongruity for which America is justly famous: sex and God and war (those helmeted and armored soldiers of the gridiron who'll run back to battle as soon as halftime is over) and ninety thousand people seat-dancing to "Just a closer walk with Thee: / Grant it, Jesus, is my plea! / Daily walking close to Thee: / Let it be, dear Lord, let it be."

The Crimsonettes are as wholesome as a glass of 2 percent milk, altar girls serving in the football minster. Yet that line of glossy-haired, cherry-lipped girls high-kicking for the Crimson Tide suggests something at once voluptuous and Darwinian: prized beauties destined to be the mates of alpha males, a reward for the purest of heart and the toughest of tacklers, sort of like the Hadith's seventy-two Virgins of Paradise.

In the stadium, we affirm a creed of violence and conquest: the Bible says God is love, but surely He likes to see a prideful quarterback taken down with a righteous sack. We sing hymns of submission to the Lord—I am weak but Thou art strong; / Jesus keep me from all wrong!"—but we pray for a king-hell open-field tackle. Hit him! Harder! No wonder throughout the South and the Midwest, you hear gospel from the marching band and singing in the stands: "Closer Walk," "I'm So Glad," and "Old-Time Religion," which I've heard played straight up and bouncy by the Florida A&M band, and syncopated with an "Indian" tom-tom beat by the FSU band. It's both a lively old Jubilee song and perfect athletic anthem celebrating the past, mama and daddy, suffering, Israel, and the coming apocalypse. "It was good for the Prophet Daniel"—Daniel, you will recall, emerged from the Babylonian lions' den as unscathed and smiling as Kenny "the Snake" Stabler from the 1967 Nebraska defense. Football is Old Testament, old-time religion, rage and ritual and miracle, an affirmation of pain given and pain received. As the song goes: "It was tried in the fiery furnace, / It was tried in the fiery furnace, / It was tried in the fiery furnace, / And it's good enough for me!"

On a wall in a Tuscaloosa bar, Bear Bryant as the God of Creation hands the National Championship's crystal football to an Adamic Nick Saban. The commandments as rewritten in a devotional volume called *Bama, Bear Bryant and the Bible*, begin with "Thou shalt have no other college teams before the Crimson Tide," go on to III, "Remember the Game Day and keep it Holy"; VII, "Thou shalt not steal, except to dishonor Auburn or Tennessee"; and X, "Thou shalt not covet another team's apparel." Bob Ufer, the Voice of the Wolverines from 1935 to 1981, used to say, "In Michigan, football is a religion, and Saturday is a holy day of obligation"; in Florida we accord football coaches the status of canonized intercessor, even while they're still alive: we drive around with genuflecting bumper stickers. HAIL, ST. BOWDEN.

Penn State folk continue to teeter on the horns of an eschatological dilemma: did the Elevator Invisible convey Joe Paterno up or down? In 2012, shortly after Paterno died, a cartoonist drew Bear Bryant welcoming his longtime rival through the Pearly Gates. Another cartoonist countered with the Bear throwing JoePa out of heaven as if he were Almighty God evicting a rebel angel. On July 4, 2013, a cloud weirdly resembling JoePa in profile appeared over Mount Nittany—a deep blue cloud, Penn State blue! A sign! True Believers tweeted and retweeted the picture as if it were an apparition every bit as holy as the Virgin Mary's famous 2004 manifestation on a grilled cheese sandwich.

God is so all over college football, you'd think He played for Amos Alonzo Stagg back in the day. In South Bend, Jesus stands tall on a huge mural at one end of Notre Dame stadium, signaling touchdowns eternal. In Tallahassee, where people use their cars to proselytize, you've got the ichthus, the classic Jesus fish; Jesus's supposed enemy, the Darwin fish (complete with little evolving feet); and, beginning in 2013, a fish called Jameis, after FSU's Heisman-winning quarterback. Seminoles who found that too subtle could also buy a T-shirt with Jameis Winston's face cack-handedly Photoshopped onto Jesus Christ's head. Sporting unfortunate hair extensions, Jameis looks like he's off to a toga party wearing a number 5 where Jesus's burning, bloodied heart should be.

When the University of Georgia Bulldogs came from behind to beat South Carolina for the SEC Championship in 2002, Head Coach Mark Richt wouldn't talk ball until he'd given "thanks to my Lord and Savior, Jesus Christ." After Alabama beat Texas in the 2010 national championship game, Longhorn quarterback Colt McCoy didn't whine, even though he had a pinched nerve in his throwing shoulder: "God's in control of my life and, if nothing else, I'm standing on the Rock," he said. "It's what was supposed to happen, and I just thank God I handled it the way He wanted me to handle it."

A college football game is at once high mass and tent revival, rich in ceremony and mystery, emotionally incontinent, unabashedly in touch with the supernatural. A receiver scoring six on a forty-yard frozen rope

causes the heavens to rejoice, the cherubim to sing praises, and the arch-
angels to high-five in jubilation. Or so we have been led to believe. The
player points to the sky: *Yo, Jehovah!* This is church, except longer—unless
you belong to one of those Holiness outfits with the two-hour sermons
and the snake handling. Divine service on Sunday and Saturdays down
at the stadium ring with hymns, chanting, creeds. We sit, we stand, we
raise our hands and testify. We weep, we wail, we're filled with the Spirit.
Some have been known to speak in tongues. And always, we observe the
time-honored rituals. In the Liturgy of the Eucharist, we sing the Sanctus.
At the First Presbyterian Church, we affirm, "I believe in God the Father
Almighty, Maker of Heaven and Earth and in Jesus Christ His only Son,
our Lord." At Reynolds Razorback Stadium, we call, "Woooooooo Pig!
Sooie!" At Temple Beth-El, we pronounce, "Hear, Israel, the Lord is our
God, the Lord is One." At Bryant-Denny, we proclaim, "Rammer Jam-
mer, Yellowhammer, / Give 'em hell, Alabama!" The "Ten Thousand Men
of Harvard," exhort the team in dog Latin:

> *Illegitimum Non Carborundum;*
> *Domine, salvum fac.*
> *Illegitimum Non Carborundum;*
> *Domine, salvum fac.*
> *Gaudeamus igitur!*
> *Veritas non sequitur?*
> *Illegitimum non Carborundum—ipso facto!*

Experiencing the Divine takes us out of our limited bodies. Experiencing football, if you truly believe, does something similar. The
game pierces our hearts the way the angel stabbed Saint Teresa with
a golden lance, over and over and over. She wrote: "The pain was so
great, that it made me moan; and yet so surpassing was the sweetness
of this excessive pain, that I could not wish to be rid of it."

That's exactly how it feels to watch FSU play the University of
Florida every damned year.

Chapter 7

CONSECRATED GROUND

I HAVE RULES: I don't wear white shoes after Labor Day. I don't do décolleté before three o'clock. I don't go casual to football games. No FEAR THE SPEAR T-shirts, no SUCKS TO BE U, no GO 'NOLES! with or without apostrophe.

People wear any damn thing to church, too. These days college game attendees blossom forth in novelty sweatshirts featuring teddy bears waving school pennants, Nike gear ('cause if I'm in a number 8 jersey, I'll channel the awesome power of Marcus Mariota!), foam hands, temporary tattoos, permanent tattoos, feathers, glitter, cowboy hats, face paint, body paint. They want to proclaim their team allegiance. They want to attract the ESPN camera. They want to be *comfortable*, though since when is comfort a component of worship?

Honorable holdouts include older alums of HBCUs, such as Florida A&M and Spelman, who still bust out the pearls and the hats for Homecoming, as well as Greeks at Alabama and Chapel Hill, Ole Miss Grovers, the Republican gentry of South Carolina, and pretty much everybody at Sewanee, who go the full 1960s country club prêt-à-porter with Sperrys and khakis, Lilly Pulitzer sheaths, and caps featuring whales, ducks, or Labrador retrievers in bow ties.

In Oxford one October Saturday, I witnessed a couple of elegant young women wrestle their outfits to a draw in the ladies' room at Vaught-Hemingway Stadium. The Rebels were up five or six touchdowns on Arkansas State, and the cocktails, which can render almost any fashion martyrdom—four-inch heels, say, or a boned bodice—tolerable, had worn off. I refreshed my lipstick very slowly, watching them in the mirror. "This scarf is driving me *insane*," said one, hauling off an Isadora Duncanish length of chiffon and shaking it like a wet towel. "It keeps whomping me in the face."

The other one, with twenty-four-karat-colored hair and a fraternity lavalier, hiked up her navy piqué shift to pull at the legs of her Spanx Skinny Britches. "These goddamn things," she said. Both girls were slim as birch saplings. "*Goddamn* things!"

Il faut souffrir pour être belle, y'all. I admired these young women for their insistence on dressing for the ball game as their mothers and grandmothers had, despite the suffering—suffering is what it's about: in the pew, on the field, in the stands. No pain, no gain, as Preacher says. Or is that Coach? Southern Protestantism is big on travails and sorrow and sinfulness and sermons on how winning in this life means nothing if you don't score in the next life. Faith must be tested, whether that test takes the form of a 320-pound tackle heading straight at you or a vicious Lycra body shaper. College football's devoted pilgrims know what it's like to flounder in the Slough of Despond. What looks like charming modesty is really self-loathing mixed with hostility. Remember, the white South long ago figured out how to glamorize losing. If we can't come out on top, we can at least pretend to be self-deprecating. Here's an Old Miss Rebel's open letter to the Longhorns in 2013, challenging Texas's lofty claims to football pitifulness:

When you inundated our fine city last year with your gaudy burnt orange apparel, your ridiculous cowboy hats, your second-rate actors and women, we smiled and politely offered you our cold chicken tenders and backup bourbon and pretended to enjoy your company.

But now you've gone too far. This we cannot abide, so let's get this straight right now: You do not shit the bed. *We* shit the bed. Read that again. Repeat it. Tell it to your friends. We scoff at your pedestrian attempts at bed shitting. So you got blown out by BYU. Well, bully for you. Now you think you get to run around whining, lamenting the fact it's been eight years since your last national championship. On behalf of legitimate bed-shitting programs everywhere: How dare you?

You want to talk about shitting the bed? Please. Perhaps you were surprised when you lost to BYU in such embarrassing fashion. We were not. It is all part of the setup: "Texas gets trounced by BYU and now a feisty 2-0 Ole Miss team, which has just entered the rankings for the first time since 2009 (that's right, 2009), travels to Austin for a winnable game against a prestigious but vulnerable program in the midst of a coaching controversy with an inept defense and a new (but still shitty) defensive coordinator and an angry fan base." We're supposed to be getting our hopes up right now, but we're old hands at this. We know how this movie ends.

So say it with me now: Ole Miss will shit the bed Saturday. We do not know the precise method of our downfall, but rest assured that the bed will be shat. The conventional wisdom among more rational Ole Miss fans is that Bo Wallace will throw between four and seven interceptions in the first half before his surgically repaired rotator cuff implodes and he's replaced by Barry Brunetti, who will promptly begin pitching forward laterals directly to your fastest defenders before stepping aside gallantly like a torero facing an oncoming bull. . . . Our offense will sputter, our play calling will be nonsensical, our defense will look like, well, like it did last year, our best players will get injured, etc. We know the drill.

Remember this prophesy Saturday night as the clock ticks down to zero and you're smiling down upon the field and your newly revived football season, wondering how it all came to pass. Your lackluster attempts at bed shitting are embarrassing, you bunch of wannabe cowboy, faux-hippie, bed-shitting amateurs. Prepare to see the real deal. We shit beds like you for breakfast.

I respect the University of Mississippi's time on the cross. I do. But Seminoles know more about real humiliation than the Rebels ever will. I'm not just talking about the way the Oregon Ducks kicked the Seminoles to death with their webbed feet in the 2015 playoff game and jeered at Jameis Winston with "No means no!" while performing the tomahawk chop, though that did hurt; I don't even mean 2012's shaming 17–16 loss to NC State (NC State!), the Gators' ignominious blowout (45–12) of FSU in 2007, or the disheartening drag-ass procession of one- or two-point "wide right" losses to Miami in the 1980s and 1990s, No, I'm talking about years in the wilderness: the 1-10 season in 1974; the 0-11 season of 1973. That was pain; that was abasement.

But suffering, along with moments of transcendence, makes the football field holy, sanctified by the sweat (always) and blood (sometimes) of martyrs, exalted by more than a century of brain-rattling, bone-snapping, ligament-ripping games, trod by the righteous cleats of heroes, graced by the satin-shod feet of Homecoming Queens, and ennobled by the ashes of the fanatical dead.

Stadiums are to college-town America what cathedrals were to the cities of Europe: assertions of engineering sophistication, power, affluence, architectural swagger, the biggest structure for miles around, the edifice for the great occasions of life: baptisms, marriages, funerals, rivalry games. The cathedral and the stadium assert the community's identity, God's majesty, the alumni's pride. "The Church of Nick Saban," an Alabama Facebook page, doesn't bother to be metaphorical: "Bryant-Denny is our Cathedral (much more awesome than the Catholic version if you ask me). Football is our ritual. Cheerleaders lead prayers. The Million Dollar Band plays our hymns. The players are our Saints. Nick Saban is our God."

In the twelfth century, French townsfolk hitched themselves to carts and dragged timber and stone to the building site at Chartres, helping to raise the great cathedral, proclaiming themselves the Blessed Virgin's number-one fans. In College Station, pious disciples of Aggie football collected several hundred million dollars to expand Kyle Field because, according to the 12th Man Foundation, it makes the "statement that the Aggies do not settle, we commit to excellence in everything we do. A redeveloped Kyle Field will amplify and honor our past and our traditions while expanding the intimidation factor."

Not to mention expanding the boasting factor: new Kyle holds 1,393 more people than Darryl K. Royal in Austin. Texas. Size fetish. Medieval France likewise: at Notre Dame de Chartres they'll point out their church is bigger than Notre Dame de Paris. Immensity is part of the full cathedral experience. You go there to experience the grand, the numinous, to glimpse immortality. Same with a football stadium. In 1994, when FSU, down 31–3 at the beginning of the fourth quarter, scored 28 points to tie the Gators, every Seminole learned the meaning of resurrection, every Seminole saw Doak Campbell Stadium bathed in the golden light of glory.

Cathedrals are all about miracles: during the first week of Lent in 1287, Edith Oldecriste went insane. Her husband carried her to Hereford Cathedral and left her tethered near the tomb of Saint Thomas de Cantilupe. By Palm Sunday, she was perfectly rational. Miracles happen in stadiums, too, as Auburn Tigers will testify. During the 2013 Georgia game, a pass ricocheted off a Bulldog receiver's hand, landing in the arms of a Tiger. Monsignor William Skonecki of the Church of Saint Michael the Archangel in Auburn declared it an "Immaculate Deflection," though in Mississippi, that term refers to the 40-mph gust of wind in 1983 that blew a sure-thing Mississippi State field goal off course, allowing Ole Miss to prevail 24–23. In any case, God seemed to love Auburn in 2013. As the clock sighed to double zeros at the end of the Iron Bowl, Tiger cornerback Chris Davis ran Alabama's missed last-tick field-goal attempt back 109 yards for the winning touchdown.

Davis's transfiguring score further hallowed the already revered turf of Jordan-Hare. After that victory, groundskeepers discovered cremated remains near the 40. Whether from human or critter no one knows, but Scott McElroy, a professor of crop and soil science at Auburn, told reporters, cremains don't make good fertilizer: "It kills the grass," said Dr. McElroy.

In the 2014 Iron Bowl at Bryant-Denny, WTVY reporter Taylor Tannebaum tweeted that a Tide acolyte "just dumped his grandpa's ashes on the field in front of me." Apparently, some of grandpa blew all over a state trooper standing guard on the sidelines. But what's a little discolored turf or bone ash up your nose compared to the person so committed to the church of RollTideRoll or War-damn-Eagle that someone sacked up the mortal remains, carried them onto the field in the heaving, joyful, post-win melee, and dispersed them? This is not evidence merely of love but of the stadium's democratic spirit. Only princesses and prelates, saints, poets, prime ministers, and famous generals get their ashes deposited in the likes of Westminster Abbey or Saint Peter's Basilica. All you need to achieve football immortality is a surviving family member with a ticket to the game and a Ziploc sandwich bag.

Same with weddings. You don't have to be royal to enter into the sacrament of matrimony in your favorite stadium: anybody with a ring and a rental fee can do it. In May 2012, Michigan alumna Elaine Ng suited up in a white strapless crinoline and walked from the Wolverines' locker room into the Big House. There she pledged her troth to Andy Li. Go Blue! You can jump the broom where the South Carolina Gamecocks play, where the Cal Bears play, and under the flagpole in the north end zone of Ohio State's horseshoe-shaped ball field, which, according to the brochure, offers "a breathtaking backdrop for a wedding with the scoreboard behind you and 105,000 empty seats around you."

Wedding parties (groomsmen in Buckeye gray, bridesmaids wearing Buckeye scarlet) pose for pictures in Ohio Stadium's Rotunda, which is, the university wishes you to know, a copy of the

Pantheon in Rome. The original was dedicated to all the gods, from Apollo, God of Reason, whose motto was "nothing in excess," to Terminus, God of Boundaries, whose motto, *Concedo nulli*—"I give no ground"—reveals him to be God of Defensive Tackles, too. The tall arches ringing the rest of OU's stadium replicate another Roman landmark, the Colosseum, proclaiming it a place of worship and of violence, reverence and sacrifice, pious devotion and gladiatorial whup-ass.

Doak S. Campbell Stadium at Florida State is Gothic to Ohio State's classical Roman, with clock towers, bar tracery, battlements, bosses, crockets, lancets, and clerestory windows. Like any self-respecting cathedral, it's rich in devotional statues, mostly located in the parking lots where five-figure boosters tailgate. There's *Seminole Family*, a sculptural group of Native American mother, father, and child depicted at the time of the Second Seminole War, when the United States government did its damnedest to run them out of Florida. There's the famous *Unconquered*, an equestrian Osceola raising high his light-up spear, and *Sportsmanship*, in which a player Extends the Hand of Gentlemanly Fair Play to the Worthy Opponent whose sorry butt he just tackled. There's Bobby Bowden, too, guarding the north end zone. People touch his bronze Nikes the way pilgrims to Santiago de Compostela caress the feet of the apostle.

The ecclesiastical look doesn't stop there: Doak Campbell's Great West Window is only slightly smaller than the North Rose Window of Washington's National Cathedral. Hand-assembled from 8,500 pieces of stained glass by fourteen artisans in the university's Master Craftsman program, it's a throwback to medieval technology. So's the design: just as the unlettered folk of the Middle Ages learned the lives of the saints in glass, the stadium window recounts the Seminoles' *Legenda aurea* in hallowed jersey numbers—16 for Heisman Trophy–winner Chris Weinke, 17 for Heisman Trophy–winner Charlie Ward, and 28, worn by both Warrick Dunn, the three-time Pro Bowl running back and philanthropist, and Florida State president T. K. Wetherell when he was a star player for the Seminoles, all

grouped around the central colossus: FSU's legendary, lauded, belau-
reled Bobby Bowden, who stands nearly three stories high. Next to
him, Oklahoma State's Pistol Pete, rendered in colored glass at Boone
Pickens Stadium, looks like a third-string angel hanging around the
lower corner of a window in a suburban Baptist sanctuary.

Chapter 8

GOD IS MY OFFENSIVE COORDINATOR

ROBERT CLECKLER "BOBBY" BOWDEN came down from the mountains to FSU in the bicentennial year of 1976. At West Virginia, they'd put For Sale signs in front of his house and hanged him in effigy. Tallahassee had kind of a genteel reputation. Besides, it was a lot closer to Birmingham, his hometown, and Tuscaloosa, the Holy See of Southern football. Bear Bryant would retire—or die—someday. Bowden would surely be in line to inherit his mentor's crimson mantle. In the meantime, he'd been hired to transform a wretched program with a record of 19-37 since 1971, an errant flock who obviously needed a firm, Pauline course correction.

Seminoles swiftly fell in love with him: *such nice manners!* a cross between Rhett Butler and Billy Graham, a Bible-witnessing, witticism-spouting, mama-complimenting, twinkly-eyed self-deprecating Southern performance artist with a first-rate line in charming bullshit. Not like the last head coach, the cerebral Midwesterner Darrell Mudra, with his PhD, his suspicious tolerance of hippiedom, and his strange habit of calling plays from the press box. Bowden endeared himself to grown folks worried about weed smoking, nakedness— Florida State claims to have invented streaking—and communist professors. Bowden didn't take much stock in that separation-of-church-

and-campus business: "I do not want our boys to smoke, drink or cut classes. And I encourage church attendance."

Bowden is extravagantly devout: he and Jesus are like *that*. He may not be on the sideline anymore, but he's still a presence in pulpits, testifying to the twin glories of God and the no-huddle offense. His 2014 book, *The Wisdom of Faith*, lauds (in this order) Faith, Family, and Football. Bowden never apologizes for lacing his football with Christianity and his Christianity with football, telling a BeliefNet interviewer in 2013, "So many coaches think you've got to kick your players in the rear end. You've got to cuss them out. You've got to hit them across the head. No. You don't have to do that. You don't have to touch a kid. You don't have to scream at a kid. But you can take the principles of the Bible and you can take the principles of Jesus Christ and transfer them right into coaching."

Which he did, never mind that his employer was bound by a constitutional prohibition on the endorsement of any particular religion. What, you want those young 'uns to burn in *hell*? In 2009, former Seminole defensive end (1993–1997) and All-American Andre Wadsworth, told ESPN: "Coach Bowden was a father figure to all of us. He told us he was going to treat all of us like his sons, and that's what he did. The first day, he told us he didn't want us sleeping with women because he thought sex should be saved for marriage. He told us he didn't want us drinking, even after we turned twenty-one."

In football's tribal lands, God and the Constitution trip over each other all the time. Ohio State coach Urban Meyer told the *Columbus Dispatch* in 2012 that he would lead Bible study for his players. The university president swiftly issued a "clarification": Meyer would not, in fact, be teaching Sunday school in the locker room. Auburn chaplain Chette Williams was a three-year letterman for the Tigers in the early 1980s. Now he reads scripture with the team. When the *Huntsville Times* asked him in August 2013 to predict how Auburn's season would go, he said, "This year, we're going to see a lot of guys cross the finish line for Jesus." In 2014, University of Connecticut running-backs coach Ernest Jones informed the *Hartford Courant* his players would "understand that Jesus Christ should be in the center of our huddle."

UConn president Susan Herbst had to flag Jones—too many men on the field: "Our employees cannot appear to endorse or advocate for a particular religion or spiritual philosophy as part of their work at the university, or in their interactions with our students." UConn women's basketball coach Geno Auriemma weighed in: "Like God gives a crap that you made eighteen jump shots."

But God has his favorites: He wanted George W. Bush to be president. He roots for Argentina (how else to explain Maradona's goal in the 1986 World Cup quarters?) and, of course, Notre Dame. On October 19, 2014, the day FSU played Clemson, a headline in the Tallahassee *Democrat* asked, all wide-eyed, "Does God Care Who Wins Football Games?"

Americans United for Separation of Church and State, the American Civil Liberties Union, and other watchdog groups regularly fuss about football coaches leading their teams in the Lord's Prayer, driving them to church, and witnessing to the faith morning, noon, and night. Such secular arguments bounce right off the adamantine walls of the Church of College Football. The Freedom from Religion Foundation repeatedly tries to get the University of Tennessee to cease public prayers before every home football game (UT says the prayers are "nonsectarian") and encourages Clemson to stop "evangelizing on the football team." FFRF charges Tiger head coach Dabo Swinney pushes his players to be born again. Swinney doesn't deny it: he's been known to place a livestock trough on the 50-yard line at Death Valley for players to be baptized in, pads and all, and tells prospects, "I'm a Christian. If you have a problem with that, you don't have to be here."

Ebo Ogundeko, a defensive end from Brooklyn, had no problem with that. On the contrary: he told *The Chronicle of Higher Education* in 2013 that he liked the way that at Clemson "most dudes on the team, they take their religion very seriously, and their relationship with Jesus Christ." Like his coach and many of his teammates, Ogundeko proclaims his faith every chance he gets, including on Twitter

@Ebenezer_O_1. Along with unstartling post-adolescent male sentiments such as, "A McChicken sounds so good right now!" (March 4, 2013) and "I'm really convinced that females are crazy!" (March 15, 2013), he witnesses via retweet: "If we say that we have no sin, we are deceiving ourselves and the truth is not in us.—1 John 1:8" and "I might not be perfect but Jesus thinks I'm to die for!"

Dabo Swinney denies that he runs a pray-to-play program: "I've had Muslims, Catholics—I've got two Mormons on this team right now."

Clemson's not Bob Jones, the private fundamentalist college up the road in Greenville, which teaches "young-earth creationism" in science class. Clemson is intellectually respectable, ranked in the nation's top fifty public institutions. Nevertheless, Jesus rules Tiger football. Jeff Davis, co-captain of Clemson's 1981 national championship team and senior pastor of FreeWay Church, is also Clemson's assistant athletic director for player relations. James Trapp is another ex-Clemson player, an Olympic sprinter, and a former NFL back so mean, so prone to personal fouls, that when he played for the Oakland Raiders— the notorious Raiders, who always reveled in their street-fighting reputation—team brass sent him to anger-management classes. Well, he's the Tigers' chaplain. Both Clapp and Davis have offices in the Athletic Department

An out-and-proud atheist could no more take the top coaching job at Alabama or Ohio State than win the White House, no matter what kind of offensive genius he might be. Maybe that would work in New England or on the West Coast. Not in football's core regions, where questioning a coach's Christian bona fides means war. Matt Wyatt, a former Mississippi State player and host of the *Head to Head* sports radio show, mentioned a rumor going around that just before Signing Day 2012, University of Mississippi coach Hugh Freeze told some hotshot recruits that Mississippi State coach Dan Mullen does not believe in God.

This rumor wasn't as bad as the ones in 2010, which held that Dan Mullen was a Scientologist. SEC chat-room snark about Mullen's operating-thetan levels sparked indignation in Starkville. Everyone blamed Ole Miss provocateurs: loyal MSU Bulldogs *knew for a fact* that Mullen belonged to a Methodist congregation. Rebels pointed out that didn't mean jack: Barack Obama sat in the pews at Trinity United Church of Christ for *years*, and everyone knows he's a Muslim Marxist bent on the destruction of America.

Dueling YouTube videos, each depicting the other college as a roiling stew of racism and ungentlemanly language, ensued. The Rebels' entry features MSU's coach (identified as "Pastor Dan Mullen") talking about faith to the plinky sound of "Amazing Grace" played on a child's piano, intercut with MSU players jumping up and down in the locker room chanting, "You niggers over there, you ain't worth shit! You ho's over there, you ain't worth shit!"

The Bulldogs countered with black-and-white footage of the Oxford riots of 1962, a hooded Klansman, and some wasted frat boy snarling, "Fuck those niggers!" as the Ole Miss band plays its famous "Slow Dixie."

There are no atheists in Division I locker rooms. Uncoupling Christianity and college football is like trying to leave butter out of cake. It might be healthier, but it wouldn't taste the same. Coach-style Christianity favors biblical literalism and puritanical self-control; coaches worry more about the bush league of the Seven Deadlies, the likes of lust, gluttony, and sloth, than the top sins of pride, anger, envy, and avarice. Pleasure freaks them out: Bobby Bowden used to warn his assistant coaches that alcohol and promiscuity would get them fired. Indeed, he once dismissed a coach for getting divorced, though he later said he regretted it.

The locker room is sanctified—*1, 2, 3, Jesus!* Now the church is strapping on its pads. Pastors now love to produce sermons equating the gridiron with this mortal coil, sermons with titles like "Football Jesus," "Faith Conditioning in the Fourth Quarter of Life" and "Get in the Game." In 2002, the Reverend Dennis Cocks of New Hope Baptist in Plano, Illinois, preached on what he saw as the striking parallels between football and the Christian life. For starters, God "expects us all to give one hundred percent: the field-goal kicker is only on the field a few times a game, yet he is sometimes the reason the team wins and also loses. We all have jobs to do for the Kingdom."

Reverend Cocks continues: in the huddle, "the preacher (QB) calls the plays from the play-book [Bible]"; you accept your assignment.

> Not everyone can be the quarterback. Not everyone can be a running back. Not everyone can be the middle linebacker. Those are the glory positions. The team needs players in all positions. It needs offensive linemen. Defensive linemen. Special team players. Every position is vital to the team if it is going to win. Without an offensive line, the defense would smother and kill the quarterback.

No shame in being a third-string placekicker. Or even a mere cheerleader. Life is the biggest of big games, and your opponent is Satan.

Football is a grand metaphor for the struggle to live virtuously, especially in a country that can't decide if it worships hedonism or an Old Testament god who inflicts suffering the way Coach inflicts Oklahoma drills on rookies. Hit; take a hit; toughen up; if Coach calls a post route, execute. Just because you think an end-around would have been more effective is no reason to get mouthy with Coach. Coach has a *plan*. Football theology is not subtle. Or nuanced. Or inclusive. It leaves out a lot of people: non-Christians, women. David E. Prince and Jimmy Scroggins, both associated with the Southern Baptist Convention, wrote a piece in 2013 in which they lament:

> Football represents one of the only major American institutions still standing that is exclusively for males and speaks unashamedly about manliness and toughness. Boys are drawn to demanding physical competition against other boys, assertive male leadership, and a cause that demands sacrifice and calculated risk. These are good things that ought to be cultivated on a pathway from boyhood to Christian manhood.

This iteration of "manhood" demands regulation of the body. Lift your weights, run your sprints, stay away from the temptations of drugs, booze, and babes. Problem is, football players tend to be young men, in their teens and early twenties—which is to say, natural idiots. They arrive on campus, testosterone surging and hormones gone anarchic, Superman bodies with Daffy Duck heads. They're not evil, they're unfinished: the frontal lobe, the part of the brain that handles judgment, is not fully connected in males until they're thirty. No matter how righteous the coach, the coach's flock is hardwired to stray.

And stray they do. Midway through Bobby Bowden's first season, after he'd promised to cultivate morals first and take care of football second, star receiver Mike Schumann got busted for cocaine possession. Since 1976, not a year has gone by at FSU (or, to be fair, any other big-time program) without some kind of scandal, from minor eye-rolling idiocy—public drunkenness, marijuana possession, shoplifting, shooting at squirrels on campus—to burglary, battery, and rape. Ron Simmons, All-American noseguard, pled "no contest" to receiving stolen goods in 1981. Deion "Prime Time" Sanders didn't bother to actually attend a class or take any exams in fall 1988. He played in the 1989 Sugar Bowl anyway, grabbing the win-preserving interception in the end zone with four seconds to go.

Maybe it was Christian forbearance and not an overwhelming desire to kick Auburn's ass that led Bowden to forgive Deion and let him play. The kid blew off *classes*, not practice. Maybe it was Christian forgiveness when Bowden wrote a character reference for former FSU running back Michael Gibson, sentenced to four life sentences for rape in 1994: "I can only account for what I know about him when I was recruiting him out of North Florida Christian High School and for the time he was on our football team at Florida State University," Bowden said.

Bowden's successor, Jimbo Fisher, demonstrates a similar moral flexibility. Hit-and-run accident? Domestic violence? Sexual assault? The football players entangled in these allegations got a one-game suspension (at most) and a head-shaking, rueful wish from Coach that they'd make "better choices."

Fisher's response was practically thirty lashes compared to the Tallahassee cops, who declined to charge anybody with anything. In July 2014, Bobo Wilson, given name Jesus, a preternaturally talented wide receiver, "borrowed" another student's Bintelli moped, wrecked it, and found himself charged with a felony. On August 1, Fisher suspended him "indefinitely." By September 1, the felony was reduced to a misdemeanor. "Indefinitely" was over. Fisher cited Bobo's "maturity" in "handling his situation," reinstating him in time for the second game of the season. Miranda Wilhelm, FSU running back Karlos Williams's girlfriend (and mother of his two children) posted photos of bruises, implying he'd hit her. Fisher insisted there was nothing in it. Williams is a "tremendous kid," said Fisher.

Then there's Jameis Winston, getting the Jesus-fish treatment one minute, accused of rape the next. Criticized for bellowing the punch line of a particularly stupid Internet meme, "Fuck her right in the pussy!" in a crowded student union, cited for stealing crab legs from the supermarket, cautioned for shooting at squirrels with a pellet gun on campus, implicated in the same autograph-selling kerfuffle that got Georgia's Todd Gurley suspended for four games, he has miraculously retained Jimbo Fisher's full confidence. OK, he got suspended for the big ACC battle at Clemson over what respectable sports journalists called his "obscene and vulgar language," but except for that one time, Winston played every game on the 2014 schedule. Won every game, too. Jimbo Fisher assures us Winston's "done nothing wrong."

A *Sports Illustrated* survey from 2010 revealed that one in every fourteen players in the top twenty-five programs had been arrested at least once. That doesn't mean they were guilty of anything; many were never even charged with a crime. Fifty percent of young African American men will be arrested for a non-traffic-related reason by the time they're twenty-three; for white men up to the age of twenty-three, it's 38 percent. These numbers tell us more about systemic racism in law enforcement than actual criminality. College football is nevertheless special. Players have a high profile, so off-field infractions get plenty of press. At the same time, it's hard to convict players: the community sympathizes with them, and sometimes cops let them off easy. The *New York Times* examined the close relationship among Seminole Boosters, FSU, and Tallahassee cops—extra pay for policing games and private security work—which meant that officers would give Coach a heads-up when one of his boys got in trouble. Coach would, in turn, vouch for the boy, give him a talking-to, and say he'll see he goes to church.

The real problem here is women. Girls. Warriors used to abstain from sex before battle; football coaches used to warn players not to go near a vagina-toter for twenty-four hours before a game. These women-creatures unman you. They're walking temptation generators. And boys can't help being boys. One night in 2012, a sixteen-year-old got so drunk at a party in Steubenville, Ohio, she couldn't stand, much less consent to anything. Two high school football players raped her. Some of their vile abuse of this girl got captured—inevitably—on some kid's phone. Yet the town, always supportive of the Big Red football team, felt she colluded in her own assault. Nice girls don't get drunk, right? At least one coach wondered what she had been wearing. In 2004, four Brigham Young football players were indicted for gang rape. BYU, run by the Church of Jesus Christ of Latter-Day Saints, is chastity obsessed: you can get kicked out for having consensual sex of any flavor. Two guys were tried. One of their teammates turned state's witness. Didn't matter: the jury acquitted both. As Jeff Benedict and Armen Keteyian relate in *The System*, their fine book on college football, the jury told the stunned prosecutor that since the boys had lost their scholarships, they'd "suffered enough."

According to the Roman Catholic Church, the only perfect woman was Mary, the mother of Christ, the Blessed Virgin and Queen of Heaven. The University of Notre Dame is dedicated to her. But if I were Mary, I wouldn't want to hang out with the Fighting Irish. In 1974, a young woman said six football players gang-raped her. No charges were ever filed; a university administrator referred to the young woman as a "queen of the slums" and said she had "a mattress tied to her back."

Tertullian, a third-century Church Father, liked to call women "the devil's gateway."

When a Notre Dame student claimed she was raped by four players in 2002, university officials discouraged her attempt to press charges; they didn't even want to give her counseling. Defensive back Abram Elam was convicted of felony sexual battery, but that didn't stop him from later playing for the New York Jets and the Cleveland Browns. Lizzy Seeberg committed suicide in 2010, after she said she'd been assaulted by a Notre Dame player and threatened by that player's friend via text: "Messing with notre dame football is a bad idea." Nearly two weeks after Lizzy Seeberg overdosed, the cops still hadn't talked to anyone involved.

It's easy to mistake official piety for actual virtue, as if invoking the name of Jesus acts as some kind of charm against reality. In 2004, Bobby Bowden went out of his way to defend Fisher DeBerry, football coach at the United States Air Force Academy, who allowed a big Fellowship of Christian Athletes banner to hang in his locker room. It said, I AM A CHRISTIAN FIRST AND LAST.

The trouble is, not everyone is a Christian, first or last. Not even all football players. Several Jewish cadets were victims of that old medieval favorite, the blood libel, blamed for being "Christ killers." Coach DeBerry presided over Academy football—perhaps obliviously—during the time when the country discovered male cadets (including football players) raped female cadets with traumatic regularity. A damning, detailed, and well-publicized report came out in 2003; nevertheless, Bobby Bowden appeared at an FCA event in Colorado Springs, loudly sympathizing with DeBerry: "He's fighting a heck of a battle because he happens to be a Christian, and he wants his boys to be saved."

Dozens of college football coaches will tell you they want to run their program the way Bowden ran his, including the part about inviting Jesus into his huddle or his locker room. Here's how Bowden described it: "Every morning that our coaching staff would meet, we started off with a devotion. We'd read scripture and end with a prayer. We'd have seventeen coaches sitting around the table and we'd take turns leading the devotion. I didn't expect them to believe what I believed, but I wanted to hear what they believed. I'm sure the ACLU would be very disappointed in me. I told our president, 'If they ever say anything about it, I'll go underground, because I'm not going to stop.' "

The Fellowship of Christian Athletes named its top player award, the one given to the student-athlete who "conducts himself as a faith model in the community, in the classroom and on the field," for Bobby Bowden.

Chapter 9

MUSCULAR CHRISTIANITY

THE CHURCH HAS NEVER made up its mind about the best way to mortify and subdue the flesh: Do you deny it, like St. Catherine of Siena, who starved herself to death at the symbolic age of thirty-three, or Saint Simeon Stylites, who lived on top of a pillar? Or do you take that leaky, stinky, sin-susceptible vessel and train the fuck out of it: crafting a buff body worthy to house your buff soul? As Paul asks in his first letter to the Corinthians 6:19, "Or do you not know that your body is a temple of the Holy Spirit within you, which you have from God?"

Football—ain't this genius?—does both. The player accepts, even welcomes, the pain he will suffer, a sacrifice for the good of the team. Just like Jesus, come to think of it. At the same time, the player begins to use his body to inflict pain. Not like Jesus, who didn't cotton to stoning, smiting, or generally hurting people. How to square this with football's de facto state church? Muscular Christianity.

The First Church of Christ Linebacker doesn't hold with gentle Jesus meek and mild. The Lord is a tough, manly dude, and football is an allegory of the soul's struggle against evil: Saint George skewering the dragon, Saint Michael kicking the devil's scaly butt. The reverends Prince and Scroggins warn against "the moral, therapeutic deism that equates Christianity with being a nice guy and views God as a benevolent being who helps us be nice guys. Laziness and intentional underachievement, along with a safety-centric worldview, are enemies to the advancement of the gospel. Likewise, there is a price to pay on the football field for laziness and lack of focus."

For fans of Football Jesus, a "benevolent" deity who "helps us be nice guys" is doctrinally suspect. Because nothing says Redeemer like an ass-whupping courtesy of some 340-pound DT. Ken Smith, former chaplain to the Seminoles, the Gamecocks, and other top-shelf teams, told *Sports on Earth*: "I think sometimes we make Jesus out to be a little bit more of a sissy than he was."

Muscles and morality have been entangled since Herodotus glued together the words for "beautiful" and "good," *kalos* and *agathos*, making *kalogathia*: the physically blessed must surely also be virtuous. Jesus and jockery go way back, too. The apostle Paul, a belligerent cuss himself, even after he got knocked upside the head by Jesus on the road to Damascus, employed lots of athletic imagery. He exhorted the young church to be in it to win it: "Train yourself in godliness" (1 Timothy 4:7).

Corinth, site of a Christian community Paul founded and recipient of his epistles, was a center of the sporting world, home of the Isthmian Games, staged every other year from around 600 BC in honor of the sea god Poseidon. "Corinthian" is an elegant, if somewhat antique, term for amateur athlete, and the name of several British and Brazilian football clubs. The Isthmian Games were still a big deal in the first century AD, so Paul, who knew that all church politics was local, wrote to his contrary congregation: "Every athlete exercises self-control in all things." He goes on: "I do not box as one beating the air; but I pommel my body and subdue it, lest after preaching to others I myself should be disqualified." Coach Paul is all about results: "Do you not know that in a race all the runners compete, but only one receives the prize? So run that you may obtain it" (1 Corinthians 9:24–27).

Paul's jock talk forms the theological underpinning of Muscular

Christianity, a movement that bounded onto the field in the mid-nineteenth century—about the same time as college football—and commenced to colonizing the Anglo-American male brain. Muscular Christianity countered what its disciples saw as creeping feminization, women breaking out of the domestic sphere, meddling in politics and society. Women led US and UK antislavery movements; women wrote novels decrying poverty and injustice and gained international fame. Nathaniel Hawthorne famously bitched to his publisher about that "damned mob of scribbling women," women such as Harriet Beecher Stowe, author of *Uncle Tom's Cabin*, and Susan Warner, author of *The Wide, Wide World*, both of whom sold way better than he. As if that weren't upsetting enough for the male ego, a woman, a little, short woman, ruled Britannia, the most powerful nation on earth.

Never mind that most women were wholly owned subsidiaries of their fathers until they married, at which time they became wholly owned subsidiaries of their husbands. Women couldn't go to university, or play sports, or enter a profession, unless it was teacher, writer, or prostitute. Women couldn't vote; women couldn't run for office. Trussed up in whalebone, hoops, and petticoats, women couldn't run, period. Yet men on both sides of the Atlantic feared "the woman peril," what a New York editor and anti-suffrage campaigner named Alexander Harvey darkly described as the "feminization now sapping the national energies." Women had got their dainty hands on religion, too, messing it up with those sentimental hymns and sermons about love and forgiveness.

In England, appalled masculinists pointed to the weedy, pale asceticism of the Oxford Movement with its virgin martyrs, its Mariolatry, its angels sweet as marshmallows, and its girly Jesus as depicted in Holman Hunt's 1854 painting *The Light of the World*. The last thing WASP Christianity needed was to get in touch with its feminine side. A ninety-eight-pound weakling Savior could never have lugged a heavy wooden cross through Jerusalem and up the hill of Golgotha, much less become a good role model for future leaders of the British Empire.

Charles Kingsley, Anglican priest, poet, novelist, hunter, hiker, and hard-shell believer in the White Man's Burden, wasn't about to take girly Jesus lying down. His popular books embraced team sport as "conducive not merely to physical but to moral health." Boys would "acquire virtues which no books can give them," including "daring and endurance," self-restraint, honor, and fair play. Indeed, the term Muscular Christianity first appeared in an 1857 review of one of Kingsley's novels, and his good friend Thomas Hughes produced one of the movement's seminal works, the 1857 *Tom Brown's Schooldays*. A lawyer, Christian Socialist, and member of the Society for the Suppression of the Opium Trade, Hughes's novel bigs up ball games as the perfect training for the young Englishmen who'll take Christianity to the far reaches of the Empire whether the far reaches like it or not.

Hughes sets his novel at Rugby School (founded 1567), somewhat spuriously giving his old headmaster Thomas Arnold credit for creating the sporting ethos of the English public school. The young toffs at Eton and Winchester had actually taken up the ancient game of mob football in the seventeenth century; other English schools soon followed, making up their own rules—insofar as there were rules. At Rugby, games could go on for days and involve a couple of hundred boys. When Queen Adelaide visited in 1839, School House (the oldest house at Rugby, with 75 boys) played against The Rest (225 boys), trampling each other like demented bison. It was more stylish than it sounds, though: the boys wore white trousers to demonstrate their indifference to the game's rampant (and perfectly legal) shin kicking.

Rugby football's origin myth tells us that in 1823, a boy by the name of William Webb Ellis "with a fine disregard for the rules of football as played in his time, first took the ball in his arms and ran with it." This cute story is every bit as accurate as the one about Abner Doubleday "inventing" baseball in Elihu Phinney's cow pasture. Sports needs legends and heroes. Ellis (who was a real person) and Hughes's Tom Brown (who wasn't), helped popularize a species of football that would conquer the Anglophone world and eventually produce one of America's signature paradoxes: the warlike sport presided over by the Prince of Peace.

Tom Brown arrives at school just in time for a big match, which his new pal Harry "Scud" East sums up as, "two collar-bones broken this half, and a dozen fellows lamed." With no regard for sanity or safety, Tom jumps into an ongoing scrummage, determined to help the "præpostor"(a senior, one of the captains) and make his mark:

> Now is your time, Tom. The blood of all the Browns is up, and the two rush in together, and throw themselves on the ball, under the very feet of the advancing column; the præpostor on his hands and knees arching his back, and Tom all along on his face. Over them topple the leaders of the rush, shooting over the back of the præpostor, but falling flat on Tom, and knocking all the wind out of his small carcass. "Our ball," says the præpostor, rising with his prize; "but get up there, there's a little fellow under you." They are hauled and roll off him, and Tom is discovered a motionless body.

Aw, he ain't dead: just got his bell rung. When he comes to, Tom realizes why he was put on earth: "This is worth living for; the whole sum of school-boy existence gathered up into one straining, struggling half-hour, a half-hour worth a year of common life."

Tom's schoolmasters agree: cricket and football, more than boxing, certainly more than book-learning, foster "discipline and self-reliance" in boys. At Rugby, Tom Brown imbibes "just enough Latin and Greek" to get into Oxford: sports and Christianity constitute his real education. The individual "doesn't play that he may win, but that his side may." Even taking into account a few concussions and some broken bones, team sports make a boy "a brave, helpful, truth-telling Englishman, and a gentleman, and a Christian." As a bonus, violent team sports distract a boy from girls, booze, buggery, and opium smoking. Kids would transfer all that pent-up sexual energy and resulting hostility to the football pitch and beat the hell out of other kids. Rugby, rowing, and cricket would exhaust boys so thoroughly, they wouldn't have the energy to sin.

Some boys managed to sin anyway: homosexual, or at least homoerotic, relations flourished at Rugby, Eton, Harrow, Winchester, and other top schools. Reginald Brett, later Lord Esher, described in his 1868 diary how Eton boys liked to "spoon," cuddle, and kiss each other, often in front of their schoolmasters. Tom Brown and his sporty mates roll their eyes at the way the "little pretty white-handed, curly-headed boys" are "petted and pampered by some of the big fellows," but don't seem morally outraged. After all, the English public school based its curriculum on pederastic classical learning: Plato's *Phaedrus* was a seminal text. God knows how much actual sex went on between boys and teachers, or boys and other boys: what's clearly true is that schoolmasters encouraged some form of "Greek love," whether fully consummated or just heavy petting. Few regarded the love that dare not speak its name as a threat to society—until Oscar Wilde not only spoke its name but shouted it from the steps of the Old Bailey. No, the key problem, as Victorian educationalists in Britain and America saw it, was masturbation. Male masturbation—apparently whatever women got up to down there was either not real or not important.

Pounding the flounder became public enemy number one in the eighteenth century: *Onania; or, The Heinous Sin of Self-Pollution*, a pamphlet published circa 1712, sold faster than backstreet gin (it went through twenty-odd editions by 1788), sparking a moral panic on both sides of the Atlantic. Onanism, especially in young men, must be stamped out, lest the nation's future husbands and fathers fall prey to "disturbances of the stomach and digestion, loss of appetite or ravenous hunger, vomiting, nausea, weakening of the organs of breathing, coughing, hoarseness, paralysis, weakening of the organ of generation to the point of impotence, lack of libido, back pain, disorders of the eye and ear, total diminution of bodily powers, paleness, thinness, pimples on the face." Physician and signer of the Declaration of Independence Benjamin Rush warned that masturbation could cause epilepsy.

Somehow, a private sexual activity that, until the early eighteenth century, wasn't even considered a sin—or not much of one, since the Old Testament makes it pretty clear that Onan's transgression was coitus interruptus for contraceptive purposes, not spanking the monkey—became a menace to British and American manhood. Learned doctors leaped into action, recommending cold baths, circumcision, or kinky devices such as penis cases, erection alarms, and shackles. In 1829, the Reverend Sylvester Graham of New Jersey invented a "wafer" (you know it as the Graham cracker) to curb a man's carrot-slapping impulses: he thought bland food tamped down sensual thoughts. Decades later, films such as *The Solitary Sin* showed masturbation as a slippery slope to madness and damnation: the protagonist, a world-class wanker, eventually loses his mind and murders his wife.

Of course, the best way to curb degenerate hand-genital action was exercise: team sports at boarding school for privileged boys, and starting in the 1840s, Bible study, strenuous games, and "hygiene" instruction at the YMCA for working-class lads. The Reverend Edward Thring, headmaster of Uppingham School in England from 1853 to 1887, fought masturbation the way Saint Anthony of Egypt fought demons in the desert. Thring discouraged solitary pursuits—like reading a book—and encouraged boys to inform on each other: anyone caught fiddling around under the bedclothes was instantly expelled. Reverend Thring's younger brother J. C. Thring, a noted footballer at Cambridge and later a housemaster at his brother's school, drew up football's first real set of standard rules. The Thring brothers figured repression was essential to manliness and thus to world order. The exemplary Englishman first subdues his own naughty passions, then subdues India and Africa.

The same goes for the exemplary American. Theodore Roosevelt's "American Boy" essay of 1900 instructs boys to play sports but not obsessively, be chivalric, and eschew anything unclean or "depraved." He ends with "in life, as in a foot-ball game, the principle to follow is: Hit the line hard; don't foul and don't shirk, but hit the line hard!"

The Duke of Wellington probably did not say the Battle of Waterloo was won on the playing fields of Eton, but the men in charge of the Empire picked up plenty of tips there, and at Oxford and Cambridge, where they became "Blues" (what Americans call lettermen) in football, cricket, and rowing, graduating to the jockocracy running colonial administrations in Africa and India. In the late nineteenth century, London wits said Sudan was a land of "Blacks ruled by Blues." Reverend J. E. C. Welldon, headmaster of Harrow School in the 1880s and 1890s, declared: "In the history of the British Empire, it is written that England has owed her sovereignty to her sports." Another cheerleader, J. G. Cotton Minchin, puffed the image of "the Englishman going through the world with rifle in one hand and Bible in the other," adding, for good measure, "If asked what our muscular Christianity has done, we point to the British Empire."

Not to mention non-masturbating, sporty, clean-limbed young men like Tom Brown, a decent, patriotic chap just learned enough to translate *Mens sana in corpore sano*, but not an egghead, a guy who'd *have a go* at pretty much anything, whether it's jumping into the middle of a mob football game or trying to turn back the Mahdist Revolt, an orthodox Anglican—if not much of a churchgoer. As Hughes says in his sequel, *Tom Brown at Oxford*, "The least of the muscular Christians has hold of the old chivalrous and Christian belief, that a man's body is given him to be trained and brought into subjection, and then used for the protection of the weak, the advancement of all righteous causes, and the subduing of the earth which God has given to the children of men."

Theodore Roosevelt couldn't have put it better himself. Indeed, he didn't try. The *Tom Brown* books were among his favorites. In 1899, Roosevelt delivered a speech in Chicago on the "strenuous life," warning that America was going soft, becoming "over-civilized" (read: feminine), and needed to man up, British fashion. In the 1873 self-help book *Getting On in the World: Hints on Success in Life*, Chicagoan William Matthews trumpeted, "That the splendid empires which England has founded in every quarter of the globe have had their origin largely in the football contests at Eton, the boat-races on the Thames, and the cricket-matches on her downs and heaths, who can doubt?" Religion was all well and good, but football, according to Roosevelt, "the greatest exercise of fine moral qualities, such as resolution, courage, endurance and capacity to hold one's own and stand up under punishment," was better. Anyway, far from being some dewy-eyed, soft-haired pacifist, Roosevelt's Jesus was physically fit, a hard-core avenging hombre kicking over the money changers' tables as if they were made of cheap papyrus.

Influenced by *Tom Brown* and the Spartan rigors of the English public school, the gospel of what Roosevelt called "rough, manly sports" spread to America. Roosevelt sent his own sons to Groton, a school modeled on Rugby and founded by Reverend Endicott Peabody. TR's cousin Franklin went there, too. Like Reverend Thring, Reverend Peabody preferred to turn out physically impressive Christian gentlemen rather than intellectually impressive freethinking types, and enforced "purity" through cold showers, no privacy, and lots of sports.

Muscular Christianity demands the body be whipped into submission, subdued, subjugated. Once it was self-flagellation or a hair shirt. Now that Muscular Christianity expresses itself most fully in the First Church of Christ Linebacker, it's monkey rolls or mat drills or, for those who transgress, stadium steps. Muscular Christianity doesn't promise an end to pain. On the contrary: it's a celebration of pain, an exaltation of the body by punishing the body.

From the founding of the YMCA in 1844 and the Boy Scouts in 1907, Muscular Christianity ruled on both sides of the Atlantic. While the Y and the Scouts are now mostly secular (or at least ecumenical), the Fellowship of Christian Athletes, their evangelical grandbaby, has become the new home of godly jockery: hands down, the most muscular of Muscular Christians, self-proclaimed "warriors" for the Lord. In words that would have made Charles Kingsley smile, the FCA insists that "just because FCA encourages athletes to compete for Christ's glory doesn't mean Christian athletes should be labeled as 'soft.' In fact, it's quite the opposite." No girly Jesus here, even if you're a girl (as about 40 percent of FCA members are). FCA-ers make like latter-day Crusaders riding off to liberate some metaphorical Holy Land from the self-indulgence, moral (and physical) flabbiness, and spiritual decadence that has seized it, declaring, "I am a member of Team Jesus Christ; I wear the colors of the Cross."

Founded in 1954 by an Oklahoma coach named Don McClanen, and helped with seed money from baseball mandarin Branch Rickey, FCA was supposed to bring young jocks to Jesus before rock 'n' roll, booze, reefer, or radical politics could get a foothold in their still-absorbent brains. FCA is now the largest sports ministry in the world, with chapters in a couple of dozen countries and more than four hundred thousand members in nine thousand high schools and colleges. One of its chief corporate sponsors is Chick-fil-A, owned by the billionaire biblical-literalist Cathy family. FCA runs summer camps and campus ministries, organizes student "Huddles," and sells Bibles, golf umbrellas, mixed nuts, FCA-logo footballs, almond bark, inspirational books by and about coaches, T-shirts proclaiming, WE AIN'T NEVA SKURED! and Christmas cards with Baby Jesus lying on some uncomfortable-looking packing material and surrounded by eager-faced young athletes in FCA gear with a Mary who looks more Tri-Delt than House of David.

In American college football, FCA is as ubiquitous as jockstraps. It pays chaplains' salaries and sponsors devotional services and counseling. Its members coach (without worrying their righteous heads about separation of church and playing field), furthering their mission to charge "coaches and athletes, and all whom they influence" with "the challenge and adventure of receiving Jesus Christ as Savior and Lord, serving Him in their relationships and in the fellowship of the church." Ole Miss coach Hugh Freeze holds worship services in the university's Manning Center, uses Christian music at practices, and tweets out Bible verses. Tommy Bowden, son of the more famous Bobby and Dabo Swinney's predecessor at Clemson, fell mildly afoul of the ACLU for transporting football players to church in taxpayer-bought buses. Unrepentant, he organized private cars to take them. He did his best to counter secular education, pooh-poohing evolution, and telling the *Washington Post* in 2014, that bringing Jesus to his players was his "No. 1 job."

Clemson boosters, largely evangelical Christians themselves, liked that about Tommy Bowden—until their Tigers started losing. In

2008, with the Tigers 3-3, he resigned. These days he keeps his hand in the proselytizing game, speaking at FCA events and showing up on Fox News when some godless types question the propriety of a coach praying all over his football team at a taxpayer-funded school.

Outside the South, FCA doesn't always have an open field. At Iowa State in 2007, Head Coach Gene Chizik wanted to hire an FCA-approved pastor named Kevin Lykins to help him foster "godly young men," as he puts it in his spiritual and sporting autobiography, *All In*. Many on the faculty, however, objected. Iowa State's a public institution; employing a team chaplain looked a lot like the university was endorsing Christianity. So ISU and Chizik renamed the position "life skills assistant" and hired Pastor Lykins.

FCA is unrepentant over its vast influence. It calls on young people to be "ready to compete for Christ," to keep Jesus in their minds as they play sports for the glory of God. FCA's "Competitor's Creed" proclaims "I am a Christian first and last . . . a member of Team Jesus Christ" playing "for the pleasure of my Heavenly Father, the honor of Christ, and the reputation of the Holy Spirit." FCA's theology is aggressively Protestant, affirming the inerrancy of the Bible and the necessity of being born again: "We believe that for the salvation of lost and sinful men (women), regeneration by the Holy Spirit is absolutely essential." Don't think you're going to get into Heaven by doing good works: the FCA is hard-core *sola fide*. Go born-again or go home.

The body is your oblation: "My sweat is an offering to my Master. My soreness is a sacrifice to my Savior." But that sweat had better be in the cause of good, clean play, blocking, running, and hitting. FCA demands its students eschew drugs, alcohol, cigarettes, and sex. The student leader "Statement of Purity" declares: "God desires His children to lead pure lives of holiness. The Bible is clear in teaching on sexual sin including sex outside of marriage and homosexual acts." The creed says, "My body is the temple of Jesus Christ" and "Nothing enters my body that does not honor the Living God. I give my all—all of the time. I do not give up. I do not give in. I do not give out."

Or put out. Football, especially college football, officially cele-brates virtue, defined as sexual abstinence. In 1995, *Playboy* magazine named Clay Shiver, Florida State's starting center, to its preseason All-American team. It wasn't a shock: Shiver'd won the ACC's Jacobs Blocking Trophy and helped FSU win a national championship the year before. Plus, Seminole chaplain Clint Purvis had a premonition. "He knew I was going to be selected," said Shiver. "It was like the Lord spoke to him."

Or something. Shiver prayed on it and turned the bunnymen down. "I couldn't see any good coming from being in the magazine," he said. Other avowedly religious players have told *Playboy* no, too, among them Mitch Donahue of the University of Wyoming in 1990, UF Heisman Trophy winner Danny Wuerffel in 1996, Tommie Harris of Oklahoma in 2002, and, no surprise here, Tim Tebow.

You'd think young, presumably straight fellows for whom puberty still looms large in the rearview mirror would love to be honored by *Playboy*. But to boys reared with an FCA understanding of the body, certain kinds of pleasure are sinful. And the *Playboy* football edition usually features a photo shoot of essentially naked college sirens: "Girls of the SEC!" "Girls of the Big Ten!" The guys are celebrated for their athleticism, their power to intimidate, their big muscles; the girls for their nubile beauty, their implied availability, their big tits. The whole point of Muscular Christianity, in contrast, is to tamp down the erotic through athletic training, kind of the way Saint Benedict of Nursia conquered lust by rolling naked in a patch of thorns.

It's a contradiction: football celebrates the body. Strength and studliness bring rewards: the NFL, money, the pick of babes like su-permodel Gisele Bundchen and AJ McCarron's missus, Katherine Webb, the one who eats the cheeseburger on TV, licking the sauce suggestively off her pretty fingers. Football also demands self-control and denial. *Sharing the Victory*, FCA's magazine, is full of tales of sex-ual sin and eventual redemption right out of a medieval morality play. Here, a Mississippi State basketball player fools around with boys, fools around with girls, then, of course, repents:

Have you ever fallen into the pit of despair, landing in a pool of your toxic mistakes and filthy sin? There in the depths you gaze in doubt at the slippery walls of consequence that rise 20 feet above you on all sides. "I sink in the miry depths, where there is no foothold," describes the psalmist in 69:2 (NIV). . . .

The story told in the Psalms is familiar to Mississippi State senior Alexandria Hagler. Plagued at one time by sexual sin, homosexuality and abortion, Alex's pit became deep and slippery. But just like the psalmist, Alex now shouts for joy that her Savior redeemed her life from the abyss. Her story reminds us no sin is too great for God's grace.

No gay sex, no straight sex, and no masturbation. FCA rarely addresses self-pleasuring as directly as the Victorians, but *Sharing the Victory* is clear that men, especially, need to tamp down any lustful thoughts, unless they're married to the object of said lustful thoughts. Single guys need to do sports: "Talk about a battle: honoring the Lord with our flesh. Since it's not likely that Christ will miraculously make us sexually pure—we'd learn nothing if He gave us the easy way out—we have to fight for it, and in the process, build our relationship with Him. So, men, are we willing to put on our armor?"

Chapter 10

GATOR GALAHAD

TIM TEBOW WEARS HIS ARMOR, the full armor of God, even in the shower. He wields the Sword of the Spirit and the Shield of Faith, too. In college, he passed for nine thousand yards and ran for three thousand. He scored eighty-eight touchdowns and thanked Jesus for every one of them, hitting the turf in that famous one-knee, fist-on-forehead pose, the gridiron genuflection the world knows as tebowing. In 2012, Tebow trademarked tebowing. Steal his move, and you'll owe him money.

Tim Tebow is the acme of godly jockhood. Football players, both college and pro, name-check Jesus about as often as they chug Gatorade, but when it comes to teeth-achingly earnest piety, he makes every man jack of them look like mere country club Whiskypalians. As a homeschooled kid playing ball, he became the subject of an ESPN documentary called *The Chosen One*. Not to be confused with all the other "chosen ones" trumpeted by the sporting commentariat since David's big score in the Valley of Elah, and despite decades of *Sports Illustrated* covers variously declaring LeBron James, Bryce Harper, Kellen Winslow Jr., and Michelle Wie as "chosen ones." They were false messiahs: Tebow's another story. Like his namesake, the apostle famous for command of the scriptures as a very young child, Tebow evangelized while still a teenager, scratching Bible verses in his eye-black at the University of Florida: Philippians 4:13 for the 2008 season, "I can do all things through Christ, who strengthens me," and James 1:2–3, "Count it all joy, my brothers, when you meet trials of various kinds, for you know that the testing of your faith produces steadfastness," at the 2010 Senior Bowl (his South squad lost 33–13). For the Gators' 62–3 scourging of Florida International in 2009, Romans 1:16, "For I am not ashamed of the gospel, for it is the power of God for salvation to everyone who believes, to the Jew first and also to the Greek." At the national championship against the Oklahoma Sooners in 2009, Tebow went with the classic—John 3:16. The newspapers said more than ninety million people googled it after the Gators beat the Sooners.

The verses proclaimed the Gospel and made a pretty good drinking game for those watching at home, too: if you found the passage in the Bible first, you took a drink; if you spotted a fan in the stands with the same verse, you took a drink; every time the TV camera cut to Tebow or the fan with the verse, you took a drink. The NCAA finally outlawed "facial messaging" in 2010. It didn't matter: in 2012, a poll revealed that 43 percent of Americans think God actually helped Tim Tebow win games. Theologian Owen Strachan unpacks the relationship between Tebow's faith, Tebow's football skill, Protestant church history, and Divine Providence in a 2012 *Atlantic Monthly* essay, calling Martin Luther "the Tim Tebow of his day" because the pope said he was "'a bull in the church's vineyard,' an apt description for Tebow's running style."

The Reverend Professor Strachan invokes Jonathan Edwards, the eighteenth-century New England preacher who brought us "Sinners in the Hands of an Angry God," to explain predestination and the perpetual problem of evil, i.e., why does God cause Tebow to win some games and lose others? "It may be that God is working through the miraculous feats of Tebow on the field to draw attention to his own glory," says Strachan. "God is regularly pleased to do such things, it seems, whether that means rebuking upper-crust Anglicans or bloated

Bible-belt Baptists by raising up believers in massive numbers in marginalized regions of the world or by giving favor to politicians and accountants and homemakers who nobody else deemed worthy."

The philosopher Bobby Bare put it even more succinctly:

> *Dropkick me, Jesus, through the goalposts of life,*
> *End over end, neither left nor to right,*
> *Straight through the heart of them righteous uprights.*
> *Dropkick me, Jesus, through the goalposts of life!*

According to Strachan, God "ordains what socks we put on in the morning." The Almighty also micromanages football games, though to what end, we cannot know. The righteous Tim Tebow won the 2007 Heisman Trophy. The arrogant hangover merchant Johnny Manziel won the 2012 Heisman, then the seafood-purloining alleged date rapist Jameis Winston won in 2013. Mysterious, indeed. One thing is surely clear: Tebow is among the elect. He won the James E. Sullivan Award, the Maxwell Award, the Chic Harley Award, and the Davey O'Brien Award. He was All-SEC, All-American, and a hot favorite for Tennysonian Grail Knight:

> *My good blade carves the casques of men,*
> *My tough lance thrusteth sure,*
> *My strength is as the strength of ten,*
> *Because my heart is pure.*

If only he could throw the ball.

Tim Tebow is not, as far as we know, a product of parthenogenesis. According to his parents, however, he is indeed a miracle. In the 1980s, the Tebows lived in the Philippines, ministering to a nation now pushing a hundred million souls, planting "Bible-believing churches where previously there were no churches." His father, Bob Tebow, is fond of pointing out that something like three-fourths of Filipinos have "never once heard the gospel of Jesus Christ." Since 80 percent of Filipinos are

Roman Catholic, it would seem they have at least a nodding acquaintance with the Lord, though to the Tebows, popery is little better than paganism.

Here's the Tim Tebow nativity narrative as Bob Tebow revealed it unto *Sports Illustrated* in 2009: "When I was out in the mountains in Mindanao, back in '86, I was showing a film and preaching that night. I was weeping over the millions of babies being [aborted] in America, and I prayed, 'God, if you give me a son, if you give me Timmy, I'll raise him to be a preacher.'"

The Tebows soon conceived, but it was a scary pregnancy. Pam Tebow contracted amebic dysentery and fell into a coma for a little while. Her doctors said the medicine that saved her life had likely deprived the fetus of oxygen, causing brain damage. Bob Tebow said, "'The placenta was never properly attached, and there was bleeding from the get-go.'"

The doctors advised Pam Tebow to have an abortion. She refused. Bob had promised God that if the baby lived, he'd call him Timothy, after Saint Paul's protégé. *Timotheos* means "honoring God." Tim Tebow sent a thank-you note to the Almighty in the form of a 2010 Super Bowl ad spot, paid for by the anti-choice, anti-sex, anti-gay, anti-Darwin outfit Focus on the Family. In it, Tebow and his mother, Pam, celebrate his life; then he pretend-tackles her.

If Tim Tebow had been born in medieval Europe, he might have been a soldier of the One True Church fighting the Ottomans, given the title Athleta Christi—Champion of Christ—by a grateful Holy See. Or he might have become a story in the *Legenda aurea*, somebody like Saint Roch, child of a supposedly barren but super-pious woman, who came out of the womb with a cross tattooed on his chest, or John the Baptist, that important surprise baby born to a geriatric couple, or Saint Kevin of Glendalough: as he emerged from the womb, all the snow in wintery Leinster promptly melted.

The holy and the heroic tend to get themselves born in some difficult and dangerous way—read your Joseph Campbell. Or your Marvel Comics. Timothy Richard Tebow arrived scrawny in August 1987 and remained scrawny as a child. He took to doing four hundred push-ups a day, and look at him now: 240 pounds and as ripped as Hercules. Or a Caravaggio Christ. While still in college, Tebow was photographed bare-chested in what one incensed commentator called "tight junk pants," ankles crossed, eyes cast down to one side, arms outstretched. In 2012, *GQ* printed the picture in black and white, emphasizing the hills and dales of his considerable brawn. Muscular Christianity had never been this buff.

Or this chaste. Even Tom Brown had a fling with a barmaid in college. Not Tim Tebow. At the 2009 SEC Media Days, Tebow answered an impertinent question from a leering reporter, saying yes, he is indeed saving himself for marriage. The reporter looked slightly taken aback. Tebow didn't. He laughed, not a bit embarrassed: "I think y'all are stunned right now."

That's pretty fly for a pure guy. Tebow's virginity is a *thing*, subject of scores of articles trying to ascertain what goes on with the junk in those tight junk pants. When the Broncos traded him to the Jets in 2012, the betting was that Tebow couldn't maintain his purity in the Wicked Metropolis. Ashley Madison, a dating site for people who want, for some dim reason, to wreck somebody else's marriage, offered $1 million to anyone who could prove she (he?) had Done the Deed with him. The *New York Times* actually ran a story on the "challenges" he faced in the naughty pleasure domes of Manhattan, overstocked as it is with strong drink, moral relativism, Jezebels, and unrepentant Magdalens. The biblical Timothy never faced such temptations, even in the pagan city of Ephesus, where they worshipped a goddess with several dozen breasts.

Tim Tebow is pretty much sui generis. Not only because of his presumably unpunched V-ticket. Other football players have been public about their virginity: Prince Kelechi Amukamara, a former Nebraska Cornhusker, now New York Giant and member of Nigeria's Igbo royal family, says he's committed to chastity before marriage. Other athletes are also devout. But Tebow's become the gold standard, the poster boy, the ne plus ultra of godly jocks. Tebow makes news simply by existing: a move from the SEC channel to ESPN regular (blowing on the smoldering embers of ACC paranoia that the network really is a cheerleader for the SEC), or a rumor that he's working out with some NFL team or other. When he shows up with a young woman on his beefy arm, the gossip mags go bonkers. Actress Camilla Belle, the sloe-eyed star of *10,000 BC* and *I Brake for Gringos*, appeared with Tebow at some parties in 2012: maybe *they're doing it!* Then she appeared at parties alone. Damn! But Tebow must be fucking *somebody*. Maybe he's gay! All those shirtless six-pack shots of his ridiculously perfect musculature, his apparent lack of interest in women, his Hugh Jackman–as–Wolverine facial hair—surely these indicate some faint pings on the gaydar.

Or not. Tebow may be as advertised: a believer in old school Pauline chastity, a temple-of-the-holy-spirit type for whom the body is not a pathway to pleasure but a means to glorify God, a modern-day Eric Liddell. You remember Eric Liddell, the great runner and rugby player, hero of *Chariots of Fire*, winner of a gold medal in the 400 meters at the 1924 Paris Olympics. The 400 wasn't even his event. But the 100 was scheduled for a Sunday, and Eric Liddell, an abstemious and tough Presbyterian, declined to run on the Sabbath. Everyone from the coaches of the British Olympic team to the Prince of Wales begged him to *just this once* compete on a Sunday. He refused. Liddell later became a missionary in China; he died of a brain tumor in a Japanese internment camp in 1945, just a few months before liberation.

Tim Tebow, on the other hand, isn't bothered about keeping the Sabbath. In fact, he really *wants* to compete on Sunday, and to play in the NFL, he'd give almost anything. Not his immortal soul, of course. In April 2015, he signed a one-year contract with the Philadelphia Eagles. It still might not be the answer to his prayers: they could release him any time.

To many culture warriors, Tebow is already a martyr, a victim of anti-Christian prejudice. On April 29, 2013, the Jets cut Tebow from the team, and Glenn Beck lamented, "Look at Tebow: you can be a good guy, lead a clean life, and be on the wrong side politically and you're doomed." The next day, Rush Limbaugh wondered aloud if Tebow would have lost his job if he'd come out as gay, then favored listeners with his falsetto "liberal" voice: "Nobody would ever believe that Tim Tebow is gay. What if he were? I'll bet it still wouldn't be enough. He's so Christian, he's so identified as a Christian, that even being gay couldn't overcome the burden of being a Christian in our culture or our society today. [laughs] Yeah, he's a flaming Christian."

A blogger calling himself "John Galt" called Tebow's pink slip "Christian persecution" by "the elitist citizenry who want to force-feed grown adults arugula and broccoli."

Also on April 29, 2013, former NBA center Jason Collins revealed that he's gay. Like Tebow, Collins is a Christian. But not the right flavor of Christian. ESPN basketball analyst Chris Broussard thundered that Jason Collins was "openly living in unrepentant sin." Broussard had previously shared with his public that he'd be "uncomfortable" taking a shower after hoops with a gay friend. When what Broussard called the "politically correct" media weighed in on Collins's side, the Fellowship of Christian Athletes wing of the jockocracy came to his rescue. Gordon Thiessen of the Nebraska FCA snarled: "Homosexual acts are forbidden by God through His Word. Scripture teaches that God intended sexual intercourse to be limited to the marriage relationship of one man and one woman. Scripture is clear. Homosexuality is a sin against God. All sin has an eternal consequence, and the only hope for any sinner is the redemption accomplished by Jesus Christ, who on the cross paid the price for our sin, serving as the substitute for the redeemed."

Scripture is also clear on not mixing wool and linen, on the rules for selling your daughter into slavery, the uncleanliness of menstruating women, and the abomination of eating shellfish. Most Americans ignore that stuff. But sex, now: we are the children of Puritans, still struggling over what virility, what masculinity, actually means. Muscular Christianity tries to elevate discipline, denial, and purity over comfort, gratification, and indulgence; Muscular Christianity tells us physical pain is spiritual gain. Physical pleasure is always suspect. Four hundred years after Plymouth Rock, and we Americans still can't untangle ourselves from the big knot we've made of Jesus, penis-in-vagina sex, and manliness.

The surgeon general of the United States and the Public Health Service concluded in a 1918 study that boys learned about sex before the age of twelve and usually from dodgy sources, such as movies, "easy women," and each other. Only sports could save America and capitalism! So in 1919, the Public Health Service joined forces with the YMCA in the Keeping Fit campaign. Part sex education and part moral pep talk, Keeping Fit was designed to combat cupidity and promote "self-control" in the young American male. The kids would learn about "the whole process of reproduction and nurture of children, the meaning of marriage, prostitution, venereal diseases, illegitimacy and the hygiene of sound recreation." Then they'd commence punching each other in a "healthy boxing bout."

The Keeping Fit program presented boys up to the age of twenty with vague (but ominous) information about their bodies, warnings against "yielding to temptation," general exhortations toward "willpower," and lists of body-taming activities, including wood chopping, snow shoveling, lawn mowing, and organized sports. The YMCA and the PHS used the terror of germs to combat syphilis and gonorrhea; they addressed (somewhat obliquely) "night emissions" and masturbation. Keeping Fit took Victorian Muscular Christianity, gave it a modern glaze of physiology and hygiene, and larded it with clean, moral, sporting exemplars: Teddy Roosevelt, the weedy kid who worked out like a Spartan, transforming himself from skinny-armed Eastern aristocrat to mustachioed Western heman; Abraham Lincoln, splitter of rails, mighty debater; Robert E. Lee, the conflicted rebel and embodiment of Christian chivalry (we don't talk about the slave-owning part); and Ulysses S. Grant. Yes, Grant: it seems he would not tolerate swearing or the telling of "dirty stories," even when the person telling them was Abraham Lincoln. He was a renowned soldier, certainly. Perhaps the Keeping Fit people figured the boys wouldn't know he was also a renowned drunk who apparently stayed plastered during the entire Siege of Vicksburg in 1863.

Still, these were American heroes—white American heroes. There were no people of color in the Keeping Fit toolkit. No Frederick Douglass—too incendiary for the South—no Jack Johnson: he boxed for money. According to scholar Alexandra M. Lord, there was a Keeping Fit for black kids, a much smaller program, more of an afterthought. For the Y and the PHS, sports were about building character. Physical fitness was also about what Teddy Roosevelt would call "building good stock," creating worthy men to make babies with all-American mothers. He hated the idea of birth control for middle-class women, telling the National Congress on Motherhood in 1905 that Americans (by which he meant white people) should have four to six children each to keep up with those breed-like-rabbits immigrants. To combat "race suicide," he instituted a national Heredity Commission to encourage "the increase of families of good blood and (discourage) the vicious elements in the cross-bred American civilization." Muscular Christianity, meet eugenics.

Back to Tebow, a credit to his race, a man whom one of his hagiographers called "God's quarterback." How can he—how can any Christian—reconcile the religion of turning the other cheek with the bone-snapping, sinew-tearing, brain-busting violence of football? Tebow, no more introspective than a frying pan, refuses to intellectualize either his faith or his game. His book, *Through My Eyes,* is a sunny-natured, pick-yourself-up-and-dust-yourself-off inspirational tale of how the Lord helps you keep playing. Yes, there's injury, there's pain, but Tebow never dwells on it—even if it's other people's injury and pain. He gets back on the field as soon as the trainer tapes him up.

Some Christians can't just shrug off the blown knees and concussions, however. Strachan, the thinking woman's evangelical scholar, has of late been fretting over the implications of constant blows to the head. In "Our Shaken Faith in Football," he cops to agonizing over football and brain damage, the subconcussive hits that can add up to early dementia, depression, and suicide. Remember, Brother Strachan here is a conservative, head of the Council on Biblical Manhood and Womanhood, a believer in men being men and women having babies, a soldier of the Lord against feminism, gay marriage, abortion, secularism, illicit sex, and all those vices gnawing like Satan's rats on the fabric of godly society. Yet this 2013 piece for *Christianity Today* suggests that the savagery has finally gotten to him: "Following Christ means avoiding unnecessary violence, no matter what macho culture and John Wayne manhood might say (Luke 22:36). It also means seeking the good of our neighbor, and remembering that the imago dei calls us to be a kingdom of ethical prophets who desire that all humanity might thrive." Football, like every other human activity, has been tainted by our fallen state.

Strachan, a self-confessed sports fanatic, admits to reading *Sports Illustrated* cover to cover, "even the golf articles." It pained him to raise questions about football; it also pained him to get a pile of pushback from fellow evangelicals, some of whom wrote responses namechecking Teddy Roosevelt and his love of "rough sports," arguing that the Bible exhorts men to train and "sacrifice" their bodies in tough competition. Strachan told Vice Sports in 2014: "Jesus believed in doing hard things. He was a hardworking carpenter who died in agony for our sins, so I think he would appreciate the physical challenges, the many virtues and risks that are all part of football, but point of fact, Jesus did not endorse aggression. He actively worked against needless violence. I'm not sure what he would think of football, but he did command us to put the sword away."

Au contraire, mon brave! Writing on the ecumenical site Patheos in 2013, Timothy Dalrymple, a former top Stanford gymnast (until he broke his neck), would have you know that Jesus liked a bit of aggro: "Within the context of football, it is okay for you to tackle me as hard as you can, within the rules, as it is for me to do to you; it's okay for you to try to intimidate and discourage me, as it is for me to do to you. This is not to say that there are no moral considerations but just that morality is applied in a context-specific way, within certain bounds. It's okay to deceive an opponent, and most Christian athletes will not speak up if a referee makes a bad call in their favor, but it's not okay to lie about the use of performance-enhancing drugs or, say, to poison the opposing team, even if you can get away with it."

Poisoning is bad; a pump fake is OK. I'm guessing this is Tim Tebow's basic understanding of Christian morality as it applies to football. Pain is part of the game; suffering serves the Lord; fame should be used to spread the Gospel. God doesn't care who wins; He cares only how the game is played—never mind the head injuries. In his book, Tebow approvingly quotes Eric Liddell: "I believe God made me for a purpose, but he also made me fast. When I run, I feel his pleasure." Tebow likewise affirms, "I always thought since God gave these gifts to me, my role in that exchange was to play as hard as I could and continue giving Him the honor and glory for it."

Lancelot was a good knight, but he screwed around, didn't train, and only glimpsed the Grail. Galahad lived pure, passed his tests, did what Coach told him, and beheld Heavenly Perfection. For the Muscular Christian, Providence is always right:

> *Make me, oh, make me, Lord, more than I am:*
> *Make me a piece in Your master game plan,*
> *Free from the earthly temptation below,*
> *I've got the will, Lord, if You got the toe.*

HALFTIME

Chapter 11

DEATH OF A DRUM MAJOR

JOE BULLARD, his voice as rich and dangerous as dark rum, introduces the band: "From the highest of the seven hills of Tallahassee . . ."

They call him the Almighty, and today it's like he's emceeing the Pentecost: "The incomparable, the fantastic, the ultimate, the magnificent—the most imitated band in the world!" Bullard is a veteran R&B DJ, a former Columbia Records executive. He's been the announcer for Florida A&M University's Marching 100 for as long as anyone can remember. Or since 1976, if you want to get technical.

Five drum majors in white furred hats taller than a grenadier's bearskin extend their long silver-topped batons in salute. They give the batons an insouciant twirl, tuck them under one arm, and advance in perfect cadence, leading the band from the sidelines, slowly, dead march pace, lifting one foot off the ground and holding it in the air, thighs so perfectly parallel to the ground you could safely rest a full glass of champagne on their quads. They repeat the step, again, again, as the drums beat starkly four hits, a thick pause, then a deep bass strike, echoing off the old brick campus buildings and the six, not quite so high, not quite so fortunate, hills of Tallahassee. The crowd is silent for a minute, then starts screaming as the 100 break into triple-time, 360 steps per minute, more run than march, more dance than run. It looks like chaos, elemental particles exploding onto the field, spinning every which way, action, reaction, accelerating, bursting into sound. It isn't chaos; in the physics of the 100, every jump and juke is choreographed. Just as abruptly as they burst into motion, the band halts and plays the 20th Century Fox fanfare. The Rattlers are on their feet now, hands lifted high in delight and praise.

Delight and joy have been scarce around here for the past few years, what with scandal, investigations, and resignations. The university's lost a president, a football coach, two athletic directors, and two band directors. Dr. Elmira Mangum, the sharp-suited and bepearled new president, was not to Rattlerdom born—she's from Cornell— nevertheless, she's been doing her damnedest, raising money, raising spirits. She leads cheers at ball games, standing on the field in Rattler orange and green, yelling, "The Rattlers will *strike, strike,* and *strike* again!" as Venom the mascot shakes his tail.

Bet they don't do it like this in the Ivy League.

FAMU is special, an old "normal school"–turned–world-class university, one of the largest HBCUs in the country, an incubator of African American brains and talent, a center of the civil rights movement. Everyone stands for the "Star-Spangled Banner" at football games; everyone actually sings James Weldon Johnson's "Negro National Anthem" at football games:

> *Lift every voice and sing*
> *Till earth and heaven ring,*
> *Ring with the harmonies of Liberty—*
> *Let our rejoicing rise*
> *High as the list'ning skies,*
> *Let it resound loud as the rolling sea.*

FAMU football has been a mighty source of pride since the days of the great Coach Jake Gaither, winner of multiple championships who became a cherished Florida institution—white people called him Coach and congratulated themselves on their broadmindedness. Jake

Gaither ran a program dedicated not only to winning but to producing dignified, cultivated young men, young men who could carry themselves in the hostile and tricky white folks' world.

But Jake Gaither died twenty years ago. And the 2014 Rattlers aren't giving the faithful much to lift every voice and sing about: they've lost five games in a row, two by five touchdowns. The team could lose again today, to Savannah State.

The band, however, never loses. Never. The band is the reason people keep showing up. On the field, the 100 move every part of their bodies, not just their feet, shaking and twisting, freaking, squatting, and kicking like funky Cossacks, diving onto the ground and leaping up, doing it all while playing tubas and trumpets, French horns and oboes, clarinets and saxophones, and drums and cymbals.

"It's a new day!" Joe Bullard calls out. "Size does not matter. The sound is clear. The 100 is back."

Back from the brink of destruction. Suspension. Disgrace. The band is smaller than it used to be: 160 today (the 100 hasn't had a mere 100 members since the early 1950s), down from the 250 they took to Paris for the two hundredth anniversary of the French Revolution, or the 300 or so who marched in both of Bill Clinton's inaugural parades and Barack Obama's first inaugural parade, way down from 2011, when the 100 numbered more than 400. That was the year the band almost destroyed the university. The year the band killed somebody.

ROBERT CHAMPION WAS a clarinetist from Decatur, Georgia. A good clarinetist, according to everyone who ever heard him, so good he made drum major the same year he got accepted to the band. The drum major is a leader; he wears the big hat, wields the big baton, and blows the whistle on the field. Still, Robert Champion felt as though some people didn't respect him. The drumline in particular. Drumline guys (and they're predominantly men) often think they're the badasses of the band, studly and cooler-than-thou. Robert Champion was a stickler for the rules, a band law-and-order type, though he was also quiet and, according to several of his friends, might have been gay. So to shut up his critics and show how tough he was, Robert Champion decided to undergo the rite of passage known as Crossing Bus C.

Like any exclusive club with three or four hundred members, the 100 had factions and sects. The rules forbid them to organize in secret, the band director makes the band members sign no-hazing pledges, police give workshops, yet no entity on earth can prevent college students from creating little cabals allowing them to lord it over everybody who doesn't know the handshake or the password, who doesn't have the wristband or the T-shirt. The tuba players join White Whales; kids from Georgia, the Red Dawg Order; clarinetists, the Clones. Then there's Bus C, not so much a clique as an initiation machine, a test of strength and seriousness. A band member tries to make his way from the front of a forty-five-foot-long bus to the back as fifteen or twenty other band members hit him with drumsticks, mallets, fists, whatever. Nobody knows how long it's been going on: Dr. Julian White, director of bands until 2012, warned students, the FAMU administration— everybody—that hazing was getting out of hand. Two weeks before Robert Champion crossed Bus C, White suspended twenty-six band members for hazing. He pleaded with band alumni, who help perpetuate the culture with their "war stories," their tales of triumph over whatever the Red Dawgs or Bus C threw at them, their assurances that once you subject yourself to these trials, your bond with the band will be deeper and more beautiful.

Naturally, nobody listened to the grown folks. Band is competitive: band versus band, section versus section, cadre versus cadre. Robert Champion and his friend Keon Hollis, another drum major, showed up to Bus C a few hours after they'd performed at the Florida Classic. It hadn't been the 100's best show: they formed a submarine for Adele's "Rolling in the Deep," then transformed it into a sailboat. Cute, but not breathtaking. When it was Bethune-Cookman's turn, their announcer asked of "the orange and green band that just left the field—what happened? You used to set the standard." Then the Marching Wildcats played "Na Na Hey Hey Kiss Him Goodbye."

In the dark parking lot, on Bus C, percussionist Lisette Sanchez went first. When she got to the back of the bus, she passed out. Then Keon Harris. He got punched and hit with a hard plastic CAUTION: WET FLOOR sign. But he got there, bruised and vomiting. Finally, it was Robert Champion's turn. He made it to the back of the bus, too, after being stomped and kicked and kneed. He couldn't seem to take in enough air. He said he couldn't see, even though his eyes were open. Somebody called 911; somebody else tried CPR. The paramedics finally arrived. A few hours later, everybody heard the news: Robert Champion was dead.

The doctors said it was hemorrhagic shock brought on by trauma to his internal organs. The band members said they never hit him that hard. A few licks, maybe. Witnesses either denied seeing anything violent (hey, it was late at night) or claimed they were actually *helping* Robert Champion cross the bus. Some swore they weren't there; or if they were there, they didn't participate: they got on the bus to retrieve their glasses or find a cigarette lighter. Everybody said they liked Robert; they said he was going to be named the next head drum major. It was an accident, they said, a terrible, terrible accident. The medical examiner ruled Robert Champion's death a homicide.

BANDS USED TO PROVIDE the backbeat to bloodlust, playing soldiers into battle. In 1777, General John Stark had his fifes and drums play all the way into British lines at the Battle of Bennington, instilling in the Continental Army such patriotic fervor that they beat the Redcoats, then ran with that momentum all the way to Saratoga, making General Burgoyne surrender, inspiring the French to send the Colonies guns and money, letting freedom, as it were, ring. The rest is history. Martial music goes right to the lizard brain, stoking that fight impulse, impelling you to kill or at least score a touchdown. Many nations over hundreds of years combined guns and musical instruments, but

America's the only one feeling the need to supply college sports with color guards, military ceremony, and emotion-roiling bands, making sure we confuse the gridiron with the battlefield.

Not that other nations go without music at their football contests. The Welsh sing hymns at rugby matches; in Italy, fans perform a range of favorites, from *Rigoletto*'s "La Donna è Mobile" to "Old MacDonald Had a Farm." At matches in Liverpool and Sunderland, the repertoire is simple but heartfelt: "Here We Go!" (that's both the title and the sum total of the lyrics) sung to the tune of John Philip Sousa's "Stars and Stripes Forever," "Who's Your Father, Referee?" (to "My Darling Clementine"), and the lively "Score in a Brothel" (as in, "You couldn't . . .") to the tune of "Guantanamera," a plaintive piece originally about a pretty girl from Guantanamo, before los Yanquis built the notorious prison on land purloined from Cuba.

College marching bands inherited their uniforms from military bands—the soutaches, sashes, shakos, epaulets, aiguillettes, plumes, gloves, lacing, boots, spats, the kind of Attic helmets last worn during the Trojan War (now sported by the University of Southern California Marching Band) and other esoteric parts of dress from the late eighteenth century, given a psychedelic makeover in bright colors, and trotted out onto a football field. As regimental bands egged on the Royal Scots Greys to charge the French Infantry at Waterloo, college bands keep the stands stoked, gin up "school spirit," play the Alma Mater, even if most of the alumni cannot remember the words, and provide a strong, hammering, adrenaline-goosing beat, urging their boys to fight, team, fight. Or fight, fight, fight, fight for victory. Or hike, hike, hike to victory. Or smash through to victory! Victory or death!

Maybe not death. But a loss means humiliation. And less television money, smaller bonuses for coaches, diminished chances of a postseason spot or a fatter Nike contract and new majorettes uniforms. Even if the football team is made up of twits, felons, and douche-noggins who couldn't beat a troop of wheelchair-bound nuns, the band should always be a credit to its college, demonstrating discipline and dedication with precision marching and fine musicianship. Sometimes the band is the only way to redeem the three or four hours sitting in the cold or the rain. The band reinforces football clan identity with sacramental songs and liturgical cheers, symbolic colors, and relentless optimism. The band keeps playing the school songs even if the team is losing by seventy-five points. The band loves. The band believes.

The band is rarely called on to display much in the way of wit, though you have to admire the time in 2011 when Rice University's Marching Owl Band taunted Texas governor and presidential candidate Rick Perry as well as rival Texas A&M, spelling out "$EC" on the field as the announcer intoned, "The next time you go to the polls, ask yourself, 'Is your candidate smarter than an Aggie?'"

Then there's Stanford, the gold standard of marching band satire, the pride of the Irony Coast. Other bands transgress every once in a while, as in 1985 when the Yale band dropped trou during halftime at the Holy Cross game, but no band embraces anarchy like Stanford. Dressed in fishing hats and wrinkled red blazers, they are a gleeful Bugs Bunny to everyone else's order-craving Elmer Fudd. For their halftime show at the University of Oregon in 1990, Stanford formed a spotted owl, then became a chainsaw, as the announcer lamented, "Your home is now a roll of Brawny and your family has flown the coop." Oregon's then-governor banned the band from the state.

The next year, Notre Dame banned them from its campus. The Stanford drum major appeared dressed as an Orthodox Jew for the pregame, wielding what looked like a menorah, but after the first quarter, he showed up in a nun's habit and conducted the halftime show with a crucifix. Some lady, an incensed Notre Dame congregant, lit out onto the field as halftime was ending and yanked off the drum major's habit, informing him he was going to hell.

Stanford alums who witnessed the 1982 Cal-Berkeley game might sometimes wish the band to hell, too. Late in the fourth quarter, the Cardinal kicked off after what looked like the game-winning field goal and the band, thinking the game was over, rushed the end zone. They began to play Free's "All Right Now," failing to notice the four seconds left on the clock. Cal's Golden Bears took the ball and threw five wild laterals until finally Kevin Moen, who had received the kick in the first place, tackled a Stanford trombone player and scored a touchdown. Somebody's knee may have been down, but the officials couldn't see clearly, what with the band scurrying around like startled squirrels.

The Marching 100 would never be so undisciplined. Moreover, while private schools like Stanford and Rice can snark out all they want, FAMU depends for much of its funding on a state legislature not known for its sense of humor. Not that the 100 aren't occasionally funny: at halftime during the Florida Classic in 2010, the band let the Bethune-Cookman Marching Wildcats know what they thought of them with a field formation reading SHUT UP.

Most of the time, though, the band business at HBCUs is deadly serious. If you're in the band, you are the public face of your school. You represent all the alumni who came before, the ones who rose up from slavery to the hope of an education, the generations who suffered violence, terror, institutionalized racism, the ones who sat in at the lunch counters, forced their elders to take Black Power seriously, became entrepreneurs and artists and educators and yes, professional sportsmen and sportswomen, earning success in a country that still forces people of color to prove themselves every minute. Making the band means you're part of an elite, a cohort with a sense of history and a commitment so intense the United States Marine Corps looks casual in comparison. At FAMU, if you make the 100, you are one of the chosen. You survived the death-or-glory audition, the sight-reading, the chromatic scales; you survived three-a-day practices in the sullen, relentless heat of a Tallahassee summer, the blistered fingers, the bruised lips, maintaining perfect tone while you dance under the vicious sun. A saxophonist in the 100 once described how he got in band form by playing scales while doing jumping jacks. Everybody knows the band practices longer than the team. If you haven't passed out, run off, or given up by July, you've made it, and you are, unquestionably, the shit.

AT HALFTIME, THE RATTLERS lead Savannah State 21–7. The Bragg crowd politely applaud the Tigers' Coastal Empire Sound Explosion, then Joe Bullard gets on the PA and says, "Savannah State, we thank you and hope you've enjoyed your *field trip*."

After a small pause, the Almighty intones, "No offense, but the difference is *clear*." Out come the 100, leaping into an old favorite, "Papa's Got a Brand New Bag." They played it dancing down the Champs Elysées on Bastille Day in 1989. The 100 have long been accustomed to center stage: they've done Super Bowls, movies, commercials, *60 Minutes*, the Grammys. The slimmed-down edition is still loud and proud, but—maybe I'm imagining things—a little less lordly, a little less joyous, the drumline's nasty beat a bit more straitlaced, the drum majors' high kicks a bit lower. It's as if the 100 know every time they march onto the field, a band of ghosts marches behind them.

NOBODY ON THE PERPETRATING END of hazing actually admits it's hazing. They call it tradition. Initiation. Things have always been done this way. Young men of the Satere-Mawé people must endure the stings of large and venomous Amazon bullet ants before they're accepted as warriors. Young men at Dartmouth used to have to drink bottles of MD 20/20 and Boone's Farm Blue Hawaiian, plus God knows what else, vomit and be vomited on, before they'd be accepted as brothers of Sigma Alpha Epsilon. ΣAE changed its ways, or says it did, announcing an end to such customs in 2014: the fraternity held the record for drug- and/or booze-related deaths, at least ten since 2006. One ΣAE, Cornell sophomore George Desdunes, died of epic alcohol consumption participating in a fraternity "kidnapping" in February 2011, nine months before Robert Champion crossed Bus C. One of George Desdunes's tormentors said, "It was meant to be fun."

The kids on Bus C replicated what they'd gone through, what generations of Marching 100 members had gone through, because, you know, *tradition*. We separate ourselves into tribes and assign rank within the tribe. In *Black Haze*, a study of African American college rites, Ricky L. Jones, professor of Pan-African studies at the University of Louisville, says that enduring torture earns a guy status: "The more punishment you can take, the more of a man you are. That means something in a world that doesn't always give black men respect."

Bands, fraternities, sororities, Freemasons, clans, even university English departments, all have their little ways of asserting otherwise meaningless hierarchies, everything from small slights to painful physical trials involving a knife, a heated coat hanger, and lifelong scarification: who gets the office with the window, who is the true brother of the crocodile, who is toughest, who demonstrates the most "sisterhood." The only hazing I ever experienced could have passed, for the most part, as normal etiquette in certain settings—Downton Abbey, say. During Hell Week, we sorority pledges had to wear huge, glitter-covered pasteboard zeros around our necks to class, signifying our worthlessness; we had to stand when a sister entered the room, speak only when spoken to, address a sister formally as Sister Jones or Sister Smith or whatever, and never turn our backs on a sister, even if that meant lying on the floor and pulling ourselves out of a room by our heels. The only physical discomfort was eating spaghetti and meatballs with our hands tied behind our backs.

The boys, the frats: they do far worse things to each other, often involving nakedness, cold water, sleep deprivation, paddles, blindfolds, and massive amounts of grain alcohol. Some of these boys probably grew up to be CIA "enhanced interrogation" specialists or advisors to Vice President Dick Cheney.

Ceremonial abuse in college is as American as blue jeans, guns, and denying evolution. In 2014, Ohio State's president fired the director of the "Best Damn Band in the Land" over what the press delicately referred to as the band's "sexualized atmosphere," new members forced to perform humiliating acts in their underwear, simulate oral sex while on the band bus, and take "rookie midterms" with exam questions such as "Who has the smallest tits?"

Some former Best Damn members felt OSU overreacted: they wanted the university president fired and the band director reinstated. Social media boiled, Best Damn alums complimented the band on preserving the "harmless pranks and songs." One sniffed, "I would have thought that the 'woosification' of America by liberals with hyphenated last names would have watered down those traditions a long time ago."

Former band director Jonathan Waters is suing.

Tradition. For a democratic republic, for a supposed meritocracy, America is obsessed with where you hang on the food chain, where you fall in the pecking order. Our strange, subtle class system depends on denying we have a class system at all. We hate the elite but watch them like mesmerized rabbits; we disdain royalty but consume every image of princesses and kings we can get our paws on; we say that we're as good as anyone else but lionize the rich—they must be smart or they wouldn't have all that money, would they?

Humans never lose a chance to establish a hierarchy. Had Robert Champion survived, he might have become head drum major. He was in line for the job. We're told by his family and close friends that he disapproved of hazing: would he have changed his mind? People do, when their ordeal is over. Maybe he would have used his leadership position to demand change, put a stop to the torture masquerading as "fun." But he might have decided that it wasn't so bad. People figure if they can hack it, so can everybody else. Lots of his bandmates clearly came to that conclusion. No matter how sweet and quiet a boy he was, Robert Champion might have transformed himself from victim to oppressor, scourging other kids on Bus C.

Tradition can be weirdly deaf to history. I can't be the only person cringing over the 100's use of a bus for their lethal *rite de passage*. A bus. A soft-seated, air-conditioned bus, much nicer than that rolling hunk of tin Rosa Parks refused to give up her seat on, but a symbol of the struggle for social justice and freedom nonetheless. In 1956, two FAMU education majors, Wilhelmina Jakes and her roommate Carrie Patterson, got arrested for refusing to go sit at the back of a Tallahassee city bus. Everybody at FAMU knows the names of Jakes and Patterson—everybody in Tallahassee knows their names. Yet here were FAMU's most important, most envied students, young African American people, beating each other over getting to the back of a bus.

The front of the bus would at least make some kind of symbolic sense.

Using a bus as a site of initiation could pass for metaphorical rec-lamation, I suppose, the way *nigger* can be dropped like a smart bomb by some singer or writer to trouble the waters of the old race para-digm, the way some fraternities—the Omegas, the Alphas—brand themselves in an act of devotion to the brotherhood, negating (I guess) the way their slave ancestors were branded to identify them as pieces of property or sometimes as punishment. Hazing appropriates the bad stuff, then transforming it, an echo of tribal marking confirming the initiate in the group. Or it might be, as Ricky L. Jones says, a "histori-cally dehumanizing practice," a "carryover from slave socialization and therefore a dysfunctional, oppressive tradition that members cannot come to grips with because of false or even double consciousness."

There's such a thing as too much forgetting.

TWO BLACK HORSES pulled the cart carrying Robert Champion's body. The program for his funeral service showed him in full green drum-major regalia, stepping high, wearing diaphanous angel wings. The five Marching 100 drum majors who survived Robert Champion led the procession. A few months later, three of those five would be arrested for killing him.

In all, 15 members of the 100 were charged with manslaughter. Felony hazing, too, a relatively new criminal category in Florida, aris-ing from the 2001 death of Chad Meredith, a Kappa Sigma pledge at the University of Miami who got liquored up with the older bros. They challenged him to swim across a lake. He did—and drowned.

A few days before Robert Champion's funeral, FAMU's president suspended the band "indefinitely." The university, the law, and the state uncovered old problems nobody had ever bothered to fix: almost one-fourth of the band's four hundred–plus members were not en-rolled as students at FAMU or anywhere else, making them ineligible to put on the uniform or claim band expenses paid by the university. The Florida Department of Law Enforcement intimated that fraud was involved. Money was missing. Old stories of beatings resurfaced: in 1998 and 2001, several band members had been hospitalized with kidney failure. In 2012, Julian White, the band director, resigned. James Ammons, president of the university, resigned too. Robert Champion's parents sued the university.

The Republicans running Florida's state government muttered about merging FAMU with FSU or cutting off the band forever, or some other dire move, implying that "those people" couldn't govern themselves. Didn't FAMU struggle with its accounting back in the 1990s? Wasn't there always some kind of scandal?

Rick Scott, who'd become governor of Florida without appearing to know anything about Florida's history, said he'd like to stop giving any state money to Florida's two private predominantly African American colleges, and wondered if FAMU, a public institution, didn't need a corporate overhaul. When hundreds of FAMU students marched to the gates of the governor's Tallahassee mansion, he tried to get down with the kids, confiding, "I lived in public housing." Compounding his gracelessness, he added, "My dad had a sixth-grade education."

To Scott, a multimillionaire, his deprivation somehow made him an honorary Negro, a brother from another (very white) mother. The students were unimpressed: "We are not all poor," one said.

From mid-November 2011 to early September 2013, FAMU had no band; no convocation concerts, no one to play Elgar at graduation (they piped in "Pomp and Circumstance"), no joyful noise at sporting events. At the Atlanta Classic against Southern University on September 29, 2012, Southern's band (known as the Human Jukebox) played Al Green's "Let's Stay Together" and spelled out FAMU in tribute. Normally, they'd be talking trash at the 100. FAMU hired acts such as Chaka Khan and Doug E. Fresh for halftime shows, but attendance still fell. The Rattlers didn't have much strike in them without the band. Some members of the 100, now under interdict, still went to games, sitting in their old seats, singing a cappella the music they should have been playing.

Every few years since the end of legal segregation, a self-renewing gaggle of white malcontents decides to wonder, loudly, why FAMU even exists: Jim Crow's dead; we're all integrated now, aren't we? Why do African Americans need a "historically black" college? They could all go to FSU! Yet they're still not satisfied. In the 1960s and early 1970s, FAMU students refused to be "colored" anymore, or even "Negroes." They informed their elders and the whole, generally nervous, white population, that they were *black*. Dig it. Stokely Carmichael came to campus in 1967, even though he'd been denied official permission to speak by FAMU's ever-cautious administration. Carmichael led seven hundred students to break into an auditorium and told them to fight for their rights. Students rioted the night Martin Luther King died in 1968, scaring the crap out of grown people. The white elite had always enjoyed attending Rattler football games—Coach Gaither and his wife were always so *welcoming*. Rattler football was often more exciting than FSU football. In the early 1960s, my parents and their friends would sit in a special section just for white people, watching the likes of Bob Hayes and Hewritt Dixon tear up the field. My mother remembers, "Everyone was so polite and nice to us. Nicer than they should have been."

But the era of genteel segregation was over. To older African Americans and most white people, all this Afro-sporting, dashiki-wearing, "by-any-means-necessary" fist raising seemed downright scary. Uppity, even. In 1968, the Florida legislature shut down the FAMU Law School, which had trained generations of African American lawyers in the South. Oblivious to the insult, they took the money that would have been FAMU's and built a new law school about three miles north—at FSU.

PRETTY MUCH EVERY MEMBER of the band who was in Orlando the night they killed Robert Champion is gone: graduated, left the university. The university says the 100 is a different institution now, leaner, saner, less of a social club. Everyone at FAMU knows the state is watching—watching the football program, the new president, the band. It's still messy. In 2014, the university trustees forced athletic director Kellen Winslow to resign seven months after they had hailed his hiring. Winslow offended Rattler alums by firing head football coach Earl Holmes four days before Homecoming. You don't fire your coach four days before Homecoming. The whole program seemed to be in disarray. Most important, the Rattlers have kept losing games.

Today, though, both the team and the band look pretty good. The 100's halftime show kicks it up from tentative to spectacular with "42nd Street." Joe Bullard says, "Hundred, the *time* is *now*—time to pull the anaconda *out*!" as they play Nicky Minaj. The drum majors bend over backward, hats touching the grass, then anchor themselves with one hand as they thrust their pelvises to the sky, jumping straight up as the band boogies and flirts all over the field, chanting, "My anaconda *don't*, my anaconda *don't*!"

FAMU's going to win this game. Finally. FAMU's going to win.

Of the fifteen young people charged with killing Robert Champion, most pleaded guilty and got some kind of house arrest, then community service and probation. One got a year in jail. Dante Martin, the "president of Bus C" and head torturer, got six years. Pamela Champion, Robert's mother, went to every hearing, every sentencing, carrying her son's cap, always standing elegant and restrained beneath an unfathomable sadness. She spoke to every defendant. She didn't sound angry or broken, she sounded like a sibyl. To one, she said, "I have no hate for you . . . you have to live with the fact that you killed my son." To another, "It will always be there haunting you. We both know that."

To Dante Martin, the president of Bus C, she said, "I just want to let you know, I forgive you. I don't hate you at all." As she held Robert's cap tight in one hand, she looked him in the eye. "And I don't want you shedding tears for my family because my fight is not over. My fight is not with you."

Drum majors in the 100 get a "band name" given to them by their peers. It's printed on their caps: THE BEAT, OLD MAN, JUICE. Robert Champion's band name was THE EXAMPLE.

THIRD QUARTER

Chapter 12

THE GENDER BOWL

FOOTBALL IS A GAME FOR MEN. Should you forget this fundamental law of the universe, men will remind you of it. Often. Teddy
Roosevelt praised football as a "rough, manly sport," even as he worried his son wouldn't be big enough to play for Harvard. "It's a man's
game, and if we keep chickifying this game, we're going to ruin it,"
lamented Rush Limbaugh, certain that "feminists" conspire even as we
speak to destroy football—and thus American manliness—by calling
attention to the epidemic of domestic abuse in the NFL.

"Playing football is a man's job," explained former Miami Dolphins lineman and champion metaphor mangler Lydon Murtha. "If
there's any weak link, it gets weeded out."

Murtha's talking about Jonathan Martin, also a former Miami
Dolphin, the young man bullied so viciously by Richie Incognito and
two other players that he contemplated suicide, eventually checked
himself into a hospital, and refused to finish the 2013 season. Somehow Martin failed to find being called a "half-nigger piece of shit"
hilarious or appreciate the boyish high spirits of texts threatening to
kill Martin's entire family and promising "to run train on your sister.
She loves me. I'm going to fuck her without a condom and cum in her
cunt."

Some people just can't take a joke.

According to keepers of the paleomasculine flame such as Murtha, Limbaugh, a nosegay of current and former NFL stars, as well as a lot of football fanboys on social media, Martin should have settled matters in the time-honored manner and beaten the living hell out of Incognito. Martin didn't do it because he's not, in football taxonomy, a real man.

Class, race, and gender—America's top three psychoses—lurk in every corner of this unseemly business. Martin's Harvard-educated parents sent him to a private prep school in California. Though he admitted he was occasionally bullied there, too, being a subliterate knucklehead wasn't the house style. His high school coach told the *Palm Beach Post* in 2013, "He's always been around Stanford, Duke, Rice kind of players," not "Nebraska, LSU kind of guys."

In other words, Jonathan Martin was accustomed to studious jocks, jocks who read books, and majored in something other than sports management.

Richie Incognito had once been enrolled at the University of Nebraska. It is unclear if he pursued an actual course of study. Martin graduated from Stanford with a degree in classics. Greek and Latin! Coy Wire, a Stanford grad who played for the Bills and the Falcons, says, "In a gladiator sport like football, intelligence can be perceived as being soft." Martin's detractors call him a sissy, a wuss. He's practically a *girl*.

Martin worried they might be right. He sent his father a despairing text: "I'm never gonna change. I got punked again today. Like a little bitch." When ESPN's *Game Day* visited the University of Southern California campus for the 2013 USC-Stanford contest, Trojan boy-wits appeared in force with their signs: variations on the theme of JONATHAN MARTIN SITS WHEN HE PEES, including one with a picture of Jonathan Martin spelling out P-U-S-S-Y with the Stanford logo S.

Pussy was one of Richie Incognito's favorite words. He kept a "fine book" in which he dinged Martin: "Pussy $100," "Pussy $100," over and over. He and the rest of the Goon Squad would tell Martin he had no balls, call him a faggot, and threaten to rape him. Incognito'd send Martin texts, first C, then U, then N, and T.

Masculinity is a precarious business, always endangered. You assume that Little Elvis or John Thomas will always be there for you, but step out of line with official manliness and that thing might go concave and turn into a dang vajayjay. Coaches displeased with their players address them as "ladies," exhorting them to "man up!" Players tell each other to quit being "pussies." What could be worse, more weak or embarrassing, than to become the organ that receives (you lucky girl!) the magisterial phallus? In a January 2014 *New York Times Magazine* piece, Steve Almond suggests it's immoral to watch the Super Bowl. The game's barbaric. It destroys bodies and brains. Almond ignited a slew of panicked responses from men, some of which he includes in his book *Against Football*, almost all of which, he swears, accused him of being endowed with a vagina. One, from a self-described "progressive," said, "change your tampon, you woman." Another insisted Almond must have "the biggest vagina."

Old Man Freud would have liked these boys. He also regarded femaleness as a debilitating condition.

As a feminist with a football problem (substitute *drinking* for *football* and you'll get what I mean), this shit makes me mad. I accept that I collude in the system. I go to games; I care who wins; I admire Kermit Whitfield's speed and revel in the way Travis Rudolph catches the ball. I do not accept that being a violent dumb jock asshole with a puerile attitude toward women should be celebrated along with football talent. But we've wrapped masculinity tight as ankle tape around football and declared that the football player is the manliest of the manly. Even a small football player is generally bigger than a normal human. And except for noseguards and linemen, they're that inverted triangle shape, a physique the Western world has cherished as the ideal masculine for 2,500 years, from the kouroi, the beautiful young male statues of Archaic Greece, to Channing Tatum: wide shouldered, narrow hipped, with muscled legs and blank faces.

Because, say it with me, people: football is a game for men. We all know women play every sport men play. Just not football. Girls and women play soccer and rugby at all levels; soccer and rugby are contact sports, too, though the culture's guardians of domestic tranquility don't manifest such anxiety over a female forward or scrum half. Maybe it's because American football's older cousins don't define masculinity for us. Maybe it's because soccer and rugby are not, in America, stand-ins for war. Boys in high school—hell, middle school—begin to weaponize their bodies, working out, piling on muscle, turning themselves into huge sinewy creatures who can both hit hard and run fast, like some advanced missile system. No wonder the idea of women playing creeps people out. Women have been in combat, but we're still not remotely comfortable with the idea of women on the front lines on purpose; we're still invested in a femininity of smallness and delicacy, or at least of sacred uteruses that must not be harmed.

Except sometimes. Every once in a while, women suit up as kickers or, in at least one case, a defensive back, but not in what the NCAA is pleased to call the "power conferences," not in the ones that get on TV. More girls try out for prep football every year: in 2013–14, according to the National Federation of State High School Associations, 1,715 girls played. Yet a young woman in a mouth guard and helmet is so exotic, she's invariably the subject of a slight but excited piece in a local newspaper, maybe on ESPN.com, even in some corner of *Sports Illustrated*, stories celebrating her athleticism and guts but also reassuring the panic-prone American public that gender as they've known and loved it is not dead. These girls aren't lesbians, they're not butch, they still want to be mothers some day; they still like skirts and makeup and boys and kittens. In October 2011, Pinckney Community High School in Pinckney, Michigan, crowned Brianna Amat Homecoming Queen during halftime at the game against Grand Blanc High. Her Homecoming Court wore sparkly gowns; Brianna Amat wore No. 12. She waved and smiled for the cameras, then pulled off her tiara and put her helmet back on. With five minutes left in the game, she booted a thirty-one-yarder to ensure the Pirates' 9–7 victory.

Americans nervous about the porous state of the gender border don't like to think of women serving in the Marines or the SEALs or even the plain old infantry, any more than they like Bruce Jenner's transformation into Caitlyn Jenner. He was a decathlete, one of the greatest champions since Cynisca of Sparta, then she went and appeared on the cover of *Vanity Fair*, all dolled up and wasp-waisted. Men of the right clutched their testicles in rage and despair: a talk-show host on American Family Radio said an America that can tolerate Caitlyn Jenner is "morally bent, morally twisted and morally bankrupt," a writer at the *American Spectator* called it "perverse," and Rush Limbaugh, predictably, got a bit hysterical, denouncing the whole thing as sick. Veteran sportscaster and fellow connoisseur of cosmetic surgery Bob Costas even had a little conniption fit over ESPN's decision to give Jenner the Arthur Ashe Courage Award. We don't want to encourage top jocks to go shifting gender on us! It's unsettling!

A lot of people don't want women encroaching onto that holy hundred-yard turf, either. Phyllis Schlafly, the ninety-something campaigner who helped kill the Equal Rights Amendment back in 1983 by raising hideous specters of women forced to register for the draft or women using the same public bathrooms as men, has spent the last ten years warning of the dire consequences of feminism. Not content with destroying the Christian family with their Free Love, their taxpayer-financed birth control, their abortions, and rape crisis centers, their insistence on equal pay, and their lack of decent foundation garments, now those godless wimmin want to wreck college football. Schlafly blames feminists for forcing Joe Paterno out of his job at Penn State and likes to point out that because by 1997, Boston University's student body had become 58 percent female, President Jon Silber's administration chose to drop football. Also, football was losing about $3 million a year, money needed to meet the Stalinist demands of Title IX. Too many women go to college, she says. The solution is enrollment quotas to assure an equal number of men on campus. How else will our girls get their MRS degree?

Moreover, as Schlafly wrote in 2005: "Men on sports teams act like men, and the feminists are hostile to the male culture. College football produces social conservatives such as Jack Kemp, Steve Largent,

J. C. Watts and the late Supreme Court Justice Byron White. College wrestling programs brought us conservative stalwarts Defense Secretary Donald Rumsfeld, Speaker Dennis Hastert, and Kansas Attorney General Phill Kline."

Schlafly might be sorry she included Hastert, called "the Coach" by his Washington colleagues, in that list, what with him now under federal indictment for bank fraud, reportedly shoveling money at a male former student to keep him quiet about past sexual misconduct. What was that about acting "like men" again, Ms. Schlafly?

Younger members of the Ladies Against Women movement, such as Charlotte Allen, who publishes in all the best newspapers as well as the *Weekly Standard*, wishes that women would just back off dissing football. Team sports are metaphors for war, a manly thing, which, while not necessarily *good*, is natural and inevitable and related to competition. Men need to compete because otherwise they'd go around destroying civilization. As Allen wrote in October 2014 in the *Los Angeles Times*, football "affords opportunities for heroism . . . because men venerate heroism as a positive channeling of the aggressiveness and competitiveness that are part of masculine nature. It's 'brutal' because it's played by men, who are generally exponentially stronger than women."

Besides, Allen says, men talking ball is kind of hot: "I'm fascinated by the detailed conversations about the nearly impossible intricacies of plays that I overhear from the male cashiers at my neighborhood Safeway every Monday morning after an NFL game."

What are women bitching about anyway? If they want to ape their gender betters, there are some semi-pro leagues in which they can play full-pad, full-contact games. In 2005, the Pittsburgh Passion and the DC Divas, two Women's Football Alliance franchises, combined to play against a male team in the Los Angeles Coliseum. The game was filmed for reality TV and billed as the Gender Bowl. The opposing team was a bunch of ex–high school ball players craving one more shot at sporting immortality. After the second practice session, the lads' head coach, former Dallas Cowboys star and Super Bowl MVP, Larry

Brown, told his team: "This game, guys, has tremendous magnitudes, and I have to come clean. It is not the type of game that you think. It is a totally different game."

Different because they were going to play against women. It seemed to make them extra angry. The assistant coach apparently had no trouble whipping them up into a good old castration-fear lather: "Let's protect this game! Protect our manhood! And protect this sport! Nobody's coming here and taking away our manhood!"

Come the fourth quarter, their manhood was more or less intact. The men beat the women, but not by much. Not by enough, perhaps. Women may have a place in football, but it's not on the field, not unless we're talking the Legends (formerly Lingerie) League, in which babes in bikini underwear, push-up bras, and abbreviated shoulder pads run, pass, and tackle while the spectators pray for wardrobe malfunctions. Otherwise, a woman's place is on the sidelines with pom-poms, as a trainer handing Gatorade to a player, or at the front of the band as a featured twirler with a fire baton. Between Title IX, Take Back the Night marches, and women becoming a majority on many campuses, girls are sucking all the air out of the room. Indeed, Phyllis Schlafly blames women for sexual assaults against women. In January 2015, she wrote a piece for WorldNetDaily arguing there'd be fewer rapes on campus if there were fewer women to be raped. Anti-rape campaigns are just part of feminism's project of man hating, and, besides, most of those alleged rapes aren't rape at all, just "casual hook-ups." Too much supply cheapens the product.

Many football-loving Americans hate even having to acknowledge sexual assaults and domestic violence perpetrated by players. Totally harshes your game-day buzz. So when Ravens running back Ray Rice punched his fiancée's lights out, then dragged her on the floor like a sack of feed, some people blamed *her*. Maybe she hit him first! He's five eight and weighs 210; she's maybe five five and weighs about 115. Thousands of fans at a Ravens game (including many women) gave Rice a standing ovation. Stephen A. Smith on ESPN's *First Take* cautioned women against "provoking" guys. Bitches get *mouthy* sometimes, and guys just can't help whomping on them.

To their credit, others in the football-industrial complex did not swallow that nonsense. ESPN's Michelle Beadle tweeted: "So I was just forced to watch this morning's *First Take*. A) I'll never feel clean again. B) I'm now aware that I can provoke my own beating." CBS sportscaster (and former Texas Longhorn quarterback) James Brown called for "comprehensive education of men of what healthy, respectful manhood is all about," reminding everybody, "When a guy says, 'You throw the ball like a girl' or 'You're a little sissy,' it reflects an attitude that devalues women, and attitudes will eventually manifest in some fashion."

People who believe that America is great because America is good, and that American football is evidence of America's special dispensation, find this discomfiting. Football represents discipline in a world of chaos, the triumph of American will. As talk radio host Steve Deace thundered in a *USA Today* piece, football "embodies everything we love about American exceptionalism. Merit is rewarded, not punished. Masculinity is celebrated, not feminized. People of various beliefs and backgrounds—a melting pot, if you will—must unify for a common goal for the team to be successful."

The college football demographic—those who go to games and, more important for the corporations who run this place, watch games on television—is white and Republican, people who like things the way they think they used to be. (The most Republican college football clan in the nation? The Crimson Tide.) These people are not keen on separation of church and state, but boy, do they cling to separation of dude and babe. They don't think women should be in combat, they don't want their daughters playing football—though it's OK for sons—and they're tired of having to consider themselves just another ethnic category in the crazy salad of America instead of unthinkingly enjoying the pleasures of hegemony without a second thought, even as they reject the notion of white privilege. Deace says, "As a people we are becoming soft—both around the waist and in the head." "Soft" is, of course, feminine. They're into personal responsibility. They give Janay Rice credit for admitting she may have colluded in her own beating, nodding approvingly when she said she "deeply regrets the role that she played the night of the incident." They embrace every dumb, testosterone-saturated stereotype of men as "naturally" aggressive, tough, rejoicing in pain—Hercules playing with a torn ACL, a broken back, six cracked ribs, a brain tumor, indigestion, and a bad case of acne. As if we fail to hang on to the most muscle-bound, nuked-up, ultracompetitive version of America, capitalism, and football, the terrorists win.

College football (pro, too) is a game predominantly played by African Americans, but predominantly controlled by white men. Yet white men have convinced themselves somehow that they've become an oppressed minority, constantly under siege from affirmative action, feminism, political correctness, doctors treating traumatic head injury, trial lawyers, and the likes of Barack Obama, who may love basketball but obviously hates America. Not only did the president say if he had a son, the boy would look like Trayvon Martin, that hoodie-wearing teenage thug who got in the way of George Zimmerman's ground-standing righteous vigilante bullet, he told the editor of the *New Yorker* he wouldn't want any boy of his to play football.

Well, Obama's no Teddy Roosevelt. He doesn't equate national virility with "manly games" or national power with beating the shit out of somebody on the field. Is this any way to run an empire? Americans have been nervous about the "feminization" of their society almost since they had a society. Before the Civil War, people fretted that religion was getting too girly; subsequently, Americans feared that educating girls robbed boys of "natural" superiority, allowing women to vote undermined the role of husbands and fathers as heads of households, working women deprived children of love, "feminazis" busted the balls of decent, innocent men, on and on unto the present hour, in which Fox News and their co-religionists blame feminism for everything from Ebola to bad hair days. On *Fox and Friends*, Elizabeth Hasselbeck ruminated on whether feminism might hurt national security. The Web site of "Joe the Plumber" stands up for men thus: "Do you ever wonder why there isn't a viable women's football league—a

WNFL? It's because women are not physically cut out to play football," and, just in case you ladies are confused, Joe says: "Who fought the bloody battles of the American Revolution that established America as a free and sovereign nation? It was men. Who drafted the Declaration of Independence and Constitution—two of the most significant documents in human history? It was men. Who went chin to chin with Hitler's storm troopers in four years of brutal battles and saved the world from Nazi tyranny?"

Certain Americans of both genders long for the innocence and prosperity somewhere back in our entirely fictional sepia-toned past, when everybody was Christian, maybe the time of "knights and their ladies fair," maybe before Social Security destroyed the national sense of initiative, maybe the 1950s, when Daddy went out to work and Mother stayed home—any era we imagine was as secure and uncontested as childhood. We long for the America in that Jason Michael Carroll song "Where I'm From":

> Where the quarterback dates the homecoming queen,
> The truck's a Ford and the tractor's green,
> And "Amazing Grace" is what we sing,
> Where there's a county fair every fall,
> And your friends are there no matter when you call.

Eden before the Fall, America before feminism, a time when boys played football and girls cheered. A time before football got chickified.

Chickification includes, of course, homosexuality. University of Missouri star Michael Sam came out to the world (he'd long been out to his teammates), got drafted by the NFL, and joyously kissed his boyfriend. Lordy! The knuckle draggers lurched out of their dunghills to object: former Jet Derrick Ward tweeted "No bueno . . . U got little kids lookin at the draft." Miami Dolphins safety Don Jones went, "horrible."

In February 2014, Sam's father, Michael Sam Sr., was at Denny's, celebrating his birthday, when he got a text from his son: "Dad, I'm gay." Mr. Sam told the *New York Times* he was so upset, "I couldn't eat no more." His distress impelled him to go drinking at a nearby Applebee's, saying, "I'm old school. I'm a man-and-woman type of guy" who doesn't want his grandchildren exposed to the homosexual lifestyle. As an example of his American values, he told the reporter that he had taken Michael Jr.'s older brother to Mexico to lose his virginity.

A Washington lobbyist named Jack Burkman claimed to be drafting a bill for Congress to take up, the "American Decency Act of 2014," which would ban gays from the NFL. "We are losing our decency as a nation," said Burkman. "Imagine your son being forced to shower with a gay man. That's a horrifying prospect for every mom in the country. What in the world has this nation come to?"

Well, whatever America may be coming to, Congress won't be coming to that bill. Same-sex marriage is now legal, and casual homophobia is going the way of casual racism—a social solecism. Except, perhaps, in NFL and NCAA locker rooms, middle school, frat houses, and certain segments of the Republican Party. Culture warriors continue to bemoan acceptance of the "homosexual lifestyle," which, they imagine, is turning everybody into women. Unless they're women already, in which case, they're turning into meddling feminists determined to destroy manly pursuits, just because those pursuits are manly. And a bit violent. In a 2014 *Grantland* essay by Bryan Curtis, Utah congressman Jason Chaffetz, once a record-breaking placekicker for BYU, says he doesn't think America needs official action on damaging head injuries: "We're turning into a society of wimps. Politically correct wimps." Stuart Stevens, a campaign strategist for Mitt Romney in 2012, said, "I think any attempts to make football a safe family sport, sort of like a low-level of volleyball, are absurd."

Volleyball is, of course, a predominantly female sport.

If women try to breach the barricades—or even sneak in the side door—of football's hypermasculine fortress, they'll be met by squealing resistance. Many men still respond to the prospect of women involved in football the way Dr. Johnson responded to the prospect of them in the pulpit: "A woman's preaching is like a dog's walking on his hind legs. It is not done well; but you are surprised to find it done at all." When women defy the natural order of things, well, there will be trouble. Thirteen years before Brianna Amat reigned over both Homecoming and the football field, Katie Hnida, a four-year starter at Chatfield Senior High in Littleton, Colorado, was also crowned Homecoming Queen, also in her football uniform. Hnida went on to become the first woman to score in a Division 1-A ball game, kicking two extra points in the University of New Mexico's win over Texas State–San Marcos in 2003. The College Football Hall of Fame now displays one of her jerseys. She's a hero, not just for her record but for her guts: enduring harassment, humiliation, abuse, and rape. In 1998, Coach Rick Neuheisel invited her to walk on at the University of Colorado. He then left for a job at the University of Washington. New head coach Gary Barnett was not enthusiastic, later saying, "None of the players wanted her on the team. Basically we were doing her a favor."

Here's what kind of favor Colorado did her: at practice, she says, the backup quarterback threw footballs at her head; the players would call her a bitch and a cunt; they'd display their dicks and grab her breasts or her crotch in huddles. One night a teammate raped her. Traumatized, suffering from insomnia and depression, she didn't tell anyone. Didn't talk about it for years. She just transferred schools.

A good team player.

But in 2004, when a slew of stories came out about Colorado players assaulting women at "recruiting parties," Hnida decided to go public. Barnett went public, too, not about her rape but her kicking skills: "It was obvious Katie was not very good. She was awful," he said. "Katie was not only a girl, she was terrible. OK? There's no other way to say it."

The same day Hnida's allegations came out in *Sports Illustrated*, Barnett sent an e-mail to Colorado's athletic director asking "how aggressive should I be re katie . . . sexual conquests by her etc."

Sexual conquests. I guess that's one way to put it—if you're an idiot. She says she was a virgin when her teammate raped her. Of course, Barnett's players followed his lead, supporting their coach, calling him an "upright, honest and moral man." Nobody stood up for Katie Hnida. The guys couldn't figure out why she didn't understand that she did not belong there with them. She crashed the men's game. She snagged a spot on the roster a guy could have had. So if she can't take care of herself, then she has to suffer the consequences.

In 2013, former college soccer player Lauren Silberman became the first woman to try out in an NFL Combine. It was not, indeed, done well. Her longest kick was sixteen yards, though she claimed to be injured, and because she was injured, she didn't warm up. Unimpressed, Katie Hnida told *USA Today*, "Her performance does not have to do with her gender, it has to do with her experience and her preparation."

The NFL hyped Silberman's appearance at the New Jersey tryouts, probably figuring women would want to see if one of their kind could hack it. The NFL's always gesturing toward women: players wearing pink for breast cancer awareness in October, the tailored jerseys they sell, the "girls night out" at the stadium. The league says women constitute 45 percent of their fan base. And men might hate-watch, hoping to see manliness validated. Judging by a wholly unscientific survey of comments on NFL sites and newspaper stories, while there were many "atta girls," supportive remarks, and assurances that one day a woman *will* play in the big leagues of football, generally Silberman's performance reaffirmed football's retrograde gender politics: "Well, the NFL teams could use a good cook." Or "We are different. Men are from Mars. Women are from Venus; period. We are different NO matter how many drugs women take, they WILL Never be as agile or strong as a Man. We are different and that is Good." Or "This lady did way more harm than good. Honestly, I think that's the point—women just don't belong in the NFL. PERIOD (no pun intended)."

IN THE 1980s AND 1990s, I wrote columns about college football for the *Florida Flambeau* newspaper, regarded by respectable people and politicians as the fell offspring of the *Socialist Worker* and *Zap Comix*. I was often the only woman in the press box, other than the employees of the university's Sports Information office, who were treated (for want of a better word) as hostesses. Men would half look in my direction and say, "Go git me a co-cola, would you, darlin'?" The first time I trooped off with them to the Seminole locker room after a game, the straight-up sports guys went rigid with horror. *You can't go in there! There's, you know, nekkid men!*

My pass didn't say anything about checking out junk and ogling muscled backsides, but it did give me access—like everybody else with credentials—to the locker room, where I interviewed several towel-clad players. We failed to discuss their genitalia, instead focusing on frivolous topics such as that fourth-quarter interception that saved a touchdown, and what about that rooskie play?

Things are different now. Kind of. Women write sports for the *New York Times, USA Today,* and the *Washington Post*; women are all over ESPN and Fox Sports television, though in college football too often relegated to the role of what the hairy-chested faithful call Sideline Babes. SBs are knowledgeable reporters, highly professional, and smart. They also (this is television) tend to be sleek-haired young women in smartly cut jackets who tote network microphones out in the rain or the heat, updating us on injuries and nabbing the coach for a thirty-second interview before halftime in which he assures viewers that everything will work out if the team can just settle down, stick to their game plan, and execute. Meanwhile, up in the climate-controlled booth, a couple of guys, less attractive than the Sideline Babes, more given to intoning sports clichés dating from the Late Pleistocene, but more, you know, XY-ish, dispense lapidary phrases about What This Game Means.

Women who do color or play-by-play on television are as rare as the Hainan gibbon. The hairy-chested react badly whenever a woman takes over the booth: "I turned to the Michigan-Purdue game on ESPN this past weekend. As soon as I heard that a woman was doing the play-by-play, I had to change the channel. Please stop putting women in that position. It's not exciting and it doesn't sound natural."

Not natural. There was a similar premature discharge in 2013 when the college football playoff barons chose Condoleezza Rice for the selection committee. Tommy Bowden declared, "If the selection committee wants to get it right, and find the most knowledgeable people about the sport of football, go get people who played the game and preferably coached the game." Former University of Georgia linebacker, ESPN analyst, and first-round bonehead David Pollack didn't think the Alabama-born daughter of a football coach, a former US secretary of state, had the right equipment for the job: "I want people on this committee—guys—that can watch tape . . . that have played football, that are around football, that can tell you different teams, on tape—not on paper." When asked if that meant no lady people, Pollack went, "I'll say it, yeah. Yeah."

But nobody wallowed more in the ole-times-not-forgotten, when men grappled on the gridiron like crazed wildebeests and women stood by clutching their parasols, than Pat Dye, the chaw-spitting former Auburn coach–turned–children's book author. Of Rice he said: "All she knows about football is what somebody told her. Or what she read in a book or what she saw on television."

He went on, "To understand football, you've got to play with your hand in the dirt. She's probably a good statesman and all of that, but how in the hell does she know what it's like out there when you can't get your breath and it's 110 degrees and the coach asks you to go some more?"

According to Pat Dye's logic, only former US presidents should pick US presidents because only they understand the job. Condoleezza Rice never played the game with her, um, "hand in the dirt," putting her in the same category as 1. two other (male) members of the playoff committee and 2. Brent Musburger, Verne Lundquist, Pete Rozelle, Anish Shroff, Paul Finebaum, Paul Tagliabue, Chris Fowler, Rece Davis, Sean McDonagh, Brad Nessler, Mike Tirico, Tony Barnhart, and Keith Jackson—Keith Jackson, y'all! Keith Jackson who called the Rose Bowl the way God *Hisself* would do it.

Oh, and about that 110-degree heat? I'd like to see Pat Dye in the wet-towel torridness of a Washington DC summer in the middle of the Iraq War try to juggle Junior, Uncle Dick, and a passel of administration lies in front of a hostile press corps while wearing pantyhose and heels.

Chapter 13

THE LADIES AUXILIARY

CHECK HER OUT, the lovely Queen of Aggieland: aristocratic nose, big eyes, and golden-highlighted hair. She never trots around campus alone or carries her own student ID and cell phone. She has a man to do that for her, a cadet in Company E-2. Just as Queen Elizabeth II is colonel-in-chief of the Grenadier Guards, the Queen of Aggieland holds the rank of honorary cadet general. Freshmen cadets must salute and greet her with, "Howdy, Miss Reveille, ma'am." Indeed, she is always addressed as "ma'am" or "Miss Rev."

Texas A&M is a tradition-minded Southern university. Miss Rev is a Southern lady, even though she's a bitch. A collie bitch.

During the 2014 Texas A&M game against SMU, Miss Rev sat on the sidelines, soaking in that Twelfth Man excitement and enjoying the September sunshine. Suddenly Aggie mascot corporal Ryan Kreider, Miss Rev's official escort, realized she was in danger: Mustang receiver Der'rikk Thompson careened out of bounds at full speed, trying to catch an overthrown pass, heading straight for her. Corporal Kreider, armed only with his natty white gloves and a leash (Miss Rev at the other end of it), leaped into action, deflecting the 190-pound Thompson away from her. My hero! Chivalry, in college football, is not dead.

Equality, however, is another animal. Gender roles in college football seem to derive from some combination of comic books and medieval romances. The players, unnaturally large, unnaturally muscled, armored in sofa-size shoulder pads and laced into tight knee-pants, look like knightly superheroes. Cheerleaders, their female counterparts, look like, well, Tinker Bell. They're tiny. They seem immune to gravity, what with all that leaping and flying, yet they're strong, too, with better abs than the offensive line. The only six-pack those dudes can claim is the one waiting for them back in the dorm room fridge. In the enterprise of college football, men strive on the field, hitting and being hit. Women stay on the sidelines or in the stands: coaches' wives, cheerleaders, dancers, majorettes. They are the Ladies Auxiliary. Football, like the Catholic Church hierarchy and the United States Marine Corps, remains largely unencumbered by feminism. Men star, women support; men get the top jobs—AD, coach, quarterback—women smooth the path and cheer them on.

At the top of the Ladies Auxiliary and at the top of the stadium, too, in their own box, the coaches' wives sit like princesses at a joust. They wear the team colors, of course: they own vast wardrobes of blue and gold or crimson and white or scarlet and gray. Whenever their husbands get a new job, they have to throw that stuff out or give it to Goodwill, or repurpose it as best they can, maybe declaring that Mississippi State maroon is really FSU garnet, or figuring out whether they can get away with leftover Tennessee Vol orange in Gainesville as long as they pair it with the right Gator blue.

A coach, like a preacher or a prince, must have a wife. She should be polished and attractive, friendly and vivacious, tough but with beautiful manners: a combination of beauty pageant winner, therapist, saint, PR expert, and lawyer. If the team is struggling, the children get bullied, her husband gets shunned, and social media light up like a Klan cross. When the coach gets fired, Mrs. Coach handles selling the house and packing up the furniture, the kids, and the dog. When the coach gets a new job, she unpacks the furniture, the kids, and the dog, deals with the insurance guy, the lady at the bank, the teachers at the new school, soccer and piano practice, and finding a dentist, as well as giving parties for the other coaches' wives, the players, and the boosters, all with a big, perfectly pink smile on her face. A few head coaches' wives manage to have careers of their own: Carol Stoops, wife of Oklahoma's Bob Stoops, is a highly successful national sales director for Mary Kay Cosmetics. Kathy Miles, wife of LSU's Les Miles, used to be a basketball coach. Mary McEnery, wife of Harry Stuhldreher, one of Knut Rockne's "Four Horsemen" at Notre Dame and longtime coach at Villanova and Wisconsin, was a writer. She expressed herself in no uncertain terms in a 1948 *Saturday Evening Post* piece titled "Football Fans Aren't Human."

The Badgers, long a top-tier team, kept losing. Harry Stuhldreher resigned. His wife said that if he didn't, she would: "Three years of keeping my chin up had given me an advanced case of stiff neck. [Stiff necks have become an occupational disease among coaches' wives.] I had neither the courage nor the strength to live through another football season, and I'd be lying in what teeth I had left if I said otherwise."

The coach's wife is supposed to keep the family in line, so that the coach doesn't get distracted. But hormones, jealousy, and alcohol happen in the best of Christian families. So it was that Terry Saban, wife of University of Alabama coach Nick Saban, woke up one morning to find that her daughter was being sued by a sorority sister. In 2010, Miss Kristen Saban and Miss Sarah Grimes, both Phi Mu's, both pretty blondes, got trashed playing a drinking game called Power Hour. An unkind Facebook posting and words regarding somebody's boyfriend resulted in a hair-pulling, nose-punching donnybrook. There were tears, howls, and at least one concussion. The case went to the Alabama Supreme Court, which kicked it back to a lower court. In an attempt to squash this thing before it made the papers, Terry Saban approached Sarah Grimes's family; they claim they were offered football tickets and parking passes and other Crimson Tide treasure, if only they'd go away. It didn't work, resulting in much embarrassment, not least of which were the sports columns ruminating on how his daughter's "plight" could prevent Nick Saban from focusing on his one job, winning 'Bama another national championship, while Kristin's face appeared on game-day signs declaring KRISTEN SABAN CAN BEAT ME ALL DAY.

In April 2015, the Sabans must have worked something out with the Grimeses: Sarah Grimes petitioned to drop her suit. Court crisis averted.

Novelist Nanci Kincaid once described herself to me as a "serial marrier of football coaches" (though it was really only two). She was the Homecoming Queen at the University of West Virginia; naturally, she married the quarterback. This sort of royal pairing is not rare: Terry Saban was a head majorette; Nick Saban was the quarterback. Nanci's husband, Al Kincaid, worked for Bear Bryant, later becoming head coach at Wyoming and at Arkansas State. They divorced, and she eventually married Dick Tomey, head coach of the Arizona Wildcats, architect of the famous Desert Swarm defense. When Nanci and I were both at the University of Alabama in the early 1990s, she was still married to Al and beginning to find her way as a fiction writer, giving voice to her observations of Southernness and the strange kingdom of football. Certain (male, old) people refused to take her seriously, this beautiful, clever woman with perfect manners. Then she began to publish. Her first novel tackled interracial friendship in segregated Florida. Her second, *Balls*, dissected the well-upholstered world of coach's wives and their discontents. In it, Dixie Carraway Gibbs, married to an assistant at an alpha football school, reflects on the boss's wife: "She's not the only head coach's wife I know who calls her husband *Coach*. I hope I die before I'm reduced to calling Mac *Coach Gibbs*. She says *Coach Bomar* like it's the only way I'll know who she's talking about, like if she says *my husband* it'll mean nothing to me, and I'll have to stop and figure out who she means. I guess nobody can really think of coaches as husbands, not even their wives after a while. It's like if she called him anything but *Coach* she'd be telling a big lie."

Mrs. Coach is the Mother Goddess, tending the hearth while Coach goes off to win glory; cheerleaders are like the battle spirits, the Machae, who hung around the aegis of Zeus, egging him on. Perkier, though. Now before the Cheerleaders' Union sends a peppy hit squad after me, let me say I know that cheerleaders are athletes first and foremost, often highly accomplished gymnasts. Many are on scholarship. They train as hard and get hurt nearly as often as football players. Maybe more often. It depends on how you cut the numbers. In 2012, the American Academy of Pediatrics found that between 1982 and 2009, cheerleading "accounted for 65 percent of all direct catastrophic injuries to girl athletes at the high school level and 70.8 percent at the college level." The total number of skull fractures and other injuries causing death, paralysis, or severe permanent brain damage was low compared to the number of girls cheering—110 out of more than three million. Nevertheless, the National Center for Catastrophic Sports Injury Research says cheerleading is the most dangerous "female sport."

And yes, I know some cheerleaders are men. The first cheerers were male: when it all started depends on how you define cheering and sports. There were war cries, of course, the Old Norse *Huer av!* ("Heads off!"), which might be an ancestor of "Hurrah!" There were joyous exhortations, like Bacchae's *Evoe!* or the *Vivat!* hollered at coronations when the throng advances the wish that the king would live forever, which has exactly the same likelihood of happening as Florida State winning back-to-back national championships. Princeton University claims credit for the first sports yell sometime around 1880:

> *Rah! Rah! Rah! S-s-s-t! Boom! A-h-h-h!*
> *Hurrah! Hurrah! Hurrah! Tiger! S-s-s-t! Boom! A-h-h-h!*
> *Hooray, hooray, hooray! Tiger siss-boom-ah, Princeton!*

In the early 1880s, a Princeton alumnus called Thomas Peebles brought the phenomenon to the University of Minnesota, where students ran with it: "Rah, Rah, Rah! Ski-U-Mah! Hoo-Rah! Hoo-Rah! Varsity! Varsity! Minn-e-so-tah!"

Soon there were organized cheering squads everywhere they played college football, mostly shouting something akin to "sis-boom-bah" but occasionally more learned. At Yale, the "Long Cheer" makes frog noises in the Classical Greek of Aristophanes, then, rather ominously, quotes Charon as he docks his boat on the far side of the River Styx:

Brek-ek-ek-ek, koax, koax!
Brek-ek-ek-ek, koax, koax!
O-op! O-op!
Parabalou!
(followed by a lot of "Yale! Yale! Yale!" "Rah! Rah! Rah!")

Cheerleading seems to be a solid stepping-stone on the path to world power. President George H. W. Bush delivered this yell while a cheerleader at Yale, just as his father, Prescott Bush, had. Presidents Franklin Roosevelt, Ronald Reagan, and George W. Bush were also cheerleaders in college or at prep school. Former Texas governor Rick Perry was a yell leader at Texas A&M. The all-male squad of five wear white semimilitary uniforms and use hand signals to exhort the Aggies in cheers mixing the agricultural with the bellicose:

Squads left! Squads right!
Farmers, farmers, we're all right!
Load, ready, aim, fire, BOOM!
Reload! A&M, give us room!

Despite the continued presence of men, college cheerleading has become a girl thing, a fiesta of mixed messages in which fit, strong, talented tumblers display their athletic prowess while presenting themselves as an All-American hybrid of jailbait sexuality and apple-pie innocence. The balance can be hard to get right: in 2008, shortly after the University of Idaho Vandals players removed the UI logo from the seat of their britches (it was thought disrespectful), UI cheerleaders blossomed forth in small black halter tops and bikini-low minis. Blushing in the stands, Vandals demanded decency. This is *Idaho*, according to the Gallup organization, the third most conservative state in the nation, after Wyoming and Mississippi, a land of easily shocked white people. Vandals cheerleaders caved and covered their navels.

Most cheerleading squads now go for a kind of wholesome Lolita look: spray-on tans, false eyelashes, and bright lipstick (you have to look good when the TV cameraman zeroes in on you—and he *will*), short skirts with box pleats or side slits to allow kicking and, particularly in the red states, gigantic bows in their hair, the kind once worn by Victorian children.

Classic bowheadery evolved from preppy ribbon headbands in the 1960s and 1970s to the pastel bows worn by sorority girls of the 1980s to the "fascinators" posh British girls wear to society weddings. While New England and the Far West aren't big-bow territory, the Midwest and the former slaveholding states of the South produce a bumper crop of large bows perched on the heads of small women. Bows the size of dinner plates flourish from the University of Miami (orange) to the University of North Dakota (green) and as far west as Lubbock, where Texas Tech cheerleaders rock bows so wide, so pert, and so forward on the head they look like jackalope ears. Bows fly as far north as Minnesota, where Golden Gophers cheerleaders tie their hair with golden ribbon, though the biggest, most pre-adolescent bows are naturally found in the Old Confederacy. The University of South Carolina squad shows more bow than hair, and the white tails of the Georgia Bulldog cheerleaders' bows are long enough to smack a girl in the eye. *Adorable!*

Bow-sporting regions roughly correlate to populations that distrust feminism and vote Republican. People in the Bow Heartland cherish clear gender-role division: a boy should be strong; a girl should be sweet, vivacious, and ladylike—even when she's holding her foot up next to her cheek and presenting her pudendum—concealed in decorous Lycra—to eighty thousand football fans.

Many colleges offer an extra dose of sideline pulchritude, a dance team, which dispenses with the presence of men and wears tighter or tinier—or both—outfits. Less concerned with gymnastics than precision booty shaking and synchronized hair tossing, they're the mildly naughty

Magdalens to the cheerleaders' Madonnas. While the varsity squad performs the ancient ritual yells of "What do we want? TD! What do we want? Touchdown!" the dance team—the University of Nebraska's Scarlets, say—get down to Taio Cruz's "Dynamite," in a fashion you'd not normally expect of the blue-eyed daughters of the prairie. The Golden Girls of Alcorn State, not to be confused with the Golden Girls of the University of Missouri, UAB, Arkansas Tech, FSU, or LSU, don't seem to stop moving their hips for four quarters. With Rockette-range high kicks and funk-ballet leaps, they perform hell-for-leather halftime shows as the Alcorn State Sounds of Dyn-O-Mite Band plays the likes of Michael Jackson's "Slave to the Rhythm" and Rick James's "Give It to Me."

Then there are the majorettes, yet another flavor of sideline dream girl, long-legged and tall-booted, graceful and deft with that oddly phallic baton. Majorettes, like cheerleaders and dance-team members, must attend summer camps, sometimes two-a-day practices (just like the football team), work on choreography, and twirl till they can twirl no more. They must be fit, tough, and, according to an adept from Bibb County, Alabama, posting advice on the Web, women of character: "Majorettes don't have bad behavior in school. They also have to be classy. If you're one of them people who get into trouble a lot in school, you might want to rethink on being a majorette."

Making a big-time college majorette line is tough. According to the University of Alabama application, you must be able to execute the following:

Turns/pirouettes   double, triple (left and right); chaine; pique, illusion
Leaps   grand jeté, attitude (calypso), axel, leap to second, arabesque leap, cabriole, stag
Flexibility   kicks and splits
Acrobatic/Gymnastics   cartwheels, backbends, front/back walkers, scorpion
Twirling   finger twirls, full-hand twirls, horizontals, tosses, multi-turns (1, 2, 3, etc.).

The application warns hopefuls that judges will look at "dance/twirling technique and skills, enthusiasm, energy & spirit, showmanship, projection, poise, physical fitness, flexibility—high kicks/splits." As for tryouts, the university cautions, "Face and hair should be 'game ready.'" That means, makeup on, hair curled, supernova smiles. If you make it, your body fat will be measured twice a year.

Courtney Dover, twirling maestra, says she knew at the beginning of her University of Alabama career it was "Crimsonette or nothing else." She made the team five years in a row—trying out again each year—wearing the glittery rigs for which the Crimsonettes are known, including the patriotic one with the red-and-white striped tap pants and the gloriously glitzy, yet Annette Funicello–chaste, two-piece with the A's cascading diagonally across the top, a costume so eye-dazzlingly sparkly, it's as if the girls brush themselves with egg white and roll in diamonds. Each is hand crafted by Sheryl Wilds of Sheryl's Custom Sewing. She's been doing Alabama's majorette couture for twenty-three years, sewing tens of thousands of genuine Swarovski crystals on by hand. Each Crimsonette costume costs more than $1,000 and features the trademark BAMA picked out in gems and sequins on the derriere. Courtney Dover's colleague, Hannah Ray, told the *Crimson White* newspaper in 2013, that when she was fitted for her first Crimsonette outfit, "I turned to my dad and said, 'I've waited my whole life to have BAMA on my butt!'"

Branded on the rump—like valuable livestock. Not that the Crimsonettes see it quite like that: they are rightly proud to have achieved the BAMA on the butt. It ain't easy. Nor is it easy to earn the big bow of Gamecock cheerleading or the shiny boots and tight pants of the Alcorn State Golden Girls. But it's as obvious as a Nick Saban third-and-short play that football celebrates the most retrograde and extreme gender roles outside a 1950s sitcom: huge muscled beasts on the gridiron, petite beauties tumbling and twirling on the sidelines, ever encouraging, ever smiling, ever faithful. A bit like Miss Reveille. Even if their boys are losing by four touchdowns, they keep their chins up and their expressions sunny. Cheerleaders never roll their eyes and flounce off to find men who can actually score. Cheerleaders never give up, even on losers. Majorettes don't hurl their batons in disgust over yet another fumble, or offer to slice off parts of the players' anatomy with their twirling knives; and the dance team never stops with the inspirational booty shaking and the Miss America grins. Football's Auxiliary Ladies embody a guy's fondest fantasy: a woman who praises him, even if he can't catch, can't block, can't run. These are strong, smart, independent twenty-first-century women who nevertheless accept a secondary role in the strange and retrograde bubble of college football.

Training for football's handmaidens starts early. Courtney Dover's mother received a tiny baton as a baby gift shortly after she was born—Christie Coggins Dover was a Crimsonette herself in the late 1980s. Little girls (and some little boys) start twirling when they're two or three. You can buy cheerleader outfits for infants less than three months old; Pee Wee cheerleading begins at age four. By the time these girls are in first or second grade, they're jumping up and down cheering for seven-year-old boys on the field. The boys are already tackling; the girls are already performing arabesques, wearing midriff-baring costumes and makeup. It's like dressing kittens as a bride, a groom, and a wedding party. Cute, but faintly disturbing.

FOURTH QUARTER

Chapter 14

JABOO WINS

FROM THE FRONT, the Pike house at FSU looks like a hedge fund manager's idea of a plantation mansion: thirty-nine thousand square feet, redbrick, white columns, veranda—very tall, very grand. Antebellum is the top frat style throughout the country, though some go for chateau, Tudor pile, or hacienda, or some other architectural manifestation of privilege. The brothers call ΠΚΑ "the most prestigious fraternity on the South's most glamorous campus."

Jameis Winston used to hang out there. He was still a redshirt freshman, a friend of E. J. Manuel, the quarterback who led the Seminoles to an ACC Championship in 2012, and a first-round draft pick of the Buffalo Bills. E. J. was also a Pike. Unlike most other traditionally Caucasian fraternities at FSU, Pike has made a point of pledging a few African Americans, especially African American football players. One early spring afternoon when they probably should have been studying for a biology exam or reading *Lord of the Flies*, Jameis and some other young 'uns were messing around at the Pike house. They got to talking about the Challenge: throw a football over the house. E. J. Manuel had tried and failed. A few years back, Christian Ponder also tried. Also failed. Jaboo, as his mama calls him, the prodigy of pig iron country, wanted to show his stuff, here and now, at FSU's biggest frat, Pi Kappa

Alpha, the fraternity of senators, generals, and governors, the fraternity of Bobby Bowden and current FSU head coach Jimbo Fisher. The fraternity with a roof thirty-five feet high.

Jameis's first try, after he had rolled from behind the recycling bins in back of the house and come sprinting from the parking lot before letting go the ball, bounced off the shingles. Giggles ensued. Jameis went again, this time with a faster run-up. He launched that mother as if possessed by the spirits of Steve McNair and six generations of Mannings, and borne on his preternatural self-confidence, it cleared the roof by a good six feet. Luckily for Internet posterity, a Pike brother caught the miracle on his phone. You see the ball disappear, hear the brothers laughing and yelling "Oh, my *Gawd*!" while Jameis, wearing black shorts and garnet pullover, jumps up and down like a little kid. Jaboo wins.

He doesn't become Famous Jameis for another few months, at FSU's 2013 spring showcase, the Garnet and Gold Game, when he comes off the bench in the second quarter and immediately throws a sixty-yard touchdown pass. He's even more Famous Jameis in the first two months of the 2013 season, with a 67 percent completion rate and an undefeated team. He doesn't become Infamous Jameis until November 2013, when the news breaks that he's been accused of rape. On the field, he's been near-perfect, beating Clemson and Miami, beating everybody, by silly scores, thirty, forty, sometimes fifty points. The "close" game was against Boston College: FSU won that one by only two touchdowns. Jameis is cruising to the Heisman, maybe to a national championship, and a glorious fat NFL contract, when the world first catches wind of the events of December 7, 2012. He and his roommates met a young woman named Erica Kinsman at Potbelly's, a binge bar on College Avenue, favored by Greeks and wannabes. She went home with them. The next day, she went to the hospital for a rape kit examination.

A friend of hers had called the cops with a confusing story about how Erica might have been hit on the head, or maybe her head just hurt because somebody spiked her drink. Erica was certainly distraught.

But the blood test turned up negative: no drugs in her system. There was semen—from two different men—on her underwear. She didn't know her assailant's name, not yet. She says she found out when she saw him in class as the professor was calling the roll: Winston, Jameis.

The FSU athletic department knew—they knew about the accusation before the police did. They didn't think it worth passing up the university chain of command. Or alerting the cops. On January 22, 2013, a Tallahassee police detective named Paul Osborn called Jameis Winston and asked him to come in for an interview. Osborn then phoned FSU's senior associate athletic director, Francis "Monk" Bonasorte, a former Seminole All-American who's had his own troubles with the law (he was sentenced to six months in prison for cocaine trafficking in the late 1980s), to let him know his star recruit had a problem.

Now, you'd think the majestic machinery of justice would start humming, and things would be investigated in the usual way. But football, especially football in towns like Tallahassee, lives inside a golden bubble, and the police treated Jameis Winston as though he traveled under a diplomatic passport. According to the Title IX lawsuit filed on behalf of Erica Kinsman against FSU, Monk Bonasorte made two calls to a cell phone belonging to Candi Fisher—wife of head coach Jimbo. Then he called lawyer Tim Jansen, a high-profile, pit-bullish defender of accused jocks; Jansen told the police that Jameis Winston declined to be interviewed. The investigation stalled for nine months: the town, the Seminole Nation, remained blissfully unaware that their miraculous quarterback was accused of rape. Then a reporter for the *Tampa Bay Times* filed a public records request, revealing, hardly for the first time, the baroque theater of major college football: the lies, the obfuscations, the virtuous rah-rah facade concealing complex but unsurprising vice, the money, the Machiavellian plotting, as the law, the coaches, the boosters, and all who worship the boys of Saturday do their damnedest to tamp down any scandal that might endanger the team's progress toward the title game.

The police became part of the performance: they said the case had gone "inactive" and the victim refused to cooperate. Erica Kinsman says that's not true, that it was the cops who refused to cooperate. Officer Scott Angulo, of the Tallahassee Police Department's Special Victims Unit, didn't do what you'd expect: get security tapes from Potbelly's or interview Jameis Winston's roommates, one of whom supposedly recorded the rape, the sex, the whatever it was, on his phone. By the time anyone asked for it, the kid had deleted it. Angulo sent an e-mail to the taxicab company that had carried Jameis, his roommates, and Erica back to the apartment. The cab company apparently didn't respond and Angulo apparently didn't follow up. He closed the case without notifying Erica Kinsman.

It doesn't inspire confidence that Angulo also works security for the Seminole Boosters, the millionaire institution that helps to pay the salaries of the football coach and the university president. An FSU criminology graduate, Angulo's social media streams had been full of FSU fanboy stuff till he shut down his Facebook and Twitter accounts.

It was eleven months before state attorney Willie Meggs got a look at the allegations. The cops "just missed all the basic fundamental stuff that you are supposed to do," said Meggs. Hell, he seemed to be saying, I couldn't get a conviction if I wanted one.

What you saw depends upon who you are. The university and much of the town—including the police—wanted to believe Jameis Winston, mostly because he plays football so, so beautifully and makes us feel, so, so happy. Winning never gets old, you see. The cop who told Erica Kinsman that she should think carefully about pursuing her accusation against Jameis because "Tallahassee was a big football town," followed up that mild threat with a condescending look to her future, perhaps disguised as avuncular concern, warning that she'd "be raked over the coals and her life made miserable." He did not lie, whether he meant that as genuine advice or further evidence of his loyalties when it came to football and the law. A survey commissioned in March 2015 by Erica Kinsman's legal team found that over half the voters of Leon County, the potential jury pool for a Tallahassee trial, think she's lying. Two-thirds say Jameis didn't do it.

Universities are supposed to foster critical thinking, questioning of authority, even a touch of rebellion. And they do. But universities are also clannish. Remember, quarterbacks are our sacred kings, lords of our fondest sporting fantasies, repositories of our sense of tribal worth. #FreeJameis ran wild online—not that he ever spent a night in jail. Strangers to Erica Kinsman labeled her white trash. Jameis's defenders posted pictures of her standing in front of a Christmas tree decorated with beer cans. They published her name before she revealed it herself in Kirby Dick and Amy Ziering's 2015 documentary *The Hunting Ground*. They called her a liar. Some Seminoles decided to blame the *New York Times*. Dadgum Yankees! They wrote a big ol' story about cornerback P. J. Williams crashing into some kid on the way home from working at the Olive Garden, totaling both his car and the kid's, and fleeing into the night. After the cops showed up (city cops and, oddly, campus cops, though the accident happened at least a mile from FSU), Williams returned. They didn't test him for alcohol. They just issued him two tickets, one for the accident; one for driving with a suspended license.

P. J. Williams is now with the New Orleans Saints.

A little more than a week before Oregon slapped FSU from one end of the Rose Bowl to the other on New Year's Day 2015, Bob Gabordi, then editor of the *Tallahassee Democrat* and shameless homer, complained: "Birds traveling south for the winter from New York to Tallahassee cover more than 900 miles. So what is it about this Florida State football team that has the *New York Times* checking up on traffic tickets issued to Seminole players, as it did earlier this season?"

Surely Gabordi knew the answer to his question. Jameis Winston was FSU's Faustian Bargain: we danced with the devil to win a national championship, lionizing a kid who may or may not be a rapist— we will never know—making excuses for him, attacking the young woman who accused him, refusing to admit that the local police treat football players differently from other young men in the community or that Tallahassee might be, as the T-shirt says, A DRINKING TOWN WITH A FOOTBALL PROBLEM.

The kid is famous; the team is famous; and we expect love but not scrutiny from people whose job it is to uncover information? Gabordi goes on, petulant and provincial: "No team in college football history has had greater media scrutiny than this one. No team has been more vilified off the field or had its on-the-field accomplishments more diminished."

Rubbish. I seem to recall a fair amount of "media scrutiny" of Notre Dame's football culture after Lizzy Seeberg killed herself in 2010. When Ponzi schemer Nevin Shapiro boasted of taking Miami Hurricane players to nightclubs and restaurants, fixing them up with prostitutes, champagne, and yacht rides, and paying them to win big games, it did not go unnoticed, even by the august *Times*.

There's no conspiracy: major college football programs teem with money, sex, and violence issues, perpetually threatening to turn septic. That's why Monk Bonasorte's probably memorized phone numbers for hotdog lawyers like Tim Jansen, who says he's proud of getting guys off date-rape charges, and thinks that some women, whether consciously or unconsciously, target athletes: "These athletes are known in the communities, they are high-profile if they are a really good athlete. You've got girls out there. And don't forget they are teenagers. It is a potent combination."

Outside the FSU Athletic Department, Jameis Winston's least conflicted and most organized defenders were fraternities and sororities. FSU football's loyal Praetorians made sure the world knew they were true to their school—and their quarterback. They voted with T-shirts: the Jesus with Jameis's face, a custom-made I ♥ JAMEIS CONSENSUALLY in deepest garnet. Guys would emerge from fraternity houses on College Avenue wearing Number 5 jerseys with INNOCENT on the back.

They spoke in signs: pictures of the Heisman statue with a broomstick saying WITCH HUNT and I AM JAMEIS WINSTON showed up on ESPN's *Game Day*. ESECPN SUX! didn't make it past the network's security. Fraternities hung banners from their houses: ATΩ won the wit prize with a nice anti–Notre Dame effort: THE LAST TIME WE LOST, MANTI TÉO'S GIRLFRIEND WAS REAL #BLAMEJAMEIS. Alpha Delta Pi sorority flew a more sober flag: "AΔΠ LOVES OUR SEMINOLES!" Kappa

Delta sorority, home of several varsity cheerleaders, painted a stretch of concrete across from their house celebrating the Seminoles' winning streak: 22–0 #BLAMEJAMEIS.

Up Jefferson Street two blocks from KΔ, Delta Zeta displayed no Jameis-defending signs. Erica Kinsman was a Delta Zeta. For a while, security guards lurked on Delta Zeta's wide veranda. ΔZs would not talk to anyone with a tape recorder or a pen and pad. They stopped wearing sorority jerseys and pins on campus. A couple of my undergraduates—I'm a professor of English at FSU—members of other sororities but sympathetic to Erica Kinsman, heard that a sister had her tires slashed and the ΔZ house got a bomb threat. No one could confirm any of this. Few seemed interested in the real story, whatever that may be. Jameis versus the ΔZ had become another rivalry game. You are with us or against us.

I don't know how often Jameis Winston visited the Pike house, scene of his early throwing triumph, during his last semester at FSU. Probably not a lot, though it's conveniently located across the street from the Publix whence he purloined the notorious crab legs, the ones he first claimed he "forgot" to pay for, then changed his story, telling ESPN in 2015 that somebody who works at the grocery story, "Club Publix," where FSU students trawl the aisles checking each other out, regularly fixed him up with free stuff. Besides, the Pikes spent much of October 2014 dealing with an accusation of sexual assault of their own, which allegedly took place during the "Pikes of the Caribbean" party. The frat drew a temporary suspension. That was nothing: Pi Kappa Alpha had been banned from 1989 to 2000, thrown off campus, charter revoked. In 1988, some Pikes gang-raped an eighteen-year-old freshman: they call it *pulling train*. This was at their old house on campus, much smaller than the current pile, but still with the white columns. She was almost lethally drunk, with a blood alcohol level nearly four times the state's statutory definition of impaired. The ringleader, a trust-fund boy from South Florida, raped her, then other boys joined in. One couldn't get it up, so he penetrated her with a toothpaste pump. They scribbled profanities and the name of another frat on her thighs, pulled some clothes on her, then took her next door to the Theta Chi house and dumped her. Two of the guys involved got probation. Daniel Oltarsh, the trust-fund boy, got one year of jail time.

I wrote a column back then about the Pikes, who fancied themselves the greatest fraternity in America, the finest of men. These models of manhood did not hesitate to blame their victim, deluging my newspaper with hate mail insulting her and charging me with being bitter because (as one correspondent put it), though he had never laid eyes on me, he was certain I "didn't have what it takes" to be a Pike Little Sister.

Dang! if only I were prettier or sexier or blonder, I might have been privileged to hang with these gents and not *care* if some "dumb chick" (as many Greeks called the victim) went and got herself drunk and "used"—they'd never say "raped." Rape is something the lower classes do. *She shouldn't have been drinking* or *she shouldn't have gone back to the Pike house with him.* Sorority women whispered that they'd heard she was *trashy.* No decent house would pledge her. When ΠΚΑ got thrown off campus, the brothers were shocked. Upset. Puzzled. "I think it's sick what those guys did," said one Pike pledge at FSU. "But the press and everybody are trying to make the girl out to be the Virgin Mary. This girl got involved in this kind of stuff all the time. I hear she liked it that way."

Not the Virgin Mary. Not even a "nice girl." She left FSU, left the state of Florida. By 1990, she had become an alcoholic, diagnosed with PTSD. Many Greeks said similarly hateful things about Jameis Winston's accuser. She may or may not have been part of a loose confederation supposedly called Cleat Chasers, girls who liked to hook up with athletes, but the Seminole believers disseminated that rumor every which way they could. An online frat-chat site called Old Row (motto: "Southern Tradition at its Finest") resorted to a slur that has nothing to do with the actual morals of FSU Delta Zetas and everything to do with jejune rhyming and what passes for fraternity humor, dissing them as "Easy-DZ."

Rape, fraternities, and football go together like Everclear, sugar, and Kool-Aid. Most football players don't rape; most fraternity guys don't rape. But of the sexual assaults committed on campus, 25 to 30 percent are committed by athletes; 20 to 25 percent are committed by fraternity members. Frats rarely do themselves any favors in the PR department. In 2013, the Phi Kappa Tau social chairman at Georgia Tech sent his brothers an e-mail titled "Luring Your Rapebait," which began: "Alright chods, some of you could use some help on how to mack and succeed at parties." Two women who say they were raped at Tech's ΦKT house are suing the fraternity. You can read the studies by the University of Minnesota, the Justice Department, Indiana University, even the NCAA, for yourself. Sociologists will tell you it's about "valorizing men over women and reinforcing patriarchal legitimacy."

No shit. The brotherhood of the frat and the brotherhood of the locker room celebrate the conquest and domination of women as central to their performance of manliness. As the frat boys sing at UVA:

> A hundred Delta Gammas, a thousand AZDs,
> Ten thousand Pi Phi bitches who get down on their knees,
> But the ones that we hold true, the ones that we hold dear
> Are the ones who stay up late at night, and take it in the rear.

Worse, women don't run screaming from these guys. They sing along with them. Virginia's "Rugby Road" is not unlike the "dirty" songs my sorority sisters and I learned on initiation night. Masterpieces of misogyny such as:

> She was a virgin in her freshman year.
> She was a virgin with her conscience clear.
> She never smoked or drank or played around:
> She was the envy of every college girl in town.
> Then she met a dashing TKE
> And lost that sweet virginitee.
> Now she's a whore in gay Paree, gay Paree
> And mother of a TKE!
> (The little bastard)
> Mother of a TKE!

We had other ones, too, about Phi Delta Theta, Sigma Chi, Sigma Nu, all celebrating getting drunk and getting "nailed" by a frat guy who would then, presumably (because we were nice girls) present us with his pin. It never occurred to us to object: we wanted to be invited to the best parties. Sigma Nu Shipwreck. Or Old South. The Kappa Alpha Order, established in 1865, throws a party now officially named "Founders' Day" but known to everyone as Old South. The boys wore Confederate uniforms until their national office nixed them. But at FSU and other campuses in the South, they still sport plumed hats and ride on horseback from sorority house to sorority house, calling out their dates with a proclamation: "Fair lady! We pray you will honor us with your presence at our gala Old South Ball!" It goes on. "Dear lady, regardless of your place of birth or where you were reared, your innate gentility, refinement, and elegance entitle you to the respectful treatment afforded to a sweet Southern lady by a true Southern gentlemen." The girls float out the front door in off-the-shoulder wedding-cake crinolines, meeting their escorts under a canopy of upraised swords.

The hoop skirt's days on some campuses, however, may be numbered. In response to the jolly japes of the University of Oklahoma Sigma Alpha Epsilons, caught on video singing (to the tune of "If You're Happy and You Know It"), "There'll never be a nigger SAE" and "You can hang him from a tree, but he'll never sign with me," the KAs and SAEs at the University of Georgia have agreed to ban "Confederate dress" at their events. "Costuming," said UGA's Panhellenic and Interfraternity Council soberly, "must be evaluated as to its appropriateness." Some students might not understand. Or they might understand all too well. At Oklahoma, All-American linebacker Eric Striker called out the privileged white kids who'd cheer for him in the stands on Saturday afternoon, then laugh about lynching people like him: "Motherfuckers talk about racism don't exist, be the same motherfuckers shaking our hands, giving us hugs, telling us how you really love us. Fuck you phony-ass, fraud-ass bitches." Striker later apologized for his language and offered to help white frat boys understand what racism is.

The sorry tale of Jameis Winston and Erica Kinsman demonstrates how college football is knotted up with history, race, and sex. Whose body is more valuable: the black athlete's or the white girl's. In a nation of white people historically jittery about black male sexuality, Jameis didn't help his cause by putting out an Instagram video in which he and a teammate sing a rapey verse from a rap song: "She said she wants to take it slow. / I'm not that type of guy, I'll letcha know. / When I see that red light, all I know is go."

According to the prevailing white paranoia, black kids wearing hoodies in the street or playing loud hip-hop are pretty much criminals, even if they haven't committed any crimes. Pants up, don't loot! Black kids who win football championships for predominantly white universities are heroes. Good guys. Maybe we should be heartened to see white boosters and white fraternity and sorority members supporting a young black man who was not, let us remember, ever charged with a crime. They will share their privilege, for a while at least, with those who bring renown to the university: football stardom can bridge the class and race divide. Jameis Winston's second lawyer, a high-priced suit who represented former Miami Dolphin Jonathan Martin and other NFL players and who is now executive director of the NFL Coaches Association, claimed in a letter to FSU that the accuser's lawyer, Patricia Carroll, offered to settle for $7 million, asserting that Erica Kinsman's "sexual encounter" was clearly rape: her niece would never sleep with a "black boy." Hogwash, he said: the young woman's boyfriend, whose DNA was, like Winston's, found on her underwear, is also African American.

Jungle Fever, they used to call it. In 1934, a mob of white citizens in Jackson County, an hour west of Tallahassee, strung up twenty-three-year-old Claude Neal for the rape and murder of nineteen-year-old Lola Cannady, a white girl he'd known all his life. They may have been lovers. Nevertheless, Neal was hanged, burned, and mutilated, his genitals cut off.

Of course, Claude Neal wasn't a Heisman Trophy winner, sure to be an NFL first-round draft pick.

Chapter 15

THE PLANTATION

THERE'S SOMETHING OF the antebellum prizefight about modern college football: "our boys" can whip "your boys." I use the possessive advisedly: in a lot of ways—too many ways—the universities own these "student-athletes." Taylor Branch caught "an unmistakable whiff of the plantation" in his ass-whipping classic *The Cartel*. To me it's more like a stench. The National Collegiate Athletic Association pretties up the whole enterprise with gooey rhetoric about Sportsmanship and Fair Play, conjuring the image of a clean-limbed young American playing the game not for the wins, not for the titles, but for the sheer transcendent glory of it. In truth, the multibillion-dollar business that is college football exploits the bodies of young men who aren't even old enough to order a beer.

The Cartel (Branch means the NCAA) dissects how universities (and Nike and Under Armour and ESPN and the whole football-industrial complex) profit from the "unpaid labor of young athletes." He suggests the vestiges of slavery are readily apparent on the field, then backs off and says maybe it's more like colonialism, talented athletes, the rich natural resource of this colony, produce football to be exploited by colleges and consumed by the spectators. A tiny percentage of players go on to make their own money in the NFL; most trade their athletic ability for three or four years of free tuition at a university plus room and board (sort of) and the so-called thrill of competition. The NCAA, in turn, makes its rules and pockets its money, all the while insisting that whatever it does is in the best interests of those naive waifs, the "student-athletes."

Branch wasn't the first to liken college athletics to Twelve Oaks or Tara. Walter Byers, executive director of the NCAA from 1951 to 1988, decried "the neo-plantation mentality that exists on the campuses of our country and in the conference offices and in the NCAA that the rewards belong to the overseers and the supervisors." Byers put together the NCAA's first nationwide television contract in 1952 and is often credited (if that is the word) with transforming the NCAA from a fig leaf into college sports' rule-concocting, bureaucratic behemoth. The more authority the NCAA got, the less autonomy the athletes had.

Yet the NCAA couldn't rein in the colleges' ungentlemanly methods of recruiting and retaining athletes. As Branch points out, freshmen players at the University of Pittsburgh actually went on strike in 1939, angry that they got paid less than the upperclassmen. Unable to do anything about real corruption, the NCAA persisted, reinvented itself, and gathered unto its bloated, pettifogging corpus all manner of byzantine standards, regulations, and strictures, most of them designed to sound, at least, as though they had something to do with a college athlete's health, education, and spiritual well-being. University sports programs now hire "compliance officers" to study NCAA dictates in rabbinical detail. For example, in a scenario imagined by *Cleveland Plain Dealer* writer Bill Lubinger, "The team's star linebacker is headed to the local banquet hall to speak (for free) at a pee-wee football dinner. He swings by the athletic offices, where the head coach notices he's not wearing a tie. The coach pulls one from his drawer, tosses it to the linebacker, and wishes him good luck with the speech."

A nice, coachly thing to do, or a crime? To the NCAA, probably the latter. First it's a tie, next it's cuff links, on the road to perdition.

If the coach gives, rather than lends, a tie to a kid, it becomes the kid's property. But a football jersey, equipment given to the player that's needed to perform his role in a game, has a different status, for some bizarre reason. In 2010 a Georgia wide receiver called A. J. Green admitted to selling a jersey he'd worn at the Independence Bowl. He needed money for spring break. The NCAA hit him with a four-game suspension. Meanwhile, as Taylor Branch points out, "the Georgia Bulldogs store continued legally selling replicas of Green's No. 8 jersey for $39.95 and up." The NCAA suspended Georgia's revved-up tail-back Todd Gurley for four games in 2014, charging that he sold his autograph—his own autograph. Five Ohio State players got in trouble with the NCAA, too—their misdeed? bartering gear for tattoos.

Licensed merchandise—sippy cups, T-shirts, pasta, ChapStick holders, golf-club covers, video games, coffins, luggage straps, Rubik's cubes, tents, cocktail napkins—rakes in $7 to $10 million per year for top programs like FSU, Ohio State, and Alabama. Woe betide anyone the athletic legal office suspects of infringing a trademark. In 2012, a lady named Mary Cesar received a rather frightening cease-and-desist letter from Collegiate Licensing Co. in Atlanta. The letter threatened damages, too. Her transgression? Cookies. Illicit cookies decorated with a University of Alabama–looking A sold in her Northport, Alabama, cake shop.

Mary Cesar isn't running some sweatshop mega-bakery; it's a cute little place across the river from Tuscaloosa. She's made cakes for the UA Athletic Department before, including one in the shape of the crystal football National Championship trophy served at UA on National Signing Day. Now 'Bama's picking on her cookies? Willita Zoellner of Tuscaloosa, holder of two degrees from UA, said, "For shame, alma mater. You are behaving like a greedy shrew defending a girlie Script 'A.'" But Collegiate's humorless, corporate robot attorneys would have sued Nathaniel Hawthorne if he'd slipped and described the A on Hester Prynne's sinful bosom as "crimson."

The University of Alabama finally apologized to Ms. Cesar and backed off. Nevertheless, they've trademarked pictures of elephants in red shirts, the phrase "Roll Tide," and the word "Alabama." Yep, they've trademarked the state's name. Watch out, Skynyrd: you're next. They guard their "brand" like a hyena guards its kill, and the NCAA is right there with them, protecting its revenues and its power—not protecting the young people who play the game. In his 1995 memoir, *Unsportsmanlike Conduct*, Walter Byers says he and the NCAA saw the obvious equivalence between player and employee as a "serious, external threat" to amateurism (and thus to their very raison d'être), so they "crafted the term student-athlete, and soon it was embedded in all NCAA rules and interpretations as a mandated substitute for such words as players and athletes."

The more refined sort of plantation owner preferred the word *servant* over *slave*. No doubt, the men at the top of the NCAA see themselves as good, kindly masters who, if they punish a university or a player, do it only for its or his own good and to protect the sacred spirit of amateurism. Michael Rosenberg of *Sports Illustrated* once tried to get the late Myles Brand, then president of the NCAA, to illuminate the genius logic behind refusing to free college athletes from the nineteenth century:

Michael Rosenberg   "What makes them amateurs?"
Myles Brand   "Well, they can't be paid."
Michael Rosenberg   "Why not?"
Myles Brand   "Because they're amateurs."
Michael Rosenberg   "Who decided they are amateurs?"
Myles Brand   "We did."
Michael Rosenberg   "Why?"
Myles Brand   "Because we don't pay them."

"Contrariwise," continued Tweedledee, "if it was so, it might be; and if it were so, it would be; but as it isn't, it ain't. That's logic."

In the weird kingdom of the NCAA, it's OK if other people profit handsomely from selling a player's image, his jersey, his name. The player himself must not sully the immaculate game with grubby money. This attitude—What you boys need with money? Ain't we feeding you enough?—is hardly new. The upstanding white men who run sport have long espoused amateurism, especially for athletes of color. Slave jockeys rode their masters' horses in steeplechases, slave runners took part in races, slave boxers in fights. The owner won as well, without ever getting out of his chair. The slave's reward for success was temporary inclusion, being a part of the family for a little while, one of "us"—as long as you're successful.

Now you hear people (most likely men) bragging that "we" will beat the hell out of "you," a by-proxy dick-size contest in which you, personally, never lay it on the table but rely on other guys, often younger, often poorer, to out-phallus the competition. That's how we humorless feminists see it, anyway. And let's not forget race: because 60 percent of the "student-athletes" now playing football for the top twenty-five colleges are African American, there's a hint of that old *Birth of a Nation* favorite, the dark rumor of black male sexual superiority, wafting around the competition like the stink off yesterday's barbecue ash. Conversation at the tailgate or the sports bar compares the height, weight, and speed of your players versus theirs. It's a casual version of what coaches do judging high school recruits or potential draftees at the NFL Combine. The whiff here isn't so much of the plantation as of the slave market. In *Twelve Years a Slave*, Solomon Northup describes sale day in New Orleans, with the merchandise told to "hold up our heads, walk briskly back and forth, while customers would feel of our hands and arms and bodies, turn us about, ask us what we could do, make us open our mouths and show our teeth, precisely as a jockey examines a horse which he is about to barter for or purchase." A kid named Randall, whose selling point was youth and strength, "was made to jump, and run across the floor, and perform many other feats, exhibiting his activity and condition."

The NCAA is wounded, deeply wounded, at the suggestion that the noble game of football treats its players like slaves. Why, they can quit any time! And coaches hardly ever check out players' teeth. But players don't quite own themselves, either. They live where they're told, eat what they're told, exercise when they're told, take vitamins and supplements or whatever else the trainers tell them to swallow—for the greater glory of the university that hands out the scholarship, the coach looking to make that conference championship bonus, and the athlete himself, the young man who might, just might, be good enough to play on Sundays.

Conversely if a player gets injured, he might lose his scholarship; the university might emancipate him, setting him free to deal with his own medical bills. The NCAA pays for insurance on athletes, but the deductible is $90,000. Up to that amount, the college or the parents must insure him. After a 2005 collision that temporarily paralyzed South Carolina's Stan Doughty, he went to the locker room for a "rest" of five minutes and some kind of perfunctory examination, then he was sent out to the field again. He didn't know he had suffered big-time neurological and spinal injuries. He's now back in Louisiana, living in his parents' double-wide, unemployed and unemployable. Neither the NCAA nor the University of South Carolina has contributed to his medical bills or even acknowledged his suffering, though he helped them beat the likes of Georgia, Alabama, and Tennessee.

Sometimes an institution does the right thing: Head Coach Nick Saban insisted on Elisha Shaw getting his full scholarship to Alabama in 2014, even though he got hurt in his last high school game and won't be playing football for the Tide or anyone else. The horror stories are more typical, though. Bob DeMars, a USC defensive lineman from 1998 to 2001, separated both shoulders, seriously hurt his neck, and tore up his knees playing for the Trojans. He says: "College athletes aren't employees, so there's no workmen's compensation. They tell us we're student-athletes because it's not a job. But it sure is a business, and it's not a nonprofit."

As if that's not enough, Ed Orgeron, DeMars's coach, berated him and called him a "motherfucker" for leaving practice twenty minutes early so he could *go to class*. Such abuse isn't new, nor is the resistance to it. For a brief moment in the early 1970s, it almost looked as though football players would rise up and fight the power. Carlos Alvarez, the

"Cuban Comet," a brilliant wide receiver at the University of Florida, led an advocacy group called the Florida League of Athletes. It wasn't a union, but given the hostility from the sporting press and his own coaches, it might as well have been a branch of the Socialist Workers Party. Alvarez had also criticized Gator head coach Doug Dickey for not seeming to give a damn about his players: "Maybe Dickey would be great for General Motors," said Alvarez, "but he didn't know how to deal with the players at Florida."

Dickey dismissed Alvarez as "immature." Others suggested he was some kind of Gator traitor and demanded he "go back to Cuba." The Alvarez family had fled Cuba in 1960 because "we couldn't speak out over there," but, as they discovered, speaking out in America wasn't often welcome, either, especially by ball players, who should suck it up and take it like men.

One of the most stomach-churning abuse cases happened at Florida State in the early 1970s as the US war in Vietnam limped toward its wretched finale. Former Seminole quarterback Tommy Warren and the *Florida Flambeau* newspaper uncovered a story about brutality in the name of winning that shows that coaches saw players as expendable, foot soldiers in the football wars who had to "get tough" or die trying.

FSU's football coaches and trainers decided their boys needed what they called "conditioning." The Geneva Conventions might use a different word for it. On November 18, 1972, head coach Larry Jones lost his temper. The Seminoles had blown a Peach Bowl invitation by losing to a cupcake, the South Carolina Gamecocks, by a field goal. Jones felt his guys hadn't tried very hard. The guys lost their tempers, too: the team had no depth to speak of, and they had to play hurt. Everybody was banged up and pissed off, so they got good and drunk on the flight back to Tallahassee, making it clear they didn't *want* to play in any goddamn bowl.

Next spring, the coaches retaliated, reinstating an illicit practice (against NCAA regulations) that had begun with the previous coach, Bill Peterson, but had been allowed to lapse. Masquerading as a "voluntary" phys ed class, some drills were conducted in chicken-wire cages; some were fistfights in what the players called The Room. Two guys would stand back to back. When Coach blew his whistle, they'd start pummeling each other. Ex-scholarship player Hod Verble told a reporter in June 1973, "You would literally fight it out until somebody won. The player who lost had to stay in and fight again. You had to stay in until you won. I've seen people with blood completely covering their shirts—me, too. You could be standing there puking blood and the coaches would just holler louder, 'Get tough! Get tough!'"

Verble got tough: he quit. Other players had it worse. A coach went berserk when promising center Steve Macaulay had a bad day in practice, kicking and punching him. Boys who had been coughing up blood were forced to practice; boys with badly swollen joints and torn tendons and strep throats were forced to practice. Everybody had to beat the hell out of everybody else. In, you know, a manly fashion. Tommy Abbott, a three-sport star, reinjured a knee but had to play anyway. By the time he got specialist medical care, his knee was in, as the doctor officially wrote, "terrible shape." FSU's head trainer, Dick Milder, begged to differ, accusing Abbott of faking the injury—never mind the two surgeries he'd just had—threatening him with being kicked off the team.

Milder, the trainer, thought the team doctor mollycoddled the players. Real men, as we know, do not get sick. Real men do not get concussed. Or if they do, they keep playing. All-American wide receiver Barry Smith was knocked unconscious in the game against Houston. He stayed out cold for a good ten minutes, lying there so long, half the stadium feared he'd broken his back. The next week team doctor Robert P. Johnson, who later resigned, refused to certify him fit to play. Coaches and trainers said Johnson was trying to sabotage the team. In the third or fourth play of the game against the University of Florida, a kid named Danny Miller broke his neck. He stayed in pretty much the whole first half—the trainers wouldn't listen to him. Finally, he collapsed. Grudgingly, they called an ambulance.

Outside the militarily tidy and vicious world of FSU football,

Students for a Democratic Society were demonstrating; the Black Student Union was raising a collective fist; women were demanding equal rights under the law; and Florida State's Center for Participant Education, a "free university," promised classes called the Homosexual and Society and How to Make a Revolution in the US. The world was spinning very fast indeed. The Florida legislature got upset about the hippies and the commies and the Black Panthers and the bra burners and the student newspaper, which was the first to tell the story of Larry Jones's chicken-wire cages and beatings. They didn't have a problem with the football program. This is how football was done at Alabama and Florida and Texas A&M. This was how you made boys into men. Coach Jones was making men, real men, American men. Not like those freaks you saw sitting under the oak trees with their long hair and bare feet.

By summer 1973, twenty-eight players had either quit or had their scholarships revoked. By then, it was a national scandal. Guys who'd played hurt with wrecked backs or knees got dumped. Coach had no use for them, so they cut them loose. Many left college. The white men in charge insisted that no rules were broken. Those drills were voluntary. Those student-athletes were just fine.

St. Petersburg Times reporter Fred Girard produced a devastating three-part series detailing the players' ill treatment and the university's "response." (Tallahassee's newspaper ignored the story.) University president Stanley Marshall was shocked, shocked and dismayed: "Our primary goal is academic excellence in every department of the university. Athletics, while they are important at Florida State and while we seek to achieve excellence in every area in which we field teams, have always been secondary to our emphasis on academic programs."

Tommy Warren told Girard, "There's nothing the football player can do. He has no union, no spokesman, no grievance committee within the student body, the athletic department or the administration."

FSU went 0-11 in 1973.

A mere forty-odd years later, players still have few rights, but some of them are fighting the power. In 2014, the National Labor Relations

Board ruled that football players at Northwestern University could vote on whether to unionize. The same year, US District Court Judge Claudia Wilken ruled in a lawsuit brought against the NCAA—by former UCLA basketball star Ed O'Bannon and other basketball and football players who weren't entirely flattered to find their images and jersey numbers in video games from which they reaped not one thin dime—that players had to be compensated for use of their "names, images and likenesses." Colleges could put up to five grand per player per year into a trust for the athletes, and the NCAA could no longer stop colleges from giving players a scholarship worth—get this!—the actual cost of going to college. When FIFA, or its hideous cousin the IOC, want to defend themselves on charges of bribery and forced work conditions, no doubt they point to the NCAA as proof things could be worse.

There's also a class action suit filed on behalf of football and basketball players headed by Clemson cornerback Martin Jenkins against the NCAA and the major conferences (the ACC, the SEC, the Big 10, Big 12, and Pac-12), demanding a free market, or at least a share of the vast revenue generated by their sports. Unlike the O'Bannon suit, which resulted in limited change, this one could actually bring down the cartel, and the cartel knows it. The NCAA's defense in both cases insists that fans would hate it if players got paid. They'd be sullied, damaged goods, no longer innocent "amateurs." Besides, paying players wouldn't be fair, since some colleges are rich and others are poor, plus other sports, especially women's sports, would be cut. This would ignite a Title IX inferno.

But the NCAA's deepest philosophical objection is actually venal self-justification dressed up in emotion and nostalgia: Amateurism must not die. Amateurism is beautiful. *Dulce et decorum est* to blow out your knee and tear up your shoulder, not for anything so sordid as money, but for higher rankings and the greater enjoyment of the boosters.

Besides, the kids do get compensated for their talents. They get a "free" education. As Seth Davis of *Sports Illustrated*, perhaps offended by Taylor Branch's plantation metaphor, wrote in September 2011: "Student-athletes earn free tuition, which over the course of four years can exceed $200,000. They are also provided with housing, textbooks, food and academic tutoring. When they travel to road games, they are given per diem for meals. They also get coaching, training, game experience and media exposure they 'earn' in their respective crafts."

Davis correctly points out that "98 percent" of scholarship players "will never make a dime" in the pros. "If anything," says Davis, "most of these guys are overpaid." Yet some of them think they're owed more, just because their "labor" generates value for the university. Ingrates. I mean, *per diem*! It's true that unlike the student-somnambulists, student-hedonists, and those rare student-students who compose most of our classroom population, "student-athletes" often haven't got enough money to go out to a movie or buy a pair of shoes or treat themselves to a non–training table hamburger. They're prohibited from doing anything to make the money to pay for such things. But what do they need money for? They've got all the Nike they can wear, and the dining hall's stocked with free snacks 24/7, plus Taco Tuesdays. Back in the 1830s, the slaves got a monthly ration of eight pounds of pork and one bushel of cornmeal.

Ed O'Bannon sighs: "I've said a million times that players aren't asking for millions of dollars a year. Just a couple of dollars to take their girlfriends to dinner and a movie."

Farewell to the gentleman amateur. And welcome to another theater in the American class war. The boosters, alumni, and fellow members of the congregation who fill the stands on fall Saturdays cheer the boys on the field, line up on Fan Day for their free autographs (which they can turn around and sell on eBay perfectly legally), and link their pride to the team's record, yet the minute a player breaks a "team rule" (which is whatever Coach says it is, from staying out too late before a game, to sassing Coach, to wearing the wrong shirt), or sports what inhabitants of the suburbs think is an outlandish hairstyle, or utters a word not approved of in polite society, he goes from hero to "thug."

Surely these kids understand that they have one job to do, *one job*. Master Cardale Jones, the quarterback who led Ohio State to a national title in 2014, knew the not-so-hidden truth but unwisely tweeted it when he was a freshman in 2012: "Why should we have to go to class if we came here to play FOOTBALL, we ain't come here to play SCHOOL, classes are POINTLESS."

Head coaches claim "playing school" is important. They could hardly do otherwise. But everyone grasped the subtext. Head Coach Bill Peterson used to hold up two fingers, barking, "Men! at Florida State, academics are number one!" Then he'd say, "Football is number two!" and hold up one finger. His players got it. There was the public face, the college charade, then there was reality. Good grades matter only so far as they govern who's eligible to play. Coaches who suggest a kid take that class in the Nineteenth-Century American Novel, Cell Biology, or Italian Art of the Fifteenth Century because it will expand and enrich his understanding of what it is to be human are, it's safe to say, about as plentiful as tulips in the desert. Keep 'em ignorant. Slavery also depended, among other things, on the slaves not knowing that the Bible and the Constitution spoke of freedom and justice. Once Frederick Douglass learned to read and devoured scraps of newspapers, bits of the New Testament, and the speeches of Cicero, Pitt, and Washington in the *Columbian Orator*, it was only a matter of time before he got in his master's face and emancipated himself.

It's not just that these kids don't read *Bleak House* or don't know that Leonardo was an artist before he was a Ninja Turtle: CNN reported in January 2015 that, based on the SAT and ACT scores of basketball and football players, between 7 and 18 percent were reading at grade-school level. In 1999, University of Tennessee English professor Linda Bensel-Meyers spoke out about how tutors "helped" athletes write papers, how grades got mysteriously changed for the better, and a school psychologist would diagnose players with a "learning disability," which allowed them to evade graduation requirements met by other students. Professor Bensel-Meyers, who had tenure, was harassed and threatened to the point that she resigned in 2003 and took a job at the

University of Denver. In 2012, Mary Willingham, a reading specialist working at UNC–Chapel Hill, found that more than half the football and basketball players from 2004 to 2012 read at a level somewhere between fourth and eighth grade. She also helped blow a very loud whistle in 2011 on the "Afro-American Studies" classes, which did not actually exist, and admitted she participated in Carolina's cheating, signing forms attesting that she'd witnessed no violation of NCAA rules. The university has attacked her research, and Carolina fans accused her of plagiarizing her master's thesis. Carolina athletics director Bubba Cunningham denied there was a problem. As he told CNN, "I think our students have an exceptional experience in the classroom as well as on the field of competition."

So that's all right, then.

My university has its own struggles with the book-learnin' aspects of its mission. In 2006, Dr. Brenda Monk, a specialist in learning disabilities, was accused of virtually writing papers for athletes (which she denies), and a "rogue tutor" supposedly gave athletes the answers to the test in an online music appreciation course. Coach Bobby Bowden rolled his eyes: "I can't believe it—a music course. It's not physiology. It's a music course, open book. Anybody can pass an open-book test."

The university investigated itself and uncovered other academic peccadilloes, involving sixty-one athletes in ten sports. Then FSU punished itself, forfeiting twelve wins and giving up five football scholarships. The NCAA put on its angry-daddy voice and demanded more punishment: one more scholarship, making six total. That'll teach 'em! The tutors and the learning-disabilities specialist lost their jobs. No coaches were even reprimanded.

JUST AS THE JAMEIS WINSTON did-he or didn't-he rape allegations hit the fan in November 2013, Adam Weinstein, a sharp young journalist also teaching in the FSU English Department (and my PhD student), published a piece in *Deadspin* illustrating that while the university shamelessly exploits football players, it still values them more than it values the graduate-student instructors trying to get these boys through Freshman Composition. On the NCAA plantation, the big, fast field hands are worth more in the market than the literate, numerate, and less-muscled house slaves. Adam Weinstein interviewed his colleagues, discovering he wasn't the only teacher to be pressured by the athletic academic advising office to go easy on a kid, maybe give him an Incomplete instead of an F, or hassled by "clipboard-wielding dudes in garnet-and-gold warm-ups who pour into the classrooms during our lectures to see whether the players are present."

Weinstein tells of a young woman in the English Department who complained to an Athletic Department handler that some football players in her class never turned in their work on time, cut and pasted essays from the Web, and acted like kindergartners in class, flipping the light switch on and off. A couple of guys later came to her office to try to intimidate her. A gay teacher got an even worse dose of football macho when a boy turned in an essay that detailed how he and his friends decided to punish "a fag" for acting like a girl, beat him up, and kicked his teeth out.

Weinstein himself taught (or tried to teach) "a gentle giant of a lineman who was new to college, and to reading, and had trouble making it to the morning class. On the few occasions he made it to class (late) and didn't fall dead asleep, his earnest writing, both in style and structure, was that of an elementary school student." When Weinstein warned the handlers that the kid was failing, "a pile of final drafts would suddenly materialize, full of fairly complex, organized thoughts and diction—thoughts that hadn't made it into earlier drafts I'd seen."

It wasn't all plagiarism, absenteeism, and stupidity on the part of the players. A graduate instructor Weinstein calls "Derek" had a defensive starter (now in the NFL) in his class a few years back, a nice, mild-mannered boy whose football overlords fed him up like a prize hog. The player said his coaches made sure he ate vast amounts of food, plus supplements, pills, vitamin drinks, and who knows what all, then sent him off to lift weights, crafting him into a man-mountain of fast-twitch muscle fiber. The huge creature looked at his teacher with "kid eyes" and said, "Mister Derek, sometimes I'm just not hungry anymore."

You wouldn't think they could break your heart, would you? Way, way back in 1983, I got a job tutoring Florida State football players. I was taking a year off between my (second) undergraduate degree and beginning my doctorate in England, working for a newspaper and trying to save some money. The Athletic Department paid the lavish sum of ten dollars an hour, far more than I made writing satirical columns about Florida politics. Man, I was going to be rich. Plus, I got to sit around with guys I watched on Saturdays, impressing them with my assessment of Miami's quarterback situation, proffering observations on Kirk Coker's hands, and introducing them to the wonders of English syntax.

They were all very polite. Almost all: there was a lineman, a big old white boy on whom God decided a neck would be surplus to requirements, who'd wait till I came into the cafeteria, where we had study hall after dinner, and sat down at a table with my dictionary and my pencils, then announce loudly that he was going to watch him some *teevee* because there wasn't nothing happening in *here*. Hassan Jones, a wide receiver who went on to play for the Vikings, would say, "Don't pay him any mind. He's kind of crazy."

Oddly enough (quite odd, considering this is Tallahassee, Florida), I wasn't the first Oxford graduate hired by FSU to tutor football players. Caroline Alexander, the distinguished author of books on the *Iliad*, *HMS Bounty*, and Antarctic explorer Ernest Shackleton, had been the first female Rhodes Scholar chosen from the state of Florida. She returned from England in 1981 to train for the Modern Pentathlon national championships in Tallahassee and got a job teaching remedial English to eight football players. In *Battle's End*, Alexander's clear-eyed, moving account of the guys she tutored and how they fared a dozen-plus years later, she says she was once asked to approach a tough professor—one of her old teachers, as it happened—in hopes that a football player's grade could be massaged upward from an F to a

D, and she tells the story of the noseguard who "turned to me with the grave concern of one who wants to correct a potentially embarrassing misapprehension. 'Didn't they tell you? We *can't* write. We ain't *got* no grammar.'

A quarter of a century later, things weren't a hell of a lot different. Brenda Monk, the learning specialist fired in the 2006 cheating imbroglio, told ESPN in 2009 that one of her first experiences at FSU was of a kid coming to her office and saying, "You might as well know right off the bat, I can't read." The football team was still made up of "student-athletes" who'd graduated from schools where homework and tests weren't allowed to interfere with football or schools with dedicated teachers who couldn't magically cure generations of underfunding, racism, and neglect in poor little towns like Belle Glade, Florida, or Albany, Georgia. These boys knew that their wretched education, often another poisonous legacy of Jim Crow days, did not equip them for life outside of football. To hear them talk, *everydamnbody* was going to hit large with the NFL and roll in riches—even though they knew better. When it was just the kid and me and the dictionary, sometimes they'd admit to being scared of how they'll handle the nonfootball world. "I can't do words, Miss D," said one. "They just don't work right for me."

These boys were then, and are now, young, disadvantaged, and as sophisticated as a potato chip. For them, football still looks like a ticket out of Belle Glade or Albany or Overtown or Hueytown, or whatever they left behind when they put on the baseball cap in the colors of their chosen university and smiled for the cameras. They've already succeeded in one way: only 3 or 4 percent of high school football players make a college team. And only 1.7 percent of college players make it to the NFL. Fear of blowing your chance animates everyone in college football from the head coach down. He gets a huge salary, a car allowance, bonuses, greens fees, and extra cash from the TV commercials for Ford trucks and plywood. He also gets lots of love, but only, *only*, if he keeps winning. His assistant coaches live in fear of screwing up, knowing that their ticket on the gravy train depends on the head coach; and the players are scared of blowing their academic eligibility;

taking a T-shirt or a six-pack from the wrong person and falling foul of the NCAA; or flaming out on the field, tearing their ACLs or sustaining a spinal injury so severe that their career is over, and it's back to the bad part of town forever.

One of FSU's offensive stars in the 2014 season knew this better than most. On the field, he never celebrated, never trash-talked, rarely smiled. He was raised in South Florida by his grandmother. His father was in prison in another state. When he played high school ball, the neighborhood drug dealers would give him money every time he scored. Then he'd hand the cash over to his grandmother.

Chapter 16

FIGHTING THE WAR ALL OVER AGAIN

IT'S 1997. That's 132 years since Appomattox, 130 years since Congress placed the eleven rebellious states under federal army rule, 35 years since the Ole Miss campus went to war over the enrollment of James Meredith. In Vaught-Hemingway Stadium, Ole Miss plays the Vanderbilt Commodores, the Pride of the South Band plays "Slow Dixie," and the people in the stands play with Confederate battle flags.

Ole Miss officials have worked to dial down the Old South rigmarole, though it doesn't help that the name everybody's used for the university since 1897, when Miss Elma Meek of Oxford suggested it, refers to the senior white lady on the plantation. It's what the slaves called the master's wife. A hundred years later, Head Coach Tommy Tuberville has asked Rebels to leave their battle flags at home. The flags hurt feelings; they hurt recruiting; they look terrible on TV; they remind the nation that Mississippi had divorced itself from the Union and gone to war over the right to own human beings. Many fans bring them anyway, the "Southern Cross," the banner not of any heritage worth hanging on to, but pure, unblinking hatred.

IT'S LATE SEPTEMBER, a shade past summer but still warm. Every time Ole Miss gets a first down or makes a big play, the Rebels thrash the air with those flags, especially in the fraternity seats, where boys in white shirts and girls in Ray-Bans hold the flags over their heads, straight-armed, as if parodying the black-power fist. The friend I'm sitting with, disgusted at the way the unlovely past still holds too many of us in thrall, says it looks like a Ku Klux Klan meeting. I don't agree. After that first, brief, mephitic eruption of ex-Confederate officers and proslavery ideologues from 1866 to 1871, the Klan became decidedly déclassé, a kind of fraternity for poor white men terrified that the Negroes and the Jews and the Catholics and the immigrants were going to take their jobs and their women. These boys and girls in their blue-and-red ties, sundresses, and Tiffany silver bracelets surely belong to the elite, many descended from the old planter families who founded Ole Miss, the important white folks who once forced an antebellum president of the university to prove he was "sound" on slavery. In 1859, F.A.P. Barnard expelled a student who'd raped his wife's slave, believing the black woman over the white man. So no, the Rebels of today don't look like the Klan, or even the White Citizens' Council, the genteel face of racism in the 1950s and 1960s. These well-brushed young people, many educated in segregation academies, are less viscerally prejudiced than the elders ever were. Indeed, they're certain they're not racist, but simply proud of their ancestors and the "Southern Way of Life." Their mothers and daddies waved the flag at the ball game: why shouldn't they?

In the end, Ole Miss beats the Commodores 15–3. Vanderbilt is a kind of anti–Ole Miss, a college bankrolled by Yankee money, originally dedicated to promoting postbellum peace between North and South, "strengthening the ties which should exist between all sections of our common country." A few weeks after this game, Ole Miss chancellor Robert Khayat, himself a former football star at Ole Miss and a stud in the NFL, banned sticks at football games. Popsicle sticks, shaker sticks, corndog skewers, umbrellas—all forbidden. You could bring in your flag (First Amendment and all that), but you had to wave it like a hanky. Not something the soi-disant heirs of Stonewall Jackson and J. E. B. Stuart, Braxton Bragg, and Jubal Early, could readily tolerate.

They called the bloodshed that erupted over the enrollment of James Meredith at Ole Miss the "last battle of the Civil War." But there have been many battles since, and each time America hoped it was the final skirmish. Each time we were wrong. The last battle wasn't in 1963, when Governor George Wallace "stood in the schoolhouse door," trying to block integration of the University of Alabama; or in 1968, when people took to the streets of Washington, Chicago, Baltimore, and Detroit in grief and rage over the assassination of Martin Luther King; or in 2009, when an African American was inaugurated president and the unreconstructed right wing impugned his citizenship, challenged his patriotism, called him a liar, and accused him of being a communist or a Muslim or some such unsavory and supposedly un-American thing. It wasn't in the summer of 2015, when the Confederate battle flag was finally taken down from the State House grounds in South Carolina, in response to the night a boy with a head full of Lost Cause lies took his stand at Emanuel AME Church, killing a librarian, a city operations manager, a recent college graduate, a track coach, a Bible study teacher, a choir member, and three pastors, because they were all black, telling them, before he pulled the trigger, "You rape our women and you're taking over our country. You have to go."

Mississippi would surely be the right place for that final fight. In July 2015, University of Mississippi coach Hugh Freeze, a native Mississippian, called for the state—the last one to flaunt the "Southern Cross" on its official banner—to change the design. Lose the battle flag. Join America. After all, no state struggled harder over segregation or symbolism than Mississippi. In 1962, Attorney General Robert Kennedy had to call in five hundred US marshals, along with troops from the Second Infantry Division at Fort Benning, Georgia, plus a slew of military police and National Guard, to keep James Meredith alive. Riots raged for days; two men died; hundreds were wounded; a white mob attacked the commanding general's staff car, setting it on fire. He and his officers escaped by crawling two hundred yards under fire to the Lyceum, the lovely antebellum building with the Ionic columns, just beyond the prize tailgating spots in the Grove.

Even complimenting local football prowess didn't calm things down. In the middle of the violence, President John Kennedy addressed the nation on television, invoking the South's "great tradition" of "honor and courage won on the field of battle and on the gridiron as well as the university campus." The day before, Ole Miss had beaten Kentucky, alums and students vowing, "Never shall our emblem go from Colonel Reb to Old Black Joe!"

In 2010, UM's mascot changed. Colonel Reb, the linen-suited, string-tied cross between Colonel Sanders and Ole Massa, lost his job to a bear. University officials banned Colonel Reb from the sidelines, but resistance remains strong, with successive students and alums wearing the costume and lurking in the Grove before games: "There's no more of a noble cause than continuing the tradition of Colonel Reb." As for the bear—a nod to William Faulkner's fiction as well as to north Mississippi's megafauna—well, as an Ole Miss professor whispered to me in mock horror, "Honey, it's a *black* bear!"

Meredith, an Air Force veteran, went to class, ate in the cafeteria, though white kids would turn their backs on him, and lived in a dorm, though students in the room above him would bounce basketballs on the floor at night trying to keep him awake. The troops camped on the football practice fields; the football team went undefeated that year. One player said, "With the entire nation focused on Ole Miss, we had to do our part to uphold the pride of Ole Miss."

Until the mid-1970s or later (much later on some campuses), the battle flag and "Dixie" at football games were as normal as boiled peanuts. The Birmingham bombings, the Selma March, the Children's Crusade, cross burnings in the country, police brutality in the little towns, and the martyrdom of Medgar Evers, Addie Mae Collins, Carole Robertson, Denise McNair, Cynthia Wesley, James Chaney, Andrew Goodman, Michael Schwerner, Viola Liuzzo, Harry T. Moore, Jonathan Daniels, Martin Luther King Jr., and so many others made the South feel besieged. But on Saturdays white people could congregate in the stadium and forget or aggressively reject the forces of justice overthrowing the ancien régime.

As it had throughout most of its history, the white South felt that the rest of the country was attacking it, ridiculing it, looking down upon it. The white South reacted by aggressively celebrating its beauty queens, its college football, and its special, reality-challenged moonlight-and-magnolias version of the plantation past, which the first two were used to support. Everybody in the stadium stood when the band played "Dixie." Eventually, "Dixie" caused such a ruckus that the bands stopped playing it, or playing all of it, slipping a few bars of the song into another musical number the way unrepentant Jacobites wore white rosebuds in not-so-covert support of Bonnie Prince Charlie's doomed revolt. The University of Florida fight song incorporated a few bars of "Dixie" until the 1990s. Alabama (the university) took to playing an Alabama (the band) hit, "Dixieland Delight": its 2/2 meter allowing for the snappy hollering of "Roll, Tide!" and "Fuck Auburn!" The university has reportedly banned it, but an enterprising soul with a decent-size speaker and an extension cord will no doubt ensure it remains part of the Tuscaloosa football experience. For years, the Ole Miss band got away with "From Dixie with Love," an Elvis-inflected version of Mickey Newbury's "American Trilogy," which begins with "Dixie" and segues into "The Battle Hymn of the Republic." That custom came into disrepute when some students (that fraternity section again) replaced "His truth is marching on" with "The South shall rise again!"

Below Mr. Mason and Mr. Dixon's lordly line, white people clung to college football like a security blanket crafted from Robert E. Lee's frock coat. Maybe we were *poor*; maybe we were *country*; maybe we didn't have no *Harvard or Yale*; maybe we lost the *War*. But we were good at football. In the heady first weeks of the Confederacy, when the silver buttons on General Beauregard's uniform still shone bright, before J. E. B. Stuart lost his plumed hat at Second Manassas, it was still an article of faith that one Southerner could whip ten Yankees. The

War provided ample evidence to the contrary. Yet, ever since, college football in the South has operated on the premise that eleven Southerners could whip one big Yankee institution—Notre Dame, Penn State, Michigan, Washington—refighting Antietam and Shiloh on a hundred-yard field.

In 1925, the Alabama Crimson Tide was invited to play the mighty University of Washington in the Rose Bowl on New Year's Day. Washington was a four-touchdown favorite. Syndicated columnist Lawrence Perry wrote, "A crushing defeat of Alabama is indicated," while others snickered: "Tuscalosers," "farmers." Alabama's team came from the dubious nether regions of the nation, a place where they put a teacher on trial for teaching the theories of Charles Darwin and argued with a straight face that evolution was wicked because it taught that humans descended "not even from American monkeys, but from Old World monkeys!"

What the un-Dixie part of the planet didn't realize was that football, like practically everything else in the South, had taken on the imprint of the Civil War: Us versus Them. The War was sixty years ago; twentieth-century America had moved on; the South had not. Veterans of the Army of Northern Virginia or the Magnolia Rifles, their butternut caps tattered, still marched on Confederate Memorial Day and the United Daughters of the Confederacy dedicated monuments in every county seat from the Blue Ridge to the bayous. Custom and politics in the South worked tirelessly, neurotically, to separate black people from white people in every possible way, from anti-miscegenation amendments to state constitutions to city ordinances prohibiting interracial dominos games. The South's sense of grievance remained strong. But football gave Johnny Reb a do-over. In 1920, when Georgia Tech and Centre College in Kentucky (home of the Prayin' Colonels) played teams from above the Mason-Dixon, a Birmingham sportswriter called it, "the most serious invasion of the North since Lee was stopped at Gettysburg." When the University of Georgia upset mighty Yale in 1929, it was like "charging up the slope at Gettysburg again."

Pickett's Charge practically entered the playbook: a regiment of Ole Miss students called the University Greys suffered a 100 percent casualty rate at Gettysburg. Yet it seemed that every time a Southern team played one from the North (or West or Midwest), it was Pickett's Charge all over. Win or lose: the South was good at romanticizing an ass-kicking. As Grantland Rice, sportswriter and grandson of a Confederate officer, said of one game: "It was a magnificent charge in a lost cause. It was Pickett at Gettysburg."

Hyperbole, grandiosity, febrile rhetoric: in the South a ball game stood in for the bloodiest, most divisive war in American history. Over Christmas vacation 1925, Alabama players were inundated with messages saying "the honor of the South" rested on their winning the Rose Bowl. Honor, sir! The South stopped dueling with swords or pistols at the end of the Civil War. Now insults to the honor of the region, and thus to everyone in it, would be settled on the gridiron. Never mind that the state of Washington had nothing to do with the War and was largely populated by Scandinavians and Native Americans. This was a chance to reassert the region's virility, for Pickett's Charge to finally succeed. When Alabama won 20–19, white folks in Montgomery poured out into the wintry darkness, hollering and singing, forming a procession down Dexter Avenue, just as they had in 1861, celebrating secession from the Union. The *Montgomery Advertiser* declared that the win had solved the South's PR problem, negating "popular illusions concerning hookworm and malaria" once and for all. Even students at Auburn (then the Alabama Polytechnic Institute) cheered. Vanderbilt's coach exulted in the *Atlanta Journal*: "I fought, bled, died and was resurrected with the Crimson Tide."

The 1926 Rose Bowl may have looked like a football game, but it was really another battle in America's unfinished war. Back in Tuscaloosa, the victorious Alabama team rode in wagons pulled by students to the Quad, the center of campus, where university president George Denny waited. Denny's father had fought at Fredericksburg and Chancellorsville; the place he stood to honor the Crimson Tide is called the Mound, a grassed-over ruin where once stood Franklin Hall, built in

1833 and, like most of the university, burned to the ground by federal troops five days before Lee surrendered at Appomattox.

Football is about land. Somebody captures yours; you try to take it back. You then march on your enemy's turf. Everyone is territorial to some extent: this is *my* body, this is *my* house, *my* yard, *our* town, *our* country. In 1865, the federal government said it would offer land, forty acres, as reparation to former slaves, who once couldn't claim their own bodies. The promise was broken. Land meant power—the American government couldn't allow black people power. As for white Southerners, deep in our unconscious minds we felt invaded. Violated. Now we take our country back ten yards at a time, as if we still can't quite accept that we lost the War. I'm not saying that people from California or Ohio might not feel something similar. But in the South, we have this overarching historical context and this highly developed vocabulary for grievance. White people failed to remake the country through armed rebellion, but we keep capturing symbolic territory on the gridiron, marching through the opponent's territory, claiming his patch, entering his sanctum sanctorum to score.

The contest need not be a Southern team versus a Northern (or Western or Midwestern) squad. The opposing team is the enemy, the alien, even if it's the team just down the road in Gainesville or Starkville or Blacksburg. They are not us. In 1962, Florida State beat the favored Bulldogs in Athens, 18–0. In an act of symbolic conquest, team captain Gene McDowell grubbed up a handful of Georgia's playing field. Ever since, a big road game, a road game in which the Seminoles are underdogs, and any game against Miami or Florida, is a "sod game." If FSU wins, they take the enemy's dirt. They carve up a hunk of his turf. Doesn't matter if it's fake: in 1989, when FSU beat Auburn in the Sugar Bowl, a defensive player chopped out a piece of the Superdome's Astroturf. He was fined $500.

They take the soil back to Tallahassee in triumph, encase it in a little wooden casket, bury it in the walled garden by Doak Campbell Stadium, and mark it with a bronze plaque. At the end of 2014, there were ninety-nine graves in the Sod Cemetery, ninety-nine victories over those who would take our land, ninety-nine little wars fought and won.

Playing football, like being a soldier, is the ne plus ultra of American manliness, so knotted together we barely separate them. The ROTC color guard presents flags as the band plays the national anthem, maybe the Blue Angels scream across the sky in their F/A-18s, or the Army Golden Knights parachute onto the field. Sometimes you don't know whether to cheer or run for cover. There's no killing on the football field, or not much, not like in the early years of the twentieth century, when dozens died on the gridiron and hundreds suffered catastrophic injuries: snapped spines, broken limbs, gouged eyes, cracked ribs, perforated lungs, and concussions. Lots and lots of concussions. Things were so bad in 1909 (twenty-six dead, five hundred–odd seriously banged up) that John Singleton Mosby, the Confederate guerrilla fighter, delivered himself of a diatribe against football, calling it a "barbarous amusement." The old colonel was no wuss: as a student at the University of Virginia in 1850, he shot a classmate who riled him, and during the Late Unpleasantness, he summarily executed Union prisoners of war (to be fair, George Custer did it first). But the death of halfback Archer Christian from a cerebral hemorrhage in the Cavaliers' game against Georgetown was a casualty too far: "Cock-fighting is unlawful in Virginia: Why should better care be taken of a game chicken than a school boy?"

Because we don't send game chickens to war. We do send young men of playing age, so it has suited America to militarize football and make battle sound like a game. In the 1890s, the service academies used football to condition cadets; by 1900 army bases fielded football teams. General Douglas MacArthur returned from World War I to head West Point and promptly had the words UPON THE FIELDS OF FRIENDLY STRIFE ARE SOWN THE SEEDS THAT, UPON OTHER FIELDS, ON OTHER DAYS, WILL BEAR THE FRUITS OF VICTORY inscribed near the entrance to the gym. World War II had Operation Goalpost and Operation Varsity; Vietnam had Operation Linebacker. Football has blitzes, bombs, pistols, and shotguns. Or as George Carlin put it in a famous routine from 1984, the object of football is for the quarterback to march "his troops into enemy territory, balancing this aerial assault with a sustained ground attack that punches holes in the forward wall of the enemy's defensive line. In baseball the object is to go home! And to be safe!"

For all that we romanticize baseball as "America's game," it isn't. Football exhibits our seemingly unstoppable impulse to war. In 1908, the *New York Tribune* said college football "assumes in the minds of players, coaches, students, graduates, and the affiliated public the importance of war." And not just any war: the Civil War. Harvard's stadium is built on land donated by a Union veteran to memorialize friends who died fighting to preserve the nation. Slavery and the constant question of how people of African descent were to live as citizens in a nation that had largely (though absurdly) deluded itself into thinking it was a "white man's country" have haunted football from the first game in 1869. This legacy still haunts us. Instead of battles between (mostly) young white men, it's young black men who fight on the football field. We sacrifice the bodies of black boys and they allow themselves to be sacrificed in the name of . . . What? Glory? Fame? A big pro payout?

Chapter 17

THE SOUTHERN WAY OF LIFE

CALVIN PATTERSON shot himself to death on August 16, 1972, at the home of the history professor who rented him a room. It was the day before football practice began. When the Tallahassee Police Department arrived, they found by his body a wadded-up FSU football schedule.

He didn't mean to commit suicide. He didn't want to die. He just wanted to make himself permanently unavailable for football. By firing a .38 at his own belly, he figured he'd end the college career that never quite got going and find some other life—a life where he wasn't a pioneer or a target or a guy whose job it was to change the world.

The 1969 *Seminole Handbook* says: "Calvin Patterson has exceptional balance and good speed. Runs to daylight and is an exciting runner. Has potential to become an above average back. Must improve blocking. Is a good receiver." The handbook doesn't mention the thing everybody at Florida State noticed about Calvin Patterson before they noticed anything else: it doesn't say he was black—the first black kid, in fact, to go to FSU on a football scholarship. He'd been a star at Palmetto High School in South Miami, what the old-timey sportswriters called "a speedster." He'd been a first there, too: bused to that school with a bunch of other black kids, a full eleven years after the Supreme

Court of the United States ordered the desegregation of public schools, the first black kid to play varsity football at Palmetto, the first black kid elected (by the faculty) to the high school's Hall of Fame, honoring his "scholarship, leadership, citizenship and service."

Outside the South, college football had been technically integrated for eighty years: Amherst's team captain in 1890 was William H. Lewis, a young black man from Virginia who went on to become an All-American playing for Harvard—while attending law school. Paul Robeson played for Rutgers 1915–1918, a two-time All-American. Robert Robinson and Charles Williams made the University of Oregon team in 1926. Not that the addition of a black athlete to a mostly white team always went smoothly. At the 1923 Iowa State–Minnesota game, the Cyclones' first African American player, a superb athlete named Jack Trice, was trampled to death by Golden Gopher players as he tried to defend his team's running back. Some feared it might have been intentional: there were so many members of the KKK on the University of Minnesota campus, they entered a float in the Homecoming parade. Opposing players used to target Fritz Pollard of Brown, in 1916, the first African American to play in the Rose Bowl. He learned to discourage late hits by rolling onto his back and sticking his cleats in the air. Other players of color were spat upon, hit high, and punched.

However tough it was up north, it was far worse down south. Yet for some reason, head coach Bill Peterson decided that 1968 would be Florida State's year. The great aunt and uncle who raised Calvin told the *Sun-Sentinel* newspaper in 1995 they were impressed with his pitch: "Coach Peterson was a gentleman. He talked like he knew us."

Calvin Patterson wasn't technically the first African American to sign with FSU. Just before Christmas in 1967, Ernest Cook, valedictorian of Daytona Beach's Father Lopez High, announced his intention to play at Florida State. Coach Bill Peterson sat next to him as flashbulbs popped. White local businessman Thomas Wetherell had helped convince Cook to choose FSU. Wetherell, father of T. K. Wetherell, a recently graduated star Seminole football player who later became president of the university, had some cred among Daytona's African

Americans. He managed the local Sears Roebuck, where he allowed black customers to try on clothes (an unusual practice in the Jim Crow South) and employed black people in positions beyond janitor. But then the Cook family started to get epithet-hurling letters, calling Ernie a "coon" and a "nigger," threatening to kill him. Cook's family was terrified, so Cook decided to take his talents up north, to the University of Minnesota, which had shed its Klan past. A black quarterback had led the Golden Gophers to two Rose Bowls in the early 1960s. Maybe he wouldn't get niggered-and-cooned up there. Plus, Minnesota had a good medical school.

Calvin Patterson's family got similar letters, possibly from the same peckerwoods terrorizing Ernest Cook. Calvin could have gone to Notre Dame or Syracuse, escaping up north as Ernest Cook did, but he stuck with FSU. Maybe he was brave; maybe he was stubborn; maybe he was naive.

Floridians like to pretend their state is nothing like Alabama or Georgia, and actually belongs to a strange kingdom of the mind called the Sun Belt, where life is a beach—a beach with no ugly racist history. This is, of course, nonsense. Florida belongs as much to the Deep South as Mississippi. It was the third state to secede in 1861; from the 1880s to the 1940s, Florida had the highest per capita rate of lynching for its black population; the Klan was active in north, central, and especially northeast Florida until the 1980s; and the state used Jim Crow–era laws to disenfranchise black voters and disadvantage majority black precincts beyond even the debacle of the 2000 presidential election. By the hundredth anniversary of the Emancipation Proclamation, you'd think breaking the color line in college football would have been a sound way to goose the Old South into the New South. It didn't quite work that way. When asked about integrating football in 1963, the athletic director at Tampa University said, "I don't think this would be good for our school, for our part of the country. The Negroes are quite happy at Florida A&M."

In 1968, there were about forty African American students enrolled at FSU, every one of them reminded daily that they weren't entirely welcome: the Confederate battle flags hanging in frat-house windows, the casual racial epithets, the hostility of the dining hall and the dorm. Calvin Patterson, a quiet boy with a white girlfriend, didn't hang around the newly formed Black Student Union much, though sometimes the black students would come just to watch him practice. He couldn't really socialize at FSU. He tried FAMU, but the kids there saw him as a sellout. FAMU was less than a mile from FSU, over there on another high Tallahassee hill. But it might as well have been in a different time zone. The Rattlers had won eight national championships; the Seminoles had none. Coach Jake Gaither was a giant in the sporting world: he'd coached Hewritt Dixon, Herman Lee, Carleton Oates, and "Bullet" Bob Hayes, the Olympian. He'd sent scores of black players to the NFL. But FAMU didn't get on television; FAMU didn't play Alabama or Georgia, LSU or Florida—the big-time Southern teams.

So there's Calvin Patterson on the JV team (this was before freshmen were eligible to play in varsity games), a student at one of the universities in the South that integrated without filling the county jail and the hospital emergency room. FSU hadn't gone in for the wholesale hatefulness of the mob that Autherine Lucy encountered in 1955 when she tried to pursue a graduate degree at the University of Alabama, or the rock-throwing when Charlayne Hunter and Hamilton Holmes registered for classes at the University of Georgia in January 1961. Maybe 1968 was late enough in America's long integration game that white people were beginning to accept having to share the country with the people whose ancestors were brought here in chains. Resistance at FSU, while palpable, wasn't violent.

Football was different, though. In the mind of the white South, the Supreme Court and the federal government had been conspiring against it since the Nullification Crisis of 1832. Now Washington was forcing traditionally white colleges to integrate, sometimes at bayonet-point. But a coach didn't have to put a black athlete on his football team. Coaches could hold firm. Starting a black player was to admit defeat, admit that the "Southern Way of Life," for which white people had defied the federal government, for which they had killed, no longer meant a damned thing. Football, at least, would stay the same. Which was good, because for a lot of people—state legislators, boosters, regular people down at the Winn-Dixie of a Wednesday afternoon—football was (and is) the university's most important function. Nobody pays money to watch a professor conduct a chemistry experiment. In Tallahassee, few knew (or cared) that Carlisle Floyd, America's most important composer of opera, taught at FSU or that Sylvia Earle, pioneering oceanographer, graduated from FSU or that Paul Dirac, Nobel Prize–winning theoretical physicist, had joined FSU's faculty. Most of the people who filled the stands at Doak Campbell Stadium wouldn't know them from Adam's house cat. It was the same all across the South (and probably in the other big football towns, too). Football was the university's best marketing campaign or, as university presidents have long been fond of saying, the university's "front porch," the first thing people see, the way into the house of higher ed. And football was the white South's way of fighting back against the national narrative of barely literate, backwoods, possum-eating, cousin-marrying rubes at whom the civilized world was inclined to sneer or despair.

While a few coaches, like Peterson at FSU and Lee Corso at Maryland, could see that the wall of separation was ill-built and shaky, white people clung to Jim Crow like the last warm thing on earth. In 1959, the University of Alabama trustees had threatened to boycott the Crimson Tide's Liberty Bowl game against Penn State because the Nittany Lions had "Negroes" on their team. They should have known this doesn't work. About a month after Rosa Parks refused to give up her seat on that Montgomery city bus, the Georgia Tech Yellow Jackets faced the Pittsburgh Panthers in the 1956 Sugar Bowl. The white South focused obsessively on one Panther in particular, the black one—Bobby Grier, a fullback and linebacker. He was pretty good, but that wasn't the problem: "The South stands at Armageddon," wrote Georgia Governor Marvin Griffin in a frantic telegram to Georgia's Board of Regents, demanding that Tech refuse to play in an "integrated" game. Griffin went on, "The battle is joined. We cannot make the slightest concession to the enemy in this dark and lamentable hour of struggle. One break in the dike and the relentless seas will push in and destroy us."

Tech played anyway and won, 7–0, partly because of an interference penalty on Grier. Game films show it was a bad call: Grier was ahead of the receiver he supposedly interfered with by pushing. Was it racial? Maybe. But Governor Griffin's "break in the dike," didn't happen until 1970, when the University of Southern California, a thoroughly integrated bunch of top-flight athletes, beat Bear Bryant's all-white Tide like a rented mule, 42–21. Fullback Sam Cunningham ran up and down the field; quarterback Jimmy Jones not only out-strategized Alabama, he sported a huge Angela Davis 'fro, and to add insult to grievous injury, one of the Trojans' stars, Clarence Davis, was an Alabamian, born right down the road in Bessemer. The heavens opened, the light of inspiration shone upon the Bear, and white Southern coaches started recruiting African American football stars.

NONE OF THIS HELPED Calvin Patterson. In 1970 and 1971, he struggled. By then, FSU had signed several more African American football players. A white teammate, quarterback Tommy Warren, volunteered to be Calvin's roommate and help him with his assignments. Professors, such as Charlotte Williams in the College of Business, also tried to help Calvin. It wasn't as if he couldn't hack it intellectually: a history professor remembers arguing with him about Voltaire's *Candide* and the nature of the good. Still, he didn't show up to class, and FSU kicked him out. Despite that, he appeared at spring practice in 1972. The new coach, Larry Jones, acknowledged his potential and disparaged his current state, as if talking of a racehorse who'd become frightened of the starting gun. Jones told the *Sun-Sentinel* in 1995: "He looked out of shape. We could've used him that fall, because we didn't have any top running backs. You could see the athletic talent there. But he was rusty."

Still, Calvin said he wanted back in, back into FSU, back into football. David Ammerman, an FSU history professor who worked a lot with football players and African American students, gave him a place to stay. Calvin started working on getting his eligibility back, taking classes at the local community college. Or that's what he said he was doing. Turns out he wasn't enrolled there, either. Late one night he called a friend in Miami and told her he'd been at a store when some guy tried to rob it. The guy shot him in the stomach, he said. He told his friend he'd be OK, but it probably meant the end of football for him.

Kris Knab, Calvin Patterson's girlfriend for two years, told ESPN in 2008 that she thought the expectations weighed on him: "When he hit the dead end and was not going to be able to play football after telling everybody he was, I think he felt like he had no other way out."

The day after he made the call to Miami, Calvin Patterson turned the gun on himself. Then he called the emergency services. When the cops showed up, he lay in the hallway, convulsed with pain. He bled to death on the way to the hospital. None of the coaches from FSU attended his funeral. Even worse, the coaches and other university officials cautioned FSU football players not to go to it. A number of them ignored the coaches: four of Patterson's African American teammates served as pallbearers. All American defensive back J. T. Thomas, who later played for the Steelers, said that when coaches heard he and the other players wore their FSU letterman's jackets, they threatened to kick them off the team. The coaches had reduced Calvin Patterson to a liability; they wanted to forget him and move on.

For a long time, the university more or less erased him from history, pretended the whole thing didn't happen, didn't speak his name, as if he'd disgraced the family. Then in 1992 his friend Tommy Warren noticed that the commemorative cups sold at FSU games incorrectly honored J. T. Thomas as FSU's first black player. Warren got busy writing letters, insisting that FSU remember and restore Calvin Patterson to his rightful place as FSU's real first. Warren, by then a civil rights lawyer, along with his wife, Kathy Villacorta (also an attorney), endowed a scholarship in Calvin Patterson's name. They never forgot him. And I'll bet those first few African American students sitting in the stands at the 1969 spring game, watching Calvin Patterson run with such beauty—I'll bet they haven't forgotten either. They chanted his name over and over again. When he came off the field, he wouldn't remove his helmet. He didn't want people to see him crying.

Forty years ago, big-time teams from big-time colleges were almost entirely white. There were a few black stars peppering the pale firmament of the SEC and the Southwestern Conference; more in the Midwest, West, and North. But the narrative had changed. If you wanted to win, you'd better cross the color line. In the early 1960s, Coach Frank Howard could assure South Carolina white folks: "I'll never have a nigra at Clemson." Gene Stallings, then head coach at Texas A&M, responded to the pressure to integrate in 1965: "What we need is a team that will work and pull and fight together and really get a feeling of oneness. I don't believe we could accomplish this with a Negro on the squad."

That feeling of unity must not have helped as much as he figured: Texas A&M under Stallings had only one winning season. When Stallings coached Alabama to the national championship in 1992, his defensive starters were all black.

Instead of black players being distractions or provocations or tokens or symbols, they became vital skilled labor, the guys with speed, strength, and endurance. In place of the old stereotype of the "shiftless Negro," the lazy no 'count lying around all day, we got the "natural" athlete. TV football commentator, bookmaker, and amateur racial theorist Jimmy "the Greek" Snyder got fired from his CBS gig for such comments, but he was only saying what a lot of Americans still believe. Just as African Americans sho' can sing and dance, they're intrinsically great at sports, too: running, jumping—it's those fast-twitch muscles, right? Maybe all that running the ancestors did back on the Dark Continent or lighting out from the Old Plantation toward Free Territory?

Not that the Old Plantation didn't also consume African American athleticism: picking cotton or cutting cane weren't real thrilling to watch, so the white men in charge got the slaves racing, wrestling, and boxing in the off-hours. Tom Molineaux, born a slave in Virginia, was such a good bare-knuckle boxer, he won his owner thousands. He won his own freedom, too. He went off to London in 1809 to challenge the acknowledged Old World boxing number one, Tom Cribb, knocking him out in the twenty-eighth round. Cribb's supporters kicked up a fuss, accusing Molineaux of cheating. This gave Cribb time to come to and fight on: it was not acceptable that a black man should whip the white champion of England. In *Forty Million Dollar Slaves*, William C. Rhoden points out, "Sports, which would become the tool of liberation for Molineaux and so many others—as well as a tool of psychological liberation for generations of black fans" were used on the plantation to "dull the revolutionary instinct." Frederick Douglass says being the fastest, fittest, or strongest gave slaves a measure of dignity and pleasure. At the same time, however, sports were a "safety-valve" to "carry off the explosive elements inseparable from the human mind when reduced to the condition of slavery," tamping down "the spirit of insurrection among the slaves," keeping them too busy competing against each other to become Toussaint-L'Ouverture or Nat Turner.

American society can't figure out what to do with young black men: the qualities that create greatness on the gridiron—size, speed, aggression, strength, and cunning—scare us to death when we meet them on the street. Rattler coach Jake Gaither liked players who were "agile, mobile, and hostile," but only on the gridiron. They had to behave like nice young Christian gentlemen away from the field. Wouldn't want to frighten white folks.

On second thought, maybe there's value in shocking the decidedly bourgeois world of college football. Despite Frederick Douglass's contention that black anger is effectively redirected in sports, sometimes little insurrections rise up. William C. Rhoden relishes the time he watched Miami brutalize the Texas Longhorns, a rebellion against the nostalgic fantasy of football as a tough but punctilious contest in which you go out to win one for George Gipp as played by Ronald Reagan, and—Tom Brown and his Muscular Christians would be proud—everyone shakes hands afterward like good chaps. The 'Canes broke free of the Uncle Tom–style, soft-spoken, self-effacing "house Negro." They were exuberantly self-confident young black men, gleefully determined to shock the white overseers of the power conferences. Longhorn players called them "gangsters" and "hooligans."

The Hurricanes' modus operandi throughout the 1980s was to freak out the pearl-clutching Miss Anns in charge of college football. Joe Paterno's choirboys turned up to team events at the 1987 Fiesta Bowl celebrations wearing coats and ties, while the 'Canes sported camo and shades. *Sports Illustrated* named the 1986 Miami team the "all-time most hated," what with the drug charges and the gun charges, disorderly conduct citations, shoplifting, and assault. *SI* said, "Miami may be the only squad in America that has its team picture taken from the front and from the side." When the undefeated 'Canes played the undefeated Irish in 1988, Notre Dame students turned out in CATHOLICS VS. CONVICTS T-shirts. In the long, nerve-shattering FSU-Miami rivalry, the 'Canes would often try to provoke a fight during the warm-up by stomping in a most disrespectful manner on the Seminole logo at midfield. Even the Miami mascot suffers from a bad attitude: just before the 1989 game in Tallahassee, cops detained Sebastian the Ibis for wielding a fire extinguisher as if to put out Chief Osceola's flaming spear, a part of FSU's opening ritual regarded by Seminoles as akin to the transubstantiation of the bread into the Body of Christ during the Eucharist. As the bird tells it, five officers slammed him up against a chain-link fence, "One wing was out to one side, the other wing held behind my back. Another guy is pulling my beak and trying to yank my head off."

The ibis is lucky he's white.

In the 1991 Cotton Bowl, the Hurricanes greeted the Longhorns with upraised "We're number one!" index fingers and upraised middle fingers, too. The 'Canes drew more than two hundred yards in penalties, largely personal fouls, for dancing, pile-up punches, taunting, and the time Randall Hill snagged a forty-eight-yard touchdown pass, took it into the end zone, and kept running, disappearing down the tunnel to the locker room. TV analyst Mike Francesa called the Hurricanes' end-zone celebrations "disgraceful." Bernie Lincicome of the *Chicago Tribune* called the 'Canes "grubby" and said they were "about as far from the college ideal as a tire iron is from an ear swab." Boston columnist Will McDonough practically needed smelling salts, lamenting that Miami's win meant "the streets" had taken over the honorable game of football, calling the 'Canes thugs, and sternly demanding, "Is this college football? Is this what we want to bring into our stadium?"

Goodness gracious! Next thing you know, the Negroes will demand to play quarterback and sit on the 50-yard line. Rhoden says traditionally white universities "wanted black muscle but not the attendant zeal and style"; he loved the way the Hurricanes wreaked havoc upon college football's dubious sense of decorum and were not remotely sorry about it. I'm with him intellectually: the ebullience, the ferocity, the sheer fun some African American athletes bring to the game do occasionally freak out white folks—who could use a good freaking out, if only we'd change our behavior in response. But—the Hurricanes. The mouthy, over-accessorized, grinning Hurricanes. Perhaps I'm too tangled in my own racial biases, my own class expectations, to fully appreciate the Hurricanes' liberating intervention into college football decorum. Or maybe I just hate the bastards. They beat FSU over and over and over, often by one point, throughout the 1980s, and then in the 1990s, with FSU suffering that outbreak of wide-right fever, about which they tormented us, wielding their stupid thumb-bottomed U sign, their *Miami Vice* tropical flash, their pally-ness with rap stars and DJs and movie stars, all of which suggested that we here in Tallahassee were distinctly lacking in all the things that mattered in life, that is: style, Luther Campbell, Club Nu, and a beach.

Or it could be that I'm one of those pearl clutchers.

The swagger of the Hurricanes and some other largely African American football stars amounts to a real demonstration of power, a real revolt. Or is it what Frederick Douglass called the "safety valve"? Sociologist Harry Edwards, professor emeritus at UC Berkeley, was one of the brains behind the protest movement that impelled American Olympians John Carlos and Tommie Smith to ignite white fainting spells when they raised their fists on the medal stand in 1968. Edwards savages the myth of sports as a black kid's way out of the projects or the dead-end little Southern town: "You have a better chance of getting hit by a meteorite in the next ten years than getting work as an athlete."

A few players out of hundreds of joyfully swaggering black athletes go to the pros: under 2 percent of college players get drafted. The others get left behind. The University of Pennsylvania published a study in 2013 looking at graduation rates for African American athletes at colleges with huge "revenue producing" sports (i.e., football and basketball) programs. Some universities did very well—many of them private or highly selective—Duke, Vanderbilt, Maryland, Wake Forest, Virginia Tech. Despite their "street" image, the University of Miami boasted a 66 percent black male jock graduation rate. And then there's the SEC and Florida State: both UF and FSU, Florida's 's "preeminent" public institutions of higher learning, graduated just 34 percent of their black male "student-athletes." The University of Alabama graduated 56 percent, the second highest in the conference after Vanderbilt. What happens to those degreeless young men once the university has used their strength and speed, gotten what it wanted out of them, and turned them loose in the big, cold world?

Of the few chosen to try for glory and fat paychecks in the pros, some will get famous and rich and stay famous and rich. Some will manage their careers with great intelligence and foresight, putting away money, getting ready for the time the ACL or the back or the knee finally gives up, and a job as a high school head coach or manager of a Toyota dealership starts to look good. A few will become actually powerful, occupying positions where they can move the culture along toward that prejudice-free place we've been promising ourselves for more than two hundred years. Most won't. Almost all the NFL owners are white. Coaches and managers, too. In 2014, there were 11 African American head coaches—out of 128 in Division I. Many of the famous names past and present, the ones lovers of the game intone like a magic charm—Richard Sherman, Deion Sanders, Cris Carter, Derrick Brooks, Teddy Bridgewater, Jameis Winston—belong to African Americans. The plantation—the land and the capital—belong to white people.

"But those guys are stars," you say, "lucky as hell, making way more money than me playing a *game*." Nobody feels sorry for elite athletes; and it can be hard to see the miasma of racism rising around the castle of football. The ubiquity of black athletes, their prominence on the field, and their apparent "brotherhood" with white team members make it look as though the Movement is over, we can check the "social progress" box, and move on to something new. Integration, y'all! Even Ole Miss and Alabama, where Jim Crow had his HQ right there in George Wallace's office, love and cherish their black ball players. The problem is, there seem to be all these black guys on the field, but African Americans are underrepresented in the operating theater, on the bench, in the lecture hall, behind the camera, in the laboratory, and certainly in the administrative offices of universities. And the very success of African Americans on the gridiron sometimes seems to contribute to the old, sneaky, nasty notion—that while black men are physically superior, they don't make it intellectually.

The worse problem is that successful black athletes get used by watchers of Fox "News" and other neoracialist idiots as evidence that all you need is hard work. Successful black athletes fit too neatly into the American class delusion that determination and gumption are all that's required to make it in America, anyone can succeed if he works really hard. And don't smoke dope. And pull up your pants. And don't get born poor. It's a cruel, inhumane lie, America's animating delusion. And demonstrably untrue.

Chapter 18

THE FALL OF THE HOUSE OF BOWDEN

THE TEAM WAS SHIT, the fans were restive, and the stadium was half-empty. The Seminoles weren't posting losing seasons, not technically, though what people there were in the stands of Doak Campbell, accustomed to life in the Top Five, felt that 7-6 and 7-6 in 2006 and 2007 must be the result of some incomprehensible dark curse. The trustees muttered that the once beloved, two-time national championship–winning coach should be replaced. The football media, from Tony Barnhart at the *Atlanta Journal-Constitution* to Lee Corso on ESPN to the slightly less distinguished bloggers at the likes of Warchant.com, debated the question whether Florida State's legendary coach should bow out gracefully or clamp down on his job like a fyce on a bear's leg. Bobby Bowden, mindful that Bear Bryant lived only twenty-eight days after he quit coaching at Alabama, said he'd go when he was good and damn ready. Ann Bowden, the coach's wife, got downright hostile: "They'll have to fire him. If they've got guts enough to do it, let them do it."

They did do it: in November 2009 FSU president T. K. Wetherell, who'd played for Bowden back in the day, told the old man he had to go. The Bowdens pitched a little hissy fit. Just because he lost some games to Homecoming fodder like Wake Forest and South Florida, just because he flouted state nepotism laws to hire his son Jeffrey, whose talents as an offensive coordinator were difficult to discern, just because the NCAA ordered FSU to vacate a dozen victories over a grade-cheating scandal and he was eighty years old and not really up to calling plays, FSU decided Bowden's services were no longer required.

The chairman of the trustees shook his head: "It's sort of like when you have to put your favorite dog down; you know it's the right thing to do, but you sure feel bad about it."

The office (I don't think "job" quite covers it) of head football coach at a major college program is something like being a medieval king. You're rich, you're powerful, and when you win important battles against neighboring palatinates (or downstate rivals), you are adored. People want to kiss the hem of your polyester trousers. It's as if you can cure what ails the land, bring the rain, make the crops grow again, heal the sick. Start losing, and you'll be deposed, sent off into exile in the Mid-Atlantic Conference, or confined to the golf course for the rest of your life.

The old man said, "After you retire there's only one big event left. And I ain't ready for that." Everybody in his position shivers in the shadow of the legend, the myth, the whatever: the Bear.

Everybody knows Paul Bryant was born in a sharecropper's cabin he helped build, officially the eleventh child of Wilson Monroe Bryant and Ida Kilgore Bryant, but in truth the offspring of Stonewall Jackson and the goddess Nike. As a boy, he chopped cotton and played football for the Fordyce High School Red Bugs in Fordyce, Arkansas, where his semi-divine athletic powers won him a scholarship to the University of Alabama. He pledged Sigma Nu. He dated an Alpha Gamma Delta. He liked to drink. He played in the 1935 Alabama-Tennessee game with a broken leg. Some confuse Paul Bryant with Davy Crockett, who, as scripture tells us, "kilt him a b'ar when he was only three." But Davy Crockett did not play football. And Paul Bryant didn't kill his bear; he boxed it at the Lyric Theatre in Fordyce, going several rounds until the bear bit him on the ear, which was cheating. Others confuse him with the hero Hercules, who whipped a lion, a boar, and a hydra but lacked the stones to take on *Ursus americanus*—or Penn State. As a coach, Bryant won 689 national championships and in 1983 ascended to Valhalla in a winged crimson Cadillac, where he sits on the right hand of Walter Camp.

Paul William "Bear" Bryant was what W. J. Cash, the great taxonomist of the South, calls a "hell of a fellow," the guy "full of chip-on-the-shoulder swagger" who'd "knock hell out of whoever dared to cross him." The "hell of a fellow" fueled himself on whisky and testosterone, regarded women as a different species, and worshiped manliness in a way that would be totally gay if it weren't so aggressively heterosexual. There's no way to separate reality and hagiography: other men are too busy hero-worshiping him, the way that Wash Jones, one of William Faulkner's archetypal poor white men, worships Colonel Thomas Sutpen, the local plantation magnate: "If God himself was to come down and ride the natural earth, that's what He would aim to look like." George Blanda, who played quarterback at Kentucky in the late 1940s, said that when he met the Bear, he thought, *This must be what God looks like.*

One person's undying loyalty is another person's rivalry irritant. In his list of "Most Retarded SEC Traditions," VolFan46205311979 writes:

> We all know the story. In 1714, a young Bear Bryant saved an entire orphanage from certain death by pissing on a 4 alarm blaze and putting it out. In 1776, he penned the Declaration of Independence. In 1887, he invented the car. And in 19-something, he won a bunch of football games. The problem is that the Bear isn't as hot as he used to be. He's still got the touch, yes, but there are reports that he has begun to slip. Ex-assistants have grumbled about his play-calling, suggesting that there are times when the Bear won't respond to questions or select a play for an entire game. Many have questioned his work ethic, as inside sources have revealed that he hasn't shown up to work in over twenty years. Bammers remain confident,

however. They continue to believe that he is the key to returning to national prominence. Some think that Bama is taking advantage of an old man, some would say that Bama should let Bryant rest in peace.

The Bear isn't as quiet as all that. He speaks from the grave, before kickoff at every Crimson Tide home game. You hear his voice, deep as a coal mine in Appalachia, rough as Arkansas moonshine, coming out of vast speakers: "I ain't never been nothing but a winner."

When asked why he left Texas A&M for the head coaching job at Alabama, Bear Bryant replied, "Mama called." But if the university is the alma mater, the "nourishing mother," the football coach is the stern traditional father, the head of the household, the guy with the wallet, the rules, and the belt. The university president, the chancellor, and the board of trustees or regents are supposed to be in charge, officially hiring and firing coaches and athletic directors. Too often, they are not. The power is with the money, and the money is with the legislature (if it's a state university), and the big donors, who are not true to their school because of its fine Latin American Studies Department or renowned particle physicists. If you gave them a choice between paying for five Nobel Prize–winning chemists or one hot-shit defensive coordinator, they wouldn't even have to think about it. Besides, intellectuals are cheap. At Florida State, the combined professorial salaries of Pulitzer-winning writer Robert Olen Butler and the prima ballerina Suzanne Farrell, Balanchine's muse and one of the greatest dancers of the twentieth century, add up to less than that of the lowest-paid coach on the Seminoles' football staff.

From the early 1960s on, the only human being in the South more revered than Bear Bryant was Elvis. The scholar Charles Reagan Wilson sees both of them as "saints" of the Southern civil religion, icons of their people—though Elvis kind of let himself go there toward the end. Judging by the depictions of the Bear walking on water or the Bear's ghostly hand helping the Crimson Tide score, his ranking in heaven is pretty high, despite the way he drank, smoked, and, according to lots of Alabamians (and not just Auburn people), womanized like a champ. At least he didn't talk a big Jesus-game. He wasn't crazy about letting the Fellowship of Christian Athletes into his locker room, lest they make his boys "soft." The Bear believed in Manliness. He believed in Hardness. Toughness. Torture.

Seriously, torture. A few months after Bryant took the job at Texas A&M in 1954, he decided Aggie players lacked rigor and endurance. They'd been accustomed to a life of ease and pleasure on campus, where there were no women and all students belonged to the cadet corps and wore military uniforms. Still, the Bear figured he'd remove his boys from the fleshpots of College Station 250 miles into the Texas hill country, a part of Texas even Texans avoided. He took them to Junction, a wretched piece of parched, rattlesnake-infested earth to violate their human rights. Or as he would see it, "separate the quitters from the keepers." They practiced in 110-degree heat on what had once been grass but in the punishing drought had become nothing but rocks, sand, and a noisome spurred plant called puncture vine. Bryant thought water breaks were for sissies. Turkey vultures circled. By day, boys collapsed from heat exhaustion and dehydration. By night, they'd sneak out of the Quonset-hut barracks and hitch back to College Station. Gene Stallings, a "keeper" who eventually succeeded to the Bear's old job as coach of the Crimson Tide, said, "We went out there in two buses and came back in one."

On October 27, 2001, the Penn State Nittany Lions beat the Ohio State Buckeyes and Joe Paterno passed Bear Bryant's record of 323 wins. Paterno won two national championships, though he never beat the Bear on the field. On the other hand, the Bear probably never read the *Aeneid*, Paterno's favorite work of literature. Pity: he would have liked the story of a guy fleeing a ruined and impoverished kingdom to make a better life for himself by founding Rome. And he would have approved of the way that even though Aeneas could have married Dido, Queen of Carthage, and lounged around in a palace by the Med, he dumped her to fulfill his destiny, which was to become the winningest major college football coach.

LIKE THE BEAR, Joe Paterno is one of college football's lares and penates, graduating between 80 and 85 percent of his players (Bryant's graduation rate was 33 percent) and endowing faculty positions, an English major from Brown, a proud nerd in thick glasses and white socks. Paterno was also Bobby Bowden's key rival in coaching victories. Yet Paterno died in disgrace, tainted by his failure in 2001 to do more than tell the athletic director that one of his graduate assistants saw one of his former coaches—Jerry Sandusky—doing *something* to a child in the Penn State team showers. Turns out, Sandusky raped or molested more than two dozen children. In 2011, in the midst of the bright, cold light on the scandal, Paterno tried to resign; the PSU board of trustees fired him instead. A couple of months later, he died. Bobby Bowden called it "a great tragedy."

Aristotle says tragedy displays "incidents arousing pity and fear, wherewith to accomplish its catharsis of such emotions." For the Renaissance boys, tragedy was about the fall of princes, the mighty laid low by the sin of pride. America is sadly lacking in princes, but we've an embarrassment of riches when it comes to football coaches, their families, their players, and nearby narratives of glittering rise and ignominious fall—"the thrill of victory and the agony of defeat," as poet and TV *Batman* writer Stanley Ralph Ross put it. Julius Caesar howls over the fickleness of the fans, King Richard offers his kingdom for a decent quarterback, Hamlet laments his torn ACL, and Oedipus rages at insufficiently deferential university presidents and the perfidy of the sporting press.

College football shares with the peerage of Great Britain a devotion to the hereditary principle. Jay Paterno played for his father at Penn State, then coached under him for seventeen years. Skip Holtz worked as offensive coordinator for his father, Lou, at Notre Dame. Steve Spurrier Jr. endures his daddy's temper as receivers coach at South Carolina. When Alabama named Mike Price head coach in December 2002, he promptly installed his sons, Eric and Aaron, as assistants.

Not that the Price dynasty lasted long enough for anyone to notice it. Seems Daddy Mike enjoyed buying drinks for sorority girls in bars on the Tuscaloosa Strip. Then in April 2003, while disporting himself on the Gulf Coast, he got entangled with several ladies, none of whom was his wife. At a Pensacola bar where he seemed surprised that everybody knew who he was, Price treated himself to several "private dances" from a stripper named Destiny Boudreaux and met up with two women at his hotel room for a little horizontal fun and games. One of the women told *Sports Illustrated* she yelled "Roll, Tide!" while they were in flagrante. Price replied, "It's rolling, baby, it's rolling!"

Alabama president Robert Witt fired Price in early May, before he coached a single game in Bryant Denny Stadium. All three Prices slunk off to football jobs at the University of Texas–El Paso, Siberia to Tuscaloosa's Vatican City. One Alabama booster said, "Mike Price never got that this ain't the Pac-10."

Lust and stupidity aren't sins much indulged in by the Bowden clan. No, the Bowdens are the family that prays together and stays together, reinforcing their mutual hubris. Middleton or Shakespeare or one of those sixteenth-century dramatists who liked to write about prideful, ruthless, scheming clans would have enjoyed them. Bobby and Ann Bowden have six children: Ginger, a prosecutor, married (and divorced) a former FSU football player; her sister, Robyn, married a football coach. Terry, Jeff, and Tommy all became football coaches, and all worked at one point or other for their father at FSU. Steve, the eldest, bilked his own parents of more than a million dollars in 2003. He pled guilty to a securities-fraud scheme and managed to avoid jail time. Tommy and Terry became head coaches at Clemson and Auburn respectively; both flew high and fell far, especially Terry, the "smart one," the one with the law degree. Tommy's the "pretty one."

Terry became the protégé of Bobby Lowder, a millionaire who ran Auburn's board of trustees the way Vladimir Putin runs Russia. Lowder handpicked Terry to become head coach after Pat Dye, the coach–cum–athletic director who presided over a pay-for-play scandal so grubby, the Tigers were banned from television and postseason play. Terry's Tigers went undefeated his first year, and kept on winning.

But Pat Dye, who was still hanging around Auburn, began publicly criticizing Terry's play calling. Terry fired an assistant coach for insubordination; Auburn AD David Housel turned around and hired the assistant coach as a "consultant." In 1998, after Auburn lost four of its first five games, the dark eminence, Lowder, forced Terry to resign.

Tommy took the head coaching job at Clemson that same year, inaugurating the yearly "Bowden Bowl," Clemson versus FSU, a cheerfully Oedipal contest beloved of sports reporters across the nation. In 2008, Tommy had to resign. Just like Terry. As for Jeffrey, he spent six years at FSU transforming a Formula 1 offense into a Chevy Nova with a clapped-out timing belt and a drag-ass muffler. In 2006, Wake Forest shut out FSU 30–0, and after years of excuses and whining, driving Seminoles mad with frustration, Jeffrey grudgingly accepted a "generous" contract buyout from the boosters.

For a good twenty-five years, Seminoles truly loved Bobby Bowden. Everybody—with the possible exception of Steve Spurrier—loved Bobby Bowden. I loved Bobby Bowden. Not his Stone Age politics, his casual sexism, his players' rotten graduation rate; I loved his line in country-boy bullshit, the way he played a slow-talking semi-simpleton on TV, even as he designed plays of dazzling creativity and complexity. We accorded him the honorific ol', used for people we feel we know (even though we don't), whom we admire, are amused by, and sometimes deplore, people we claim as our own. We reveled in his bravura calls, the long bomb on first down, his courtly shout-outs to players' hometowns and their "mamas and daddies" on his television show, and the rooskies—the fumblerooskie, the puntrooskie—the trick plays that dazzled the nation and won FSU games.

But not too long after that second national championship, around the time he hired the lamentable Jeffrey as the Seminoles' offensive coordinator, Bobby Bowden started believing his own press. That worked fine as long as FSU beat up on UF and got invited to the Sugar Bowl and the Orange Bowl and the like, but when the team lost five games in 2005, Seminoles started grumbling. Yes, we were spoiled, hugely spoiled: we'd been a top team for as long as a lot of people could remember. It might have helped if those people could remember a little further back, say, to the epically god-awful 0-11 season of 1973, the season with two shutouts and one game (against Houston) in which we scored only a field goal. Nose to tail, a debacle, so bad that in 1974, when the team went 1-10, you'd have thought we'd contended for a championship.

We'd become accustomed to better things—or at least intelligent play calling. When the Bowdens blamed the rainy weather for FSU's loss to Miami in 2003, somebody put a big sign up on Monroe Street, Tallahassee's main drag, saying, JEFF, A POOR EXCUSE IS WORSE THAN NONE AT ALL. Seminoles circulated a petition calling for Bobby to shed Jeffrey. Peter Tom Willis, a former Seminole quarterback turned radio color guy, said that FSU had a "high school offense." All-everything FSU linebacker Derrick Brooks bemoaned his team's fall from fortune: "Florida State has been humbled," he said. "But now that we've been humbled, what are we going to do about it?"

What Bobby Bowden did was get mad—at the fans. When some hapless person on his call-in show expressed reservations about Jeff's future, Bowden barked, "I can't believe a guy asked me, am I going to fire my son. I can't believe that." Petulantly referring to Jeff's critics as "cowards," Bowden blamed a loss to the Gators on his players. Bad tackling. Lack of "execution."

Maybe Bowden was sorry he didn't try harder for the Alabama job, once his dream, when he had the chance. Alabama governor and part-time Amway salesman Guy Hunt told Bowden he was UA's first choice (yes, governors in Alabama get involved in hiring university football coaches, even governors like Hunt, who never went to college). Bowden assumed the job was his. When he got to Tuscaloosa, however, he realized he was one among several being considered. Worse still, he got asked impertinent questions. Walter Lewis, the Bear's last quarterback and the Tide's first starting African American QB, wanted to know how Bowden felt about black quarterbacks. Bowden had started two black QBs at West Virginia—in 1973 and 1974. Back in Tallahassee, he was besieged by television camera crews and sports reporters. He said: "Nobody offered me the Alabama job," he said. "I will not go chasing after it."

Three years later in 1989, he had another chance with 'Bama. He decided the hell with it. Or the heck—Bowden rarely swears. He told Joe Posnanski in December 2014 that if they wouldn't take him on his own terms at Alabama, then he figured "maybe we can make our own Alabama" at FSU.

Perhaps it was his age, pushing eighty. He was spry, but no longer the indefatigable charmer he'd been in 1976 when he first came to Tallahassee. Maybe he just couldn't admit he'd made a mistake hiring Jeff. He got sulky. Downright mean. Arrogant, too. When Seminoles disparaged his son, he warned they'd "better be glad I'd like to keep this job."

Seminoles started talking trash about their own, once immaculate, once beloved Bowdens. Restaurateurs grumbled that Ann Bowden almost never paid for the nice lunches she enjoyed around town. People complained Jeff had dumbed down the once mighty playbook. Even the most loyal began to suspect the whole family was in it for the money. By 2009, the college football planet was practically begging Bowden to retire before he further compromised his image and sullied his exceptional football record. FSU beat number-seven BYU, then barely beat tiny Jacksonville State and lost to the University of South Florida. USF, a college that had been playing football for twelve years. The big donors, the fans, the trustees—everyone knew it was time. In early October 2009, trustees chair Jim Smith told a local newspaper reporter, "My hope is frankly that we'll go ahead and . . . let the world know that this year will be the end of the Bowden Era."

Smith, a former state attorney general, and FSU president T. K. Wetherell realized the politics of the thing were tricky. Tallahassee—like Tuscaloosa or Athens or Oxford or College Park or Madison or Clemson or any other capital of college football—is like the court of Louis XIV, a place of carefully leaked information, gossip, an excess of public good manners, and mendacious language. FSU's football coach isn't just another university employee; he's a community icon, a lordly figure for whom thousands and thousands of Seminoles (and others) felt a deep emotional attachment. Smith and Wetherell knew they needed to get the faithful ready for a big change. Bowden's Dauphin, his designated successor, Jimbo Fisher, was ready to sign a contract. Fisher had already been "coach-in-waiting" (that is seriously what they called him) for two years. Now they just needed to get it in Bowden's head.

It didn't quite work. Ann Bowden, Lady Macbeth to Bobby's King Lear, made her disdain clear. She felt the university should have done more for him. She hated the way Jeffrey, her youngest son, had been knocked out of the succession and exiled. Florida State belonged to the Bowdens the way Massachusetts belonged to the Kennedys or Monaco belonged to the Grimaldis. Terry left Auburn and said, only partly joking, he might quit coaching. Unless, of course, the king designated him the heir: "If Dad wants to give me Florida State when he retires, I'll officially go back in. And to make everybody mad, I'll keep Jeff as my offensive coordinator."

Florida State no longer wanted Terry or any other Bowden princeling. The university offered to make Bobby Bowden "coach emeritus," a sort of constitutional monarch—lots of pomp, little power. He refused. As he told the *Tampa Bay Times*, it was "something below my dignity." Then he recovered some of his old humor, saying, "It reminded me of Barney Fife. They gave him a gun, but they won't let him put the bullet in there."

FSU had named the football field after him, erected a statue, put up a huge stained-glass window. From the university's perspective, they'd given him all they needed to; from Bobby (and Ann) Bowden's perspective, FSU was ungrateful and ungracious. The abdication was ugly. He didn't get a going-away present. He didn't get a party. He coached the bowl game in Jacksonville. The Bowdens took a dozen kinfolk with them to the hotel and ordered an astonishing amount of top-price room service. He won. Then decamped, leaving the bill for FSU to pay.

Once Bowden was gone, many of the very Seminoles who'd been

clamoring for his ouster suddenly fell back in love with him. If they were younger than fifty, he was the only coach they'd ever known: "The Riverboat Gambler," "ol' Bobby," "Saint Bobby." They forgot the scandals, the tolerance of player criminality. If they remembered it at all, they blamed the media. *Sports Illustrated* reminded everyone of FSU's long line of transgressions in a 1994 piece called "Tainted Title." Bobby Bowden complained: "I have not had one chance to enjoy the national championship." Seminoles shrugged off the cheating scandal of 2009: that wasn't Coach Bowden's fault—it was the tutor who gave the kids answers for that dumb Music Appreciation course. After all, Coach Bowden put FSU on the map! Nobody had ever heard of the joint till he came along!

Bowden didn't go mad and wander the blasted golf course behind his house in northeast Tallahassee. He wrote yet another devotional book, this time with his fraudster son, Steve. His jokey cheer seemed to return to him (didn't ol' Jesus say something about turning the other cheek?), Lady Macbeth cooled off some—enough, at least, to allow him to attend an FSU game in 2013. By then, T. K. Wetherell had also retired. Jimbo Fisher was winning games. And the university had cut another deal with the old man: a quarter-million dollars per annum for licensing rights and personal appearances for fund-raising. Bowden also gets almost half the royalties from the licensing rights.

Not exactly the fall of princes, unless princes fall up.

POSTGAME

IN THE END, Jameis Winston got all the crab legs he could ever want. He got a four-year, $23 million contract with Tampa Bay as well, and a new jersey in Buccaneer red and Buccaneer black. A new number, too—3.

This time the crab legs were a present. Captain Keith Colburn, skipper of the FV *Wizard* out of Seattle, Washington, and star of *The Deadliest Catch*, mailed him twenty-five pounds of king crab legs to serve at his NFL draft celebration. Seems ol' Jaboo helped Captain Keith with a children's charity event—I mean, who better to auction off a crab the size of a truck tire than Jameis Winston? Jameis's kinfolk, friends, and coaches there at the party in McCalla, Alabama, felt it was a nice gesture.But Jameis being Jameis, he sent out a photo of himself with a new Bucs hat sitting high on his head, a yee-haw grin on his face, and a tray of dismantled crustaceans on his lap. Oh, how *dare* he? Doesn't he realize he's still on worldwide Double Secret Probation for his many acts of gross depravity: the swearing, the attempted squirrel shooting, that time he didn't pay for the Coke at Burger King, that time he couldn't throw worth a damn against Oregon?

That time he was accused of rape. Yeah, that, too.

And the kid has the gall to be photographed goofing over crab legs, his girlfriend—long-suffering, elegant Breion Allen, a guard on the Rice

University basketball team—looking quizzically over his shoulder. Has he no shame? Did he not realize he'd just been invited into the National Football League, that band of bros whose virtue and moral fiber is renowned, home of men such as Richie Incognito, David Meggett, Aaron Hernandez, Ray Rice, Ben Roethlisburger, and Michael Vick? Sports columnists from LA to DC fretted over Jaboo's "character issues," his insouciance, his incessant smiling. Many called him immature. Some called him fat. Fat! How could the once powerful, now pitiful, Tampa Bay Bucs (4-12 in 2013, 2-14 in 2014, a team named after made-up Gulf Coast pirates with a mascot who, though he's called Captain Fear, looks like a confused hipster on his way to an ironic Halloween party) throw away their number-one pick on a fat, decapod-eating, possible sexual-assault perp from Hueytown, Alabama?

SEVENTY-FIVE YEARS AGO, W. J. Cash charged that the University of Alabama was less interested in "the increase of knowledge and thoughtfulness and tolerance than in the reduction of the academic department to the status of an appendage of fraternity row and a hired football team." Cash could have said that about Georgia or Florida or Florida State—or Ohio State or TCU or Mizzou or the University of Oregon. However fraternity row may behave when knee-walking drunk, its denizens officially embrace the values of the old elite: decorum, tradition, honor (which for men means unthinking loyalty to your class and caste and for women, avoiding the appearance of being a "slut"), and being true to your school. They're a bit like the pre–World War II British upper classes who drank like fish, did drugs, swore like sailors, and would have sex with anyone or anything they liked as long as it was discreet, but they would still sit in the front pew at church every Sunday as an example to the peasants.

If Cash were around today, he'd expand his definition of fraternity row to include the booster clubs, the boards of trustees, the season ticket holders, and the NCAA. For them, the university is simply a beard, a necessary collection of professors and books and labs more or less randomly assembled to allow football to look "educational," a beloved tradition rather than a vast corporate enterprise, an amateur sport. There's an order to preserve. And profits to protect.

The NCAA, like the Vatican, the British monarchy, the United States Senate, the Augusta National Club, and other elderly institutions forced to adapt to social change under threat of being laughed into irrelevance, is committed to the order it created but no longer controls. The end-times are coming: surely some rough beast is slouching toward the stadium to be born, or at least, increasing understanding of postconcussion syndrome and chronic traumatic encephalopathy in college players will soon demand a different, less lethal, game. If general outrage over broken bodies and broken minds won't do it, lawsuits will. Players will unionize, demand a share of the proceeds, and maybe choose to turn college football into an NFL farm system that happens to use university facilities, relieving it of the necessity to "play school," as Cardale Jones says. Think of how much training they could do if they never had to show up for freshman English.

Of course, the necessity for the NCAA would then disappear, and the NCAA will fight that like a crazed mink. The NCAA is self-fueling, secretive, arbitrary, and morally flexible. A former chief legal counsel for a big football college compared the NCAA to the church before Martin Luther, in which the priest "tells people what God wants, it's in a language they don't know, and it's chained to the church wall so very few people can even look." The rules aren't circulated to dues-paying member institutions. Sins against amateurism are defined after you confess to them. The former counsel notes: "The NCAA's attitude is tell 'em what you did, and they'll let you know if you screwed up."

By 2009 a penitent Florida State had investigated itself and even punished itself reasonably severely over the discovery that a "rogue tutor" had been (depending upon whom you ask) either giving exam answers to athletes or providing them "inappropriate help" on essays and tests. The university saw no reason not to be up-front about the scandal: Florida's open-government statutes require that university documents be available to citizens. The NCAA threw a tantrum, demanding secrecy. Pay no attention to the man behind the curtain! News organizations had to sue both the university (which wanted to release the documents) and the

NCAA to get a look at material that was, under the law, already public.

I say the end-times are coming for college football, but maybe that's not true. The game has managed get away with largely ignoring feminism and pretending that there are only a few—one, maybe two!—gay guys on the gridiron. Maybe college football will become a museum of ancient masculinity; as long as there is war, there will probably be football. Perhaps we'll go whole hog on the gladiator thing, deciding that it's OK to create a well-paid and willing class of athlete who agrees to accept dementia, depression, and madness by the age of forty-five and drooling, empty-brained death by the age of sixty.

BACK IN TALLAHASSEE, tumbleweeds roll down the avenues and a whistling wind blows around the turrets of Doak Campbell Stadium.

All right, that's not quite the case, but town and campus are a bit subdued these days. Season ticket sales have slowed down. For the last couple of years, Tallahassee was the capital of the college football kingdom, the Court of the Sunny King of Quarterbacks. Now, despite recruiting the third-best class of freshman athletes in the country, Seminoles feel a bit of elegiac sadness—sadness coupled with exhausted relief. Jameis has gone, though not very far. Just down the road to Tampa. We're happy for him—mostly. FSU's own interception genius and byword for bad student-athlete, Deion Sanders, said of watching the boys get drafted into the NFL, "It's awesome to see the joy. It's awesome to see the emotion, the whole family at the table when they receive that phone call."

Deion smiled like a seraph: "Finally your dreams just called you," he said. "All you have to do is answer the phone." Bucs general manager Jason Licht was just as dewy eyed: "Somebody asked me if it was like Christmas and I said, 'No, it's more like your wedding day without the cold feet.'"

So the story ends like all good romances, with a contract. Reader, they signed him. Jameis is somebody else's problem now. We'll not have to worry about waking up to news of another indiscretion, another potential criminal issue. Not committed by Jaboo, anyway. In June 2015, certain young Seminoles engaged themselves in bar fights. With women.

Dalvin Cook, one of the best running backs in the nation, is accused of punching a woman outside Clyde's, a Tallahassee watering hole. On another night, in another saloon, freshman quarterback DéAndre Johnson laid a right hook on a girl who apparently objected to his rooting ahead of her in the drinks line. DéAndre appeared on *Good Morning America*, insisting that though she threw a "racial epithet" at him, he knows there's no excuse for what he did. His mama did not raise him that way.

Both were charged with misdemeanor battery. FSU suspended Dalvin Cook "indefinitely"; the university dismissed DéAndre Johnson from the team. The difference is there's a video of DéAndre whomping on the young lady.

It's not all bad news for FSU players: the state attorney dropped the DUI charges against cornerback P. J. Williams. Insufficient evidence. One early, early morning in April 2015, he was driving a little erratically, making an illegal left turn, and swerving over the lane divider, but we've all been there, right? The New Orleans Saints drafted him in the third round.

No, now the problem is waking up to the bleak reality of losing. We will lose games. Except for the epic beat-down by the Oregon Ducks on New Year's Day 2015, Seminoles haven't had to feel the gut-bit pain of defeat since November 24, 2012, and that was against the Gators, so we were used to it.

But now Fortune's Wheel has spun and FSU's not at the top anymore. We don't know if we're on our way back up. Or down at the bottom of the circle, depicted in medieval illustrations as some poor bastard in the process of being crushed under the weight of the Wheel itself, marked with the legend *Sum sine regno*, "I have no kingdom."

Yet we will greet each game with hope and anticipation, many of us with a naggy ambivalence we try to drown out by asking, "How do you like our chances against Clemson (or the Wolfpack or the Gators or the Tide)?" College football can't last—can it? At the moment, Bevo continues to graze, Big Al swings his gray plush trunk, Uga IX lies on his bag of ice wearing his Georgia sweater, and Sparty dusts down his armor. College football endures—for a few more years, anyway. Me, I'll still care way too much, even though I know better. This is my tribe. These are my people.

ACKNOWLEDGMENTS

EFFUSIVE, HEARTFELT, damned near embarrassing thanks first to Barry Harbaugh, who read an essay I wrote for the *Oxford American* and detected a lurking book, and to David Hirshey who, despite his perverse love of the old game, the one Americans call "soccer," and the rest of the planet calls football, coached and drilled this project into shape. Thanks, too, to Sydney Pierce and everyone at HarperCollins.

I'm enormously grateful to Bob Shachochis for his friendship, for the privilege of watching games with him over the years, and for introducing me to the wonderful Gail Hochman, who, though mystified as to why any sane human would play or watch such an absurdly violent game, took me (and it) on. Tommy Warren and Kathy Villacorta, forces for good in the universe, tolerated endless football conversations. Special thanks to Tommy for sharing his memories and insights into how the game worked in the early 1970s, with its cruelty and racism—not so much different from now.

Roger Hodge indulged me by publishing my football piece in the *Oxford American*. Thanks to him and to Mark Smirnoff, who printed my first large-scale attempt to capture the weirdness of college football, way back in 1998, and to the editors of the *Florida Flambeau* (Michael Moline, Eileen Drennen, Moni Basu), who got me press passes for FSU games during the 1980s and 1990s. As for *Flambeau* sports guys Rodney Campbell and David Lee Simmons: what were y'all thinking, running my columns and getting yourself in trouble with the respectable sporting press? Thanks to venerable *Flambeau* editor David Bedingfield, former Seminole pitcher and now the greatest British jurist ever to come out of Vidalia, Georgia, for all the conversations over the years about FSU sports. It's a weird yet important pleasure to sit in London over a glass of really good Burgundy and complain about poor play calling in the Florida game.

I am grateful to my father, who bequeathed to me a demented love of the game; my mother, Betty Roberts, who taught me the rules (and made great tailgate fried chicken and a chocolate concoction we call football cake throughout my childhood and beyond); my brother, Bradford Roberts, who actually played the game; and Charlotte and Ernest Williams, who have been watching FSU football since 1947 and should get some kind of medal for that.

Thanks to my colleagues at Florida State: Eric Walker, Bob Butler, Erin Belieu, Elizabeth Stuckey-French, Jimmy Kimbrell, Anne Coldiron, and Skip Horack. Y'all never rolled your eyes or backed away when I came at you yapping about football. Ned Stuckey-French deserves a big thank-you for the slightly surreal stories about his playing days at Harvard—concussions and all. My dear friends at Alabama, especially Joe and Anne Hornsby, who let me sit with them at football games in Bryant-Denny Stadium, as well as Nanci Kincaid, Kathy Starbuck, and Harold Weber, cured me of any notion that being obsessed with college football was incompatible with being "literary." Thank you, Joe, for talking football with me endlessly and for letting me try on your fancy UA National Championship ring, and thank you, Anne, for putting me onto the great Irvin Carney "throw-up orange" video—not to mention your twenty-five years of friendship. My students at FSU are not only terrific, they helped with this project just by being clever, engaged, and critical. Adam Weinstein is one of the smartest and funniest writers on God's green earth. He's also an excellent reporter, and has shed much light on the relative importance of academics and athletics at a major football school. Jesse Goolsby is not only an extraordinary novelist, but I have him to thank for the fun fact that Hitler used the rhythms of Harvard cheers for Nazi rallies. Katie Burgess Steenerson, a daughter of the South who can't stand college football, said a lot of hilarious stuff about the game—some of which I stole. Chris Mink, in exile from Tuscaloosa, kept me up on the lows and highs of the Tide. My Sports and Culture seminar in fall 2014 proved a great source of information about how undergraduates understood the Jameis Winston scandal. For example, when we heard that Jameis had "stolen" crab legs from Club Publix on Ocala Road, they all rolled their eyes and informed me it wasn't shoplifting: athletes get free stuff from that grocery store all the time, and everyone knows it.

Finally, great thanks to all of you who host football parties or come to mine or go to games with me and manage to ignore the swearing: Pam Ball and Gary White, Tyler Turkle and Jesslyn Krouskroup, Jan Pudlow, Mark Pudlow, Matt Williams, Bob and Catfish, and Amy and Mark Hinson. Mark Hinson gets a special shout-out for being the Gator with the grace to sit with me through the epic 1994 Choke at Doak, watching UF's 28-point lead melt into air. The pain for him was mitigated somewhat by later interviewing Burt "Buddy" Reynolds, former Seminole halfback and Southern film icon.

I love you all.

DKR

THERE ARE THOUSANDS and thousands of books and articles on every aspect of college football, from what repeated subconcussive hits do to your brain to the best dip recipes for your tailgate. Here are just a few. James P. Jones's *FSU One Time* (1983) is a comprehensive account of Florida State football. Samuel G. Freedman's *Breaking the Line: The Season in Black College Football That Transformed the Sport and Changed the Course of Civil Rights* (2014) is an excellent account of black college football, Florida A&M, Grambling, and the great coaches Jake Gaither and Eddie Robinson. *The System: The Glory and Scandal of Big-Time College Football* (2013) by Jeff Benedict and Armen Keteyian dismantles what the "glamour" of the college game conceals—it's worse than you think. *Season of Saturdays: A History of College Football in 14 Games* (2014) by Michael Weinreb is much more cheerful.

"The Harvard Nazi," in *Boston Magazine* (March 2005), by John Sedgwick about his distant cousin, one of Hitler's right-hand guys, might put you right off the game. Buzz Bissinger and Malcolm Gladwell are among those who have called for a ban on football at least in high school, maybe even in college. Bissinger's May 8, 2012, piece in the *Wall Street Journal* is particularly cogent.

There's no lack of material on the Bowdens. See especially: "Ann Bowden Says Bobby Bowden Is Set on Returning as Florida State Seminoles Coach," by Brian Landman, *Tampa Bay Times*, November 18,

2009. The Toomer's Oaks saga was also much covered: the *Auburn Plainsman* managed to straddle outrage and satire in its comprehensive accounting of the atrocities, from Harvey Updyke's first confession on Paul Finebaum's radio show to the installation of the new trees in 2015.

There are histories of the game to suit every ideological bent: *A Whole New Ball Game: An Interpretation of American Sports*, by Allen Guttmann, 1988; *Sports in American History*, by Gerald Gems, Linda Borish, and Gertrud Pfister, 1983; *American Football: How the Game Evolved*, by James E. Herget, 2013; and *The Real All-Americans*, by Sally Jenkins, 2008—this is the amazing story of how the Native American football players of the Carlisle Indian Industrial School invented the fast modern style. And Michael Oriard's excellent *Reading Football: How the Popular Press Created an American Spectacle* (Cultural Studies of the United States), 1998. Critics of the game began early: see Philip Stubbes, *Anatomie of Abuses*, 1583. So did fans: James I and VI, *The King's Majesty's Declaration to His Subjects Concerning Lawful Sports to Be Used*, 1618.

Charles Reagan Wilson's *Judgment and Grace in Dixie* (1995) remains one of the best accounts of the way the secular becomes the holy. And Warren St. John's *Rammer Jammer Yellowhammer* is the most accurate account of the collective madness that is the Alabama football season. I know: I lived in Tuscaloosa for fourteen years.

A more scholarly account of the football-faith complex can be found in *Game Day and God: Football, Faith, and Politics in the American South* (2009), by Eric Bain-Selbo; *Muscular Christianity: Manhood and Sports in Protestant America, 1880–1920* (2003), by Clifford Putney; and *The Opening Kickoff: The Tumultuous Birth of a Football Nation* (2014), by Dave Revsine.

For insight into how coaches and Jesus work together on game plans (or whatever), see anything by Bobby Bowden, Tom Osborne, Peyton Manning, Gene Chizik, et al. For help in understanding the weird world of white Southern masculinity, read Bertram Wyatt Brown's *Southern Honor*.

But what about all that sin? Jon Krakauer's *Missoula: Rape and the Justice System in a College Town* (2015) tells of how University of Montana Grizzly players (and others) have seemed to be able to assault young women with impunity. There's also Katie Hnida's *Still Kicking* (2006), the pieces by Stassa Edwards in *Ms.* magazine (2014) about Steubenville and Jameis Winston, and *The Hunting Ground*, a 2015 documentary by Kirby Dick and Amy Zierling featuring interviews of Erica Kinsman and other young women who experienced campus sexual assaults.

Jameis Winston's rape accusation was first reported by Matt Baker in the *Tampa Bay Times*, then subsequently by everyone on the planet. *Grantland* had a good overview: http://grantland.com/features/how-media-handled-leaks-florida-state-qb-jameis-winston-case, in late November 2013.

The most comprehensive coverage of the Jameis Winston case and the ways the university and the local cops (at minimum) dropped the ball on a real investigation can be found in the *New York Times* stories by Walt Bogdanich and Mike McIntire, especially "At Florida State, Football Clouds Justice" (October 10, 2014).

On race and football, see Horacio Ruiz's forthcoming account of how Calvin Patterson integrated the Seminoles, *The White Knight: The Calvin Patterson Story and the Integration of FSU Football*, the fullest and most authoritative history of the player and his life and struggles as a black kid on a white team. Other good sources include *The New Plantation: Black Athletes, College Sports, and Predominantly White NCAA* (2013), by Billy Hawkins; and *Turning the Tide: How One Game Changed the South* (2008) by Don Yaeger, Sam Cunningham, and John Papadakis. Dave Zirin of the *Nation* reads sports politically in *What's My Name, Fool? Sports and Resistance in the United States* (2005) and *Game Over: How Politics Has Turned the Sports World Upside Down* (2013).

INDEX

ABOUT THE AUTHOR

DIANE ROBERTS is a contributor to NPR, the *Guardian*, and the *Oxford American*, among many other publications. She is the author of three books, and her work has been anthologized in *Best American Essays* and *Best American Food Writing*. She holds a PhD from Oxford University and teaches literature and creative writing at Florida State University in Tallahassee.